Just a Bunch of Facts

Glen Alan Cheney

Other Books by
Glenn Alan Cheney

Quilombo dos Palmares:
Brazil's Lost Nation of Fugitive Slaves

Thanksgiving: The Pilgrims' First Year in America

Journey on the Estrada Real:
Encounters in the Mountains of Brazil

Journey to Chernobyl:
Encounters in a Radioactive Zone

Love and Death in the Kingdom of Swaziland

His Hands on Earth: Courage, Compassion, Charism,
and the Missionary Sisters of the Sacred Heart of Jesus

Promised Land: A Nun's Struggle against Landlessness,
Lawlessness, Slavery, Poverty, Corruption,
and Environmental Devastation in Amazonia

How a Nation Grieves: Press Accounts of the Death of Lincoln,
the Hunt for Booth, and America in Mourning

Be Revolutionary: Some Thoughts from Pope Francis

Frankenstein on the Cusp of Something

Passion in an Improper Place

Law of the Jungle: Environmental Anarchy
and the Tenharim People of Amazonia

Acts of Ineffable Love

Potshots from the Left

Poems Askance

Neighborhood News

They Never Knew: The Victims of Atomic Testing

Mohandas Gandhi

El Salvador: Country in Crisis

Revolution in Central America

Television in American Society

Life in Caves

Teens with Physical Disabilities

Drugs, Teens and Recovery

Nuclear Proliferation: Problems and Possibilities

Translations

Ex Cathedra: Stories by Machado de Assis

Trio in A-Minor: Five stories by Machado de Assis

The Best Chronicles of Rubem Alves

Tender Returns (Rubem Alves)

To the Ends of the Earth:
Memoir of a Missionary Sister of the Sacred Heart of Jesus

Just a Bunch of Curiosities
is excerpted from the following books:

*Dr. Jamoke's Little Book of Hitherto Uncompiled
Facts and Curiosities Regarding Bees*

The Cat Caboodle: A Litter Box of Cat Facts and Curiosities

Lurking Doubt: Notes on Incarceration

The Merry Burial Compendium

*Bangs & Whimpers:
The End of the World and Other Catastrophes*

Just a Bunch of Facts

Glenn Alan Cheney

New London Librarium

Just a Bunch of Facts
by Glenn Alan Cheney

Copyright © 2018 Glenn Alan Cheney
Cover art by Glenn Alan Cheney

Published by
New London Librarium
Hanover, CT 06350
NLLibrarium.com

ISBNs:1947074261
Paperback 978-1-947074-26-2

Printed in the United States

Contents

A Merry Burial Compendium

Bangs & Whimpers

Facts and Curiosities Regarding Bees

Gods, Goddesses, Nymphs,

Saints & Suspicions

Your Lord revealed to the bees: 'Build dwellings in the mountains and the trees, and also in the structures which men erect. Then eat from every kind of fruit and travel the paths of your Lord, which have been made easy for you to follow.' From inside them comes a drink of varying colors, containing healing for mankind. There is certainly a Sign in that for people who reflect.

Qur'an, 16:69

My son, eat thou honey, because it is good; and the honeycomb, which is sweet to thy taste: So shall the knowledge of wisdom be unto thy soul: when thou hast found it, then there shall be a reward, and thy expectation shall not be cut off.

Proverbs 24:13-14

The tears of the Egyptian god Ra became bees as they fell.

The Egyptian goddess Nut could manifest herself as a bee, and for all anybody knows, she still can.

Bubilas and Austeéja were the Lithuanian god and goddess of bees.

Bhramari was the Hindu god of bees.

Colel Cab was the Mayan goddess of bees.

Samson, of Biblical fame, was not only strong but clever, and honey-bees came to play a part in an interesting event. Samson, it seems, had seen the woman of his dreams, but she was from among the uncircumcised Philistines who ruled over Israel. He took his parents to meet her. Along the way, he encountered a lion in a vineyard. He tore the lion apart with his bare hands, though apparently the altercation didn't create enough noise for his parents to hear. He never told them about it.

They met the girl, and, according to the King James version, "She pleased him well." He came back later and married her. On his way home, he looked for the carcass of the lion. He found it full of bees and honey! He dug right in, ate some, and took some home to his parents, though he never told them or his wife where he got it.

Later, he took his father to see his new wife. As was customary, he held a feast for his Philistine family. Thirty uncircumcised men were assigned to be his groomsmen. They befriended him. But not a lot. Sampson offered them a cruel riddle and told them that if they answered it in seven days, he would give all thirty of them a set of sheets and garments. But if they failed to answer it, they would have to give him thirty sheets and as many garments.

The offer was undoubtedly both intriguing and disturbing, but they agreed. And Samson said unto them, "Out of the eater came something to eat, and out of the strong came something sweet."

They couldn't figure it out. Desperate, they asked his wife to tease it out of him. His wife cried for a week and "lay sore upon him." She said, "You do but hate me, and love me not: you have put forth a riddle to the children of my people, and have not told it me."

Samson, nagged raw, finally told her, and she told them. And they told Samson the answer. And Samson said, "If you had not plowed with my heifer, you would not have solved my riddle."

The Bible does not mention how the wife felt about being called a heifer or exactly what Samson meant by "plowed," but it didn't matter because that marriage was effectively over. Samson, infused with the spirit of the Lord, went and killed 30 uncircumcised Philistines and took their garments.

And his wife? She was given to one of Samson's groomsmen. End of story? Certainly not. It got even more complicated. But that's the end of the part that involved bees.

The Talmud is very specific about how big a beehive one may throw in the street without culpability. It's not as simple as one might think. For a while it was believed that if it was less than six spans (that is, six hand-widths) wide, the thrower was culpable. If wider than that, it was not a Talmudic problem. But upon further thought, it was decided that if the hive is thrown with its mouth down and it's a trifle over seven spans high (as opposed to wide), the verdict is *guilty*.

Nothing in the Talmud *requires* the throwing of beehives into the street, and local ordinances may take precedence over the Talmud, so Dr. Jamoke's advice is: *Just don't*.

Mellona was the Roman goddess of bees. Her name derived from the Greek Melisseus of Crete, the "Bee Man" whose daughters (one named Melissa) hid the infant Zeus when his father, Cronus, was coming to eat him. The daughters hid the babe in a cave and nursed him with goat milk and honey. When four men discovered them, bees chased the mwn away. For this favor, the bees were rewarded with the gift of asexual reproduction. When Cronus found out that Melissa had thwarted his brephophagous repast, he turned her into an earthworm. Zeus, still enjoying milk and honey atop Mt. Olympus, rescued her by turning her into a bee.

Potnia, the Mistress Goddess of the Minoan-Mycenaeans, also known as "The Pure Mother Bee," named her priestesses Melissae, or bees, after Melissa, an elderly priestess of Demeter, the goddess of agriculture and harvest. When Melissa refused to tell other women her priestly secrets, they tore her to pieces. Demeter avenged her by causing a plague of bees to rise from her body.

Deborah is Hebrew for *bee*. Deborah's parentsmay have named her that for the desirable qualities of the bee: hard-working, unselfish, untiring, intelligent, and with a sting for her enemies. Deborah grew up true to her name, becoming a prophetess and the only female judge of the Israelites. She rendered her judgments and prophecies beneath a palm tree. Her army of 10,000 men defeated an enemy force that included 900 iron chariots. Like most hard-working female bees, she never bore a child.

Dubious Wisdom

When bees to distance wing their flight
Days are warm and skies are bright
But when their flight ends near their home
Stormy weather is sure to come.

From beavers,
bees should learn to mend their ways.
A bee works;
a beaver works and plays.

A swarm of bees in May
is worth a load of hay;
A swarm of bees in June
is worth a silver spoon.
a swarm of bees in July
is not worth a fly.

No bees,
no honey.
No work,
no money.

When you shoot an arrow of truth, dip its point in honey.

Arab Proverb

Where the honey, there the bees.

Latin Proverb

One bee is better than a handful of flies.

English Proverb

Bees that hae honey in their mouths hae stings in their tails.

Scottish Proverb

A man doesn't escape from bees with a lump of honey in his hand.

African Proverb

Bees do not become hornets.

Spanish Proverb

Bees touch no fading flowers.

French Proverb

The buzzing of flies does not turn them into bees.

Georgian Proverb

To be rich with bees and mares is to be rich and have nothing.

Sicilian Proverb

Three things you cannot comprehend: the mind of a woman, the working of the bees, and the ebb and flow of the tide.

Irish Proverb

He who would steal honey must not be afraid of bees.

Danish Proverb

Boys avoid the bees that stung them.

German Proverb

Not a single bee has ever sent you an invoice. And that is part of the problem—because most of what comes to us from nature is free, because it is not invoiced, because it is not priced, because it is not traded in markets, we tend to ignore it.

Pavan Sukhde

The bee is more honored than animals not because she labors but because she labors for others.

St. John Chrysostom

I don't like to hear cut-and-dried sermons. No, when I hear a man preach, I like to see him act as if he were fighting bees.

Abraham Lincoln

Every saint has a bee in his halo.

Elbert Hubbard

That which is not good for the beehive is not good for the bees.

Marcus Aurelius

Everything takes time. Bees have to move very fast to stay still.

David Foster Wallace

If bees disappeared off the face of the earth, man would have only four years to live.

Maurice Maeterlinck

Handle a book as a bee does a flower. Extract its sweetness but do not damage it.

John Muir

The keeping of bees is like the direction of sunbeams.

Henry David Thoreau

In the village, a sage should go about like a bee, which, not harming flower, color, or scent, flies off with the nectar.

Anonymous

To be successful, one has to be one of three bees: the queen bee, the hardest working bee, or the bee that does not fit in.

Suzy Kassem

For better or worse, honey bees are often much too busy to be bothered with personal reflection.

Susan Brackney

We think we can make honey without sharing in the fate of bees, but we are in truth nothing but poor bees, destined to accomplish our task and then die.

Muriel Barbery

Hope is the only bee that makes honey without flowers.

Robert Green Ingersoll

• In Central Europe, a bride-to-be will walk her groom past a bee-hive to test his faithfulness. If a bee stings him, the marriage is best called off.

• The Vikings believed that mead mixed with the blood of Kvasir created the Mead of Poetry. Whoever drank it would receive the gifts of poetry, wisdom, and immortality.

• The ancient Greeks considered bees "the birds of muse." They were also considered souls of the dead in transit between death and the next world.

• Ancient Greeks dabbed honey on lips of babies to promote eloquence and song—ideally even prophecy.

• If a bee landed on an ancient sleeping Greek child's lips, the child would become a poet or, at the very least, incapable of speaking or writing anything other than truth. Such was the fate of Plato, Pindar, and St. Ambrose, the saint of beekeepers,

• In the British Isles it is believed that bees hum a special hymn on Christmas Eve.

• In ancient Egypt, the bee represented the pharaoh's sovereignty over Lower Egypt.

• The Egyptian Temple of Neith, goddess of the night, was known as

"The House of the Bee."

• The Sanctuary of Osiris, god of the underworld and death, was "The Mansion of the Bee."

• There was a time when people believed the queen bee was a king.

• In Poland, Michel Wiscionsky was chosen king because bees landed on him during the election.

• In ancient Lithuania, Austeja was the bee goddess. Her husband, Bablilos, was the bee god.

• Hindus believe in Madhu-Vidya, the "Wisdom that Reveals Delight," or "Secret Honey" of the Creative Spirit or the Absolute. Madhu is Sanskrit for "honey." The word comes from the same Indo-European root as mead.

• In Britain and Ireland it was believed that if a bumblebee buzzed around your house or window, a visitor was coming. If anyone killed the bee, the visitor would bring bad news.

• In Wales it was believed that if bees made a home near yours, you would be prosperous. If a bee landed on your hand, you'd have good luck. If a bumblebee died in your home, it meant bad luck.

• A bumblebee on an English ship meant good luck.

• Lethargic bees augur misfortune; busy bees, good fortune.

• If you dream of getting stung by a bee, you will be betrayed by someone you know.

• In Britain, bees were invited to weddings and funerals, and if they didn't come, a piece of the wedding or wake cake was left at their hive.

• In England, a girl could prove her virginity by walking through a swarm of bees without getting stung.

History

The ancient names beginning with "Mel-" (Mellona, Melissa, Melisseus, etc.) go back to the Greek word *melitta*, bee, which descended into such words as mellitology (the study of bees), melliferous (producing honey), mellifluous (sounding smooth, like honey), and words meaning honey in other languages, such as *miel* (Spanish and French), *mel* (Portuguese), *miele* (Italian), *meli* (Corsican), *miere* (Romanian), мед (Russian), and *siwo myèl* (Haitian Creole).

Before there were beekeepers, bee hunters roamed the earth. As long as 25,000 years ago they were drawing pictures of the hunt on rocks in Spain, India, Australia, and southern Africa. The Cueva de la Araña in Valencia features drawings from 10,000 years ago depicting honey collection, bee swarms, and men on ladders to get at hives.

Medieval doctors recommended pouring honey in the ear to treat ear ailments. If honey didn't work—and it wasn't necessarily the first thing to try—other recommended ear douches included oil, vinegar, bile of rabbits and pigs, human milk, eggs of ants in onion juice, smoked seven-day-old goat urine, horse urine, warm water with entrails of spiders, and eel fat. None of these treatments are recommended by modern medicine, not even the goat urine, not even the honey. Not even on an in-law.

The queen bee was once presumed to be useless for she had no way to carry pollen, her tongue was too short to lap up nectar, and she could not produce wax. This apparent uselessness led Aristotle to conclude she was a king, not a queen.

Propolis, also known as bee glue, comes from the Greek *pro*, meaning *in the front of* and *polis*, meaning *city*.

Propolis has been used for medicinal purposes since at least 300 BC. The gummy, intensely flavorful substance was used by ancient Greek, Roman, Arab, and Incan physicians. Egyptians used it to embalm mummies. It is vaguely and uncertainly referred to in the Bible as balm and balsam.

Antonio Stradivari is believed to have used propolis as a varnish on his violins, some of which are over 300 years old.

No one knows when the first honey bees were brought from Europe to the New World, but it was certainly in the days when it took a sailing ship two months or more to make the crossing. The bees had to be confined the whole time. Since ships avoided sailing in the winter, when ice could ruin sails, the bees were awake and lively during the whole trip. They couldn't be released because as soon as the ship sailed a few feet, they'd never find their way back to the hive. When they finally reached the New World, they, like the passengers, were no doubt itching to see a flower.

Pre-Columbian Americans had no *Apis mellifera,* but they cultivated the *Apis melipona.* The melipona was a stingless bee, but a colony produced only a kilo of honey in a year, one-fiftieth that of the mellifera. Cortés made an interesting observation about the Americans of Cozumel, Mexico, in 1519:

> The only trade which the Indians have is in bee hives, and
> our Procurators will bear to Your Highness specimens of
> the honey and the bee hives that you may commend them
> to be examined.

Archeologists later determined that the Maya had been cultivating bees since about 300 BC. They had a bee god named Ah Mucan Cab. In modern times, peasants in Yucatán were using the same means to raise bees that the ancient Egyptians had used: hollow logs stacked on a rack.

April 28, 2013, was a big day for bees and beekeepers, at least in Europe. On that day, the European Union voted to ban neonicotinoid pesticides, which are deadly to bees, for at least two years. But with stiff corporate and agricultural resistance, only 15 of 27 voting nations voted for the ban. Opposition alleged weak science, the need for pesticides, and other possible explanations for a decline in bee populations, including climate change, disease, and loss of habitat.

Bees have less reason to celebrate in the United States, where neonicotinoids are still used, and 44 percent of all hives died in the winter of 2015-16. The next spring, pro-bee activists delivered 2.6 million dead bees to the U.S. Congress. But it takes more than 2.6 million dead bees to motivate Congress. There was no legislative response.

Aristotle, Plato, Virgil, Seneca, Erasmus, Shakespeare, Marx, and Tolstoy all considered the possibility that bee society might be a model for human society.

Said the ancient Greek Pappus: "Bees...by virtue of a certain geometrical forethought, knew that the hexagon is greater than the square and the triangle and will hold more honey for the same expenditure of material."

Gaius Plinius Secondus (23 AD - 79 AD), more commonly known as Pliny the Elder, author of *Naturalis Historia*, a set of 37 volumes that attempted to record the entire knowledge of the Roman Empire, described migratory beekeeping along the River Po in the 1st century AD. Hives were tubes of pottery, wicker, or wood that could be loaded on pack animals and boats. When food for bees was lacking in the immediate neighborhood, the inhabitants put their hives in boats and took them, by night, five miles upstream. The bees emerged at dawn, fed and by end of day returned to the boats. They changed the position of the boats until they sat low in the water under the weight of the honey. Then the boats were taken back and the honey harvested.

The same was done in ancient Egypt, where beekeeper petitions on papyrus requested that hives be moved by donkey instead of boat due to flooding.

Bees arrived in North America on ships from Europe. They moved west at about the same pace as settlers. By 1811, they were 600 miles up the Missouri River. By then, Indians already recognized bees as a bad harbinger. Wherever they were found, white settlers were soon to follow.

Rev. Charles Butler (1560-1647), a.k.a. the Father of English Beekeeping, a logician, grammarist, author, and Vicar of Wootton St. Lawrence, beekeeper, and author of The Feminine Monarchie (i.e. the queen bee) said: "The Drone which is a gross hive-bee without sting, has been alwaies reputed for a sluggard, and that worthily: for howsoever he brave it with his round velvet cappe, his side gown, his great paunch, and his lowd voice, yet is he but an idle person living by the sweat of others' brows. For he worketh not at al, ether at home or abroad, and yet spendeth as much as two labourers; you shal never finde his maw without a good drop of the purest nectar." Butler also spoke out against the inconsistency in spelling in the English language.

Nature

The study of bees is melittology.

The honey bee is classified thus:

Kingdom: *Animalia* (because they are multicellular, can move of their own volition, and ingest organisms or their products)

Phylum: *Arthropoda* (because they have an exoskeletons and no spines, segmented bodies with a pair of joined appendages for each segment)

Class: *Insecta* (because they have compound eyes, two antennae, and three body sections, one of which is a thorax with a pair of legs on each of three thoracic sections.

Order: *Hymenoptera* (because they have membranous (*hymen*) wings (*ptera*)

Family: *Apidae* (because it's a bee)

Subfamily: *Apinae* (because it has a pollen basket)

Genus: *Apis* (Latin for bee)

Species: *Apis mellifera* (from the Greek, *meli*, meaning honey, and the Latin, *fero*, meaning carry.

Officially—that is, nomenclaturally—*honey bee* should be two words, though less picky dictionaries tend to recognize *honeybee* as a word. The Integrated Taxonomic Information System of the Entomological Society of America, lists the *Apis mellifer*a as "honey bee." The term isn't like *dragonfly* and *butterfly*, which are each one word because they aren't flies.

The genus Apis can be divided into three branches based on how they nest.

Open nest bees: *Apis dorsata* and *Apis laboriosa*

Dwarf, single-comb bees: *Apis florae* and *Apis andreni-formis*

Cavity nest bees: *Apis cerana, Apis koschevnikovi, Apis nuluensis, Apis nigrocincta,* and *Apis mellifera.*

Bees are found throughout North America, from Arctic Alaska to tropical Florida and southern Mexico. They live in deserts, forests, meadows, and cities. The only places free of bees are the tops of high mountains.

Of the 20,000 species of bees in the world, about 4,000 species are native to North America.

The honey bee isn't one of the natives.

Honey bees forage from morning until evening. (Beekeepers often orient the hive opening to the east so the early sun shines in the door, all the sooner to tell the bees it's time to get to work.) Bees can remember what time higher food sources were available on a previous day, so on the subsequent day, they will forage more at that time. They generally spend less than five minutes at a foraging site.

Busy as a bee? Which bee? How about busy as bee researchers at the University of Illinois who set up five hives, each with about 2,000 day-old bees. They fastened tiny transponders to a bunch of the bees so they could count, with scanners, how many were going out to forage. They found that 20 percent of a hive's bees accounted for 50 percent of the foraging activity. In other words, there were a lot of less-busy bees. When the scientists killed a number of bees who had been going out to forage, other bees were replacing them within a day. Whether the less-active bees were lazy, occupied with indoor activities such as housekeeping and child-rearing, or just held back for emergencies was not determined. In any event, not all bees are as busy as beavers.

Pre-adult honey bees raised in high-aggression environments were found to be 10-15 percent more aggressive as adults. However, unlike humans and many other animals, the socially induced high aggression made the bees more resilient rather than less resilient to immune stressors such as, in the bees, neonicotinoid pesticides. Humans raised under high aggression would be more, not less, likely to suffer health problems.

Bees' lives are measured in days, not years. During the first three days of a bee's life, a worker bee is a chamber maid cleaning brood cells, but she will spend 20 percent of her day resting and 20 percent walking around. After age four, as her hypopharyngeal glands start secreting brood food, she becomes a nurse. By age 12, she knows how to sting and she goes to work in food storage, evaporating nectar to make it honey, packing pollen, building comb, and helping guard the hive entrance. At age 20, she's ready for dangerous work outside the hive, gathering pollen, nectar, water, and resin. By the time she's 28, she has worn her wings ragged and worked herself to death.

Isopentyl acetate (a.k.a. amyl acetate) is one of two alarm pheromones a honey bes can emit. She does so under two circumstances: when she takes a stinging posture, typically on the hive's front porch (tail raised and pointed outward, wings buzzing viciously), and when her stinger is ripped from her body. The alarm pheromone alerts other bees and hails guards to the entrance. But not all available bees show up to guard. Why not? One study determined that it might be a matter of individual personality.

The queen of the Arctic bumblebee *(Bombus polaris)* wears a thick coat and leads a hard life. Her workers die come winter. For the next nine months, she has to live alone in an almost lifeless torpor in a mouse nest or other underground burrow. She's pregnant the whole time. When the first Arctic poppies, Arctic roses, and Arctic willows blossom in the spring, she has to forage for herself. She warms herself with the exertion. Every day she has to go out for more food. She builds a little nest and a hatching chamber of pollen and wax. She covers the floor with a plug of dust and nectar and therein lays some 20 eggs. She shuts it up with more wax and dust. To keep it warm, she presses her belly to it and quivers her flight muscles. Ten days later, she does it again. By June, she has a colony, but by October, everybody's dead but her.

Africanized honey bees (AHB) cannot be distinguished from the common honey bees of North America with the naked eye. They fly at about the same speed—12-15 mph, depending on urgency. The AHB sting is no worse than that of the European bees most common in the United States. However, in defense of their hive, AHBs are ten times more likely to sting, will meet an attacker farther from the hive, and will chase him, her, or it a quarter mile or more.

The smallest bee, *Perdita minima*, is half the size of the eye of its largest cousin, the carpenter bee (*Xylocopa varipuncta*).

Honey bees flap their wings 230 times per second when hovering.

Flies have just one pair of wings; bees have two.

When a bee consumes nectar from a flower, she swallows it into a "honey stomach." This organ is not part of the digestive system. It has no exit other than the entrance.

Back at the hive, she regurgitates the nectar repeatedly, taking turns with other worker bees to lap it up and heave it out. This ingestive-regurgitative process, which can take 20 minutes, uses digestive enzymes to hydrolyze the sucrose of the nectar to form a mixture of glucose and fructose. Yes, honey is bee barf...but natural!

Honey bees are excellent pollinators, but since they evolved in Europe, they aren't especially adept at pollinating many North American food crops. Pumpkins, cherries, blueberries, and cranberries are all better pollinated by native bees.

Three-quarters of the fruits, nuts, and vegetables in North America are pollinated by bees. Corn is not one of them. Corn is pollinated by the wind, which is why planting just one row of corn won't lead to much of a crop.

The best bee for pollinating blueberries would be the *Habropoda laboriosa*. And laboriosa she is. Known among friends as the southeastern blueberry bee, she may pay a visit to 50,000 blueberry flowers in her lifetime, lugging around enough pollen to produce 6,000 blueberries—thirty to forty pints.

Matinal bees go out at dawn in search of flowers that bloom in the early hours. Crepuscular bees go out at twilight. Nocturnal bees fly by the light of the moon.

The *Habropoda laboriosa*, like the bumblebee, pollinates through buzz pollination, also known as sonication. Sonication is the only way some flowers can release their pollen, yet the technique is beyond the capability of honey bees. About eight percent of the world's flowers—some 20,000 species—hold their pollen tightly inside their tubular anthers. Among them are those of the eggplant, the potato, the tomato, the blueberry, and the cranberry. Wind might work with a tomato, and with a little luck and elbow grease, a honey bee might knock off a little pollen from berry flowers. But buzz pollinators are better at it. They know how to grab anthers with their jaws and twitch their flight muscles fast enough and hard enough to shake the pollen out of the anther. The action creates a buzz, but it's not the familiar flight buzz. It's more like the sound of a raspberry blown on the belly of a child. It has to be at just the right cycle to cause the pollen to vibrate inside the anther and shoot out the open end.

Bees are herbivores. Wasps, whose ranks include the yellow jacket and the hornet, generally life off nectar, but they need to feed their young meat, most often insects or spiders. Wasps came before bees, appearing in the Jurassic period when the first marine crocodiles were crawling from the sea, pterosaurs ruled the skies, and the first mammals crept meekly in forests of fern.

The life of wasps began to change about 125 million years ago, during the Cretaceous period. Today's continents were all one landmass called Gondwana, where the climate was warm and dry. Flowering plants began to appear. They developed colors and petals that attracted insects, which were better than the wind at pollination. Wasps, hunting for prey in blossoms, discovered the sweetness of nectar and the protein of pollen. Nectar and pollen put up less of a fight than animal prey, so wasps, pursuing an easier, sweeter life, gradually evolved into fuzzier insects with pollen baskets, longer tongues, and colonies adept at storing food for the future, the industrious little buggers we came to know as honey bees.

Some species of bees live independent of a swarm. They reproduce with a mate and raise their brood without the help of others. Other species, including the honey bee and bumblebee, can live only in societies reproduced en masse by a queen and raised by a crew of workers. In that these societal bees cannot survive alone, it can be said that the actual animal isn't the bee—it's the hive as a whole.

Cuckoo bees of various species are not known for their melodious song. Rather, like the cuckoo bird, they lay their eggs in the nests of others. In other words, they are parasites. Some cuckoo bee species kill the larva of their host bee, then insert their own in its place. Tthe larva eats the host's honey, maybe even the host's larva. Cuckoos are so dependent on the efforts of other bees that they have evolved out of their capacity to collect pollen, though they might stop by a flower for a sip of nectar.

Some species of bees have long tongues, others have short tongues. The former, which include honey bees, are adapted for probing into deep flowers. Those with shorter tongues would have to pass up a lily for the shallower florets of a sunflower.

After a queen lays an egg into a comb cell, worker bees pack it with a loaf of nectar, pollen, and spit. The nectar and pollen are food for the larva. The spit prevents bacterial and fungal infection.

The queen bee's stinger is not barbed, enabling her to sting other queens without getting her stinger ripped out, which would cause her death. Other than that, she isn't likely to sting anybody. But she could if she wanted, and more than once.

Queen bees are created at the discretion of worker bees.

The queen bee stays in her hive except to mate, which she may do 15 or 20 times during a single mating flight. She is not a queen in any sense of leadership, power, or privilege. She is more like a slave to those whom she has borne, fulfilling her sole function in life as fast as she can until she weakens, at which point her progeny gather round and kill her with suffocation and heat.

Male bees—the big, fat ones known as drones—have no known function other than sex. Even so, few of them will ever experience it, and those that do tend to have nothing but negative feelings about the brief relationship. Drones do not forage for food, care for the nest, raise the young, or defend the hive. Unlike females, they often leave the hive to take a nap outside. When winter comes, they assume they'll be welcome indoors, but there will be no mating until spring, so who needs them? Nobody. The females haul them outside and toss them over the edge, into the cold.

Drones mate with a queen during her mating flight. A fellow lucky enough to insert his endophallus into the queen and ejaculate therein will, upon retraction, have his endophallus and part of his abdomen ripped out. Sex is fatal to drones.

Bee bread is made by worker bees. The recipe calls for pollen, honey, and a dash of glandular secretion. Tucked into the comb, it ferments. The fermentation releases nutrients from the pollen and creates antibiotics and fatty acids that inhibit spoilage. One job of younger bees is to eat this bee bread, then secrete it through their hypopharynxes. The hypopharynx is a tiny globular gland near the jaw. This secretion is essentially bee spit, but it is known as royal jelly.

All bee larvae are fed a bit of royal jelly to get them going. Then they live on nectar and pollen. However, if workers build a special enlarged cell for a given larva, and pack it with royal jelly, the larva will grow larger and develop ovaries, becoming a queen capable of laying eggs. Humans can manipulate a hive to have more queen cells produced and thus more royal jelly. Royal jelly is typically collected when the larva is four days old. Carefully managed and harvested, a hive can produce a pound or more of royal jelly in a year. A pound of the stuff sells for around $65.00.

Royal jelly is reputed to improve human health, but there is little, if any, scientific evidence of such benefits.

Whenever possible, bees carry waste, including their dead, away from the hive. If, however, a large intruder, such as a mouse, dies in the hive, removal is not an option. The bees will therefore encase the corpse in propolis, embalming it so that it does not rot, stink, or fester. If you were to bite into such a mummy at room temperature, you would find it gummy, and it would stick to your teeth. At cooler temperatures it would be crunchy on the outside, chewy on the inside.

The chemical makeup of propolis varies widely depending on available local plants. The color and content of propolis varies according to local vegetation and time of year. Tree resin, whose function is to seal wounds and prevent infection in trees, is a favorite among bees. In temperate climes, bees look for conifers and poplars. In tropical regions, certain flowers offer banquets of resin. Propolis does for hives what resin does for trees. It seals cracks against intruders and inhibits the growth of bacteria. It also strengthens the hive, secures comb to a frame or other surface, and deters mites.

Propolis is about 50 percent resins and balsam, 30 percent beeswax, 10 percent essential and aromatic oils, five percent pollen, and 5 percent impurities. Among the over 300 botanical chemicals that can be found in propolis, depending on the season and the location of the hive, are lipophilic acaricides, polyprenylated benzophenones, viscidone, naphthoquinone epoxide, prenylated acids, 4-hydroxy-3,5-diprenyl cinnamic acid, sinapinic acid, 3-hydroxy-8,9-dimethoxypterocarpan, medicarpin isoferulic acid, caffeic acid phenethyl ester, chrysin, galangin, and pinocembrin.

A pound of worker bees numbers a little over 3,000 individuals.

A queen bee can lay 2,000 eggs a day.

A hive's bees will fly a total of 40,000 miles to produce a pound of honey.

A pound of honey has about 1,382 calories.

A pound of Honey Nut Cheerios has about 1,680 calories in about 4,160 Cheerios.

Apitoxin is what makes bee stings hurt so much. The most abundant active ingredient in apitoxin is melittin, but the most destructive ingredient is phospholipase A2. Mellitin is the same toxin present in snake venom. Apitoxin is stored in a venom sac that is attached to the stinger. When a bee stings, both stinger and sac are ripped from her abdomen. The stinger in honey bees (and only honey bees) is barbed, so it tends to stay in the victim's skin as the sac continues to pump venom through the stinger into the skin.

An experiment showed that bees, despite having brains no bigger than a sesame seed, can recognize human faces. The bees were presented with photographs of two faces. One face had sucrose in front of it, the other a quinine solution that is bitter to bees. Later, when the reward and punishment were removed, bees tended to go to the face that used to offer a reward. One bee got the "right answer" 93.9% of the time on the first day of training and 75.9% two days later. However, if the photos were turned upside down, performance declined significantly.

One ounce of honey would be enough to fuel a honey bee for a trip around the world. A 7-11 Super Big Gulp™ cup of honey would be enough to get two bees around the world once and then to the moon and back. A Super Big Gulp of Mountain Dew, on the other hand, would most certainly kill them both.

Is altruism genetic? An experiment with bees indicates the possibility.

Bees inherit certain genes from their mother, the queen. These are called matrigenes. Other genes, called patrigenes, are inherited from one of her several mates.

When a queen dies, some worker bees take their sisters' existing eggs and try to nourish them into queens. They don't know which of those eggs come from full sisters who had not only the same mother but the same father, and which had a different father. Odds are about 20:1 an egg carries the genes of a different father. They aren't, in other words, selfishly trying to pass on their own genes.

Other worker bees start to lay their own eggs, though they will inevitably become drones, i.e. males with the genes of their fathers. They aren't, in other words, altruistically doing what's best for the hive. They're doing what's best for propagaing their own DNA.

It turns out that workers who forego laying their own eggs carry matrigenes, while workers who lay their own eggs have the patrigenes.

In other words, genes seem to be directing this altruistic or self-promoting behavior. Matrigenes direct workers to altruistically reproduce someone else's genes for the good of the community. Patrigenes direct workers to pass on their own genes, the ones they inherited from their fathers.

Now the question is: Are there human genes direct people in the same way?

Studies have linked various stressors—pathogens, pesticides, malnutrition—to colony collapse. But scientists still wonder why the collapse sometimes happens so quickly. Two scientists looked into the question by using radio tracking to follow thousands of bees during their entire lifetimes.

They found that in hives under stress, bees went foraging at an earlier age rather than sticking to in-hive tasks until they were two or three weeks old. These "precocious foragers" completed fewer sorties in their lifetimes and died at an earlier age. That disrupted the hive's finely balanced social structure and division of labor. Hives were left with plenty of brood and food but too few adults. Child labor, it seems, is not a good idea even if it seems necessary.

Or maybe it's the manganese. People need a bit of it to stay healthy, but it doesn't take much more to cause people to suffer symptoms like those of Parkinson's disease. Manganese used to be pretty rare, but now it's a common industrial pollutant, so bees end up eating it, too. The same two scientists found that manganese affects bee brains, causing them to grow up sooner and start foraging at a younger age. But they end up making fewer trips to flowers before they die. It's too soon to say whether humans suffer similar symptoms from environmental manganese, but if manganese is harming bees, ultimately it's going to harm people who eat fruits and vegetables pollinated by bees.

Health

Honey should never be given to infants under the age of 12 months due to the possibility of infant botulism. Though most bacteria cannot survive in honey, honey can support *Clostridium botulinum* endospores. In infants, the spores produce endospores in the small intestines and from there pass into the bloodstream. One fifth of infant botulism is attributed to honey. Soil is a much more common source. The disease is readily treated under clinical care. Infant mortality rate is less than one percent among hospitalized infant patients. Symptoms first manifest as weakness in the facial muscles that control chewing, swallowing, eye movement, and eyelid support. The weakness then spreads to the arms and legs and can eventually impair respiration. So: no honey for the baby!

For millennia, honey has been used for medical treatment. Modern analysis confirms that honey is antibacterial. Oonly in 2010 A.D. did scientists figure out why. The antibacterial component is a compound called defensin-1. The bees put it in there. It comes from their own immune system.

Anaphylaxis, or anaphylactic shock, is a severe allergic reaction to any of many substances, including goods, medications, and the venom of bees and wasps. A first exposure does not result in an allergic reaction, but any subsequent exposure can do so. Symptoms can include rash, itchiness, swelling of the tongue or throat, and a drop in blood pressure with a consequent quickening of the heart rate. Loss of consciousness may result. In the United States, 500-1,000 people die of anaphylaxis each year. Treatment is an injection of epinephrine into the thigh muscle, often with an autoinjector. EpiPen is a common brand. Injection is followed by a quickening of the heart rate, a rise in blood pressure, and a feeling of chilliness in the blood. Additional injections are often necessary. Immediate medical attention is essential.

Though there are no clinical studies to prove it, honey may alleviate allergies to pollen. The theory is that the small amounts of pollen in honey can trigger an immune response that produces antibodies that deal with pollen. After repeated doses, the body may become accustomed to the pollen and therefore might produce less histamine and thus experience less allergic reaction. Such honey treatment should be with raw honey that has not been pasteurized or filtered to remove "impurities." *Do not, however, give honey to an infant under the age of one. See the note on page 74 regarding honey and botulism in infants.*

Honey, being high in antioxidants, may prevent cellular damage in the brain. One study showed that menopausal women taking 20 grams of honey a day had better short-term memory than similar women taking hormone pills.

Honey also helps the body absorb calcium, which is something the brain needs to function properly. Honey may prevent or delay dementia, though there are no studies to prove it.

A 2010 study ("Effect of Honey on Nocturnal Cough and Sleep Quality...") found that honey was more effective than a placebo in reducing a persistent cough in children. In other words, honey was better than nothing. The childre in the study received ten grams of honey half an hour before bedtime.

Another study with children age two and up with upper respiratory infections found that two teaspoons of honey was just as effective as dextromethorphan, the common over-the-counter cough medicine. *Note, however, that due to a risk of infant botulism, a very serious food poisoning, honey should never be given to a child under the age of one.*

Can honey treat dandruff and hair loss? Here's the abstract from a study in the European Journal of Medical Research, "Therapeutic and prophylactic effects of crude honey on chronic seborrheic dermatitis and dandruff."

Honey has antibacterial, antifungal and antioxidant activities and has high nutrient value. In this study we investigated the potential use of topical application of crude honey in the management of seborrheic dermatitis and dandruff. Thirty patients with chronic seborrheic dermatitis of scalp, face and front of chest were entered for study. Twenty patients were males and 10 were females. Their ages ranged between 15 and 60 years. The patients had scaling, itching and hair loss. The lesions were scaling macules, papules and dry white plaques with crust and fissures. The patients were asked to apply diluted crude honey (90% honey diluted in warm water) every other day on the lesions with gentle rubbing for 2-3 minutes. Honey was left for 3 hours before gentle rinsing with warm water. The patients were followed daily for itching, scaling, hair loss, and the lesions were examined. Treatment was continued for 4 weeks. The improved patients were included in a prophylactic phase, lasting six months. Half of the patients were treated with the topical honey once weekly and the other half served as control. All the patients responded markedly with application of honey. Itching was relieved and scaling disappeared within one week. Skin lesions were healed and disappeared completely within 2 weeks. In addition, patients showed subjective improvement in hair loss. None of the patients (15 patients) treated with honey application once weekly for six months showed relapse while the 12/15 patients who had no prophylactic treatment with honey experienced a relapse of the lesions 2-4 months after stopping treatment. It might be concluded that crude honey could markedly improve seborrheic dermatitis and associated hair loss and prevent relapse when applied weekly.

Honey has also been found to help people sleep. It causes a rise in insulin and serotonin. Serotonin is a neurotransmitter that improves mood and happiness. The body converts serotonin into melatonin, which regulates sleep. Honey also contains tryptophan, the same soporific component found in turkey that results in sleepiness after a Thanksgiving meal. The body converts tryptophan into serotonin and then serotonin into melatonin. So why cook a turkey on Thanksgiving? Just have some honey!

A clinical review in the British Medical Journal, "Oesophagus: Heartburn and Honey," reported that honey can help prevent gastro-oesophageal reflux and may relieve heartburn.

In general, the darker the honey, the stronger its antibacterial and antioxidant power.

Aside from its nutritional value, honey is no better than white sugar or brown sugar for people on diets or people with diabetes. In terms of calories, the sugar part of honey has the same effects as cane sugar.

Beekeeping

Bees are the only domesticated insect and the only insect that produces food for humans. The closest thing to exceptions would be in cultures where people eat actual insects, such as ants and grasshoppers. There have also been flea circuses involving actual fleas trapped in harnesses. Ants have also been used for entertainment and observation purposes in "ant farm" toys. But bees are the only real insect farm animals.

Yao honeyhunters in modern Mozambique follow a woodpecker-like bird known as the honeyguide. Honeyhunters and honeyguides communicate with each other as the bird leads the hunter to hives that are high in trees. The Yao, a Bantu Muslim people of southeast Africa, first recruit the birds by trilling *brrrrr* and then grunting *hmmm*. When the honeyguide finds a hive—easy for them thanks to their extra large olfactory bulb—it finds a Yao and flies low, singing a *Let's Go* song. The hunters follow the guide until it sings a *Here It Is* song and flicks its white tail. Then the hunters wrap dry wood in a banana leaf attached to the end of a long pole. Then they ignite leaf and wood and extend the pole up to the hive. Once the bees are smoked out, the hunters chop the tree down. The hunters get the honey and leave the wax for the bird. This is a rare case of wild animals helping humans hunt in return for payment.

The type of hive used by most modern beekeepers is called a Langstroth hive, named for its inventor, Lorenzo Lorraine Langstroth (1810-1895). Langstroth patented his invention in 1851. The hive design induces bees to build comb on frames that can be individually moved, removed, or replaced. The hives and frames are of standard measurement, making the parts interchangeable.

Typically a Langstroth hive has two brood chambers—two boxes each of which are 9-9/16 inches deep. Ten frames, 9 inches deep, hang from a rim near the top of the box. One brood chamber sits atop the other. This combined space is mostly dedicated to the laying of eggs and rearing of brood.

One or more supers sit atop the brood chambers. These medium-depth boxes, typically 6-5/8 inches deep, hold ten frames that are dedicated to the storage of honey.

A medium-depth frame holds about six pounds of honey. A deep frame from the brood chamber holds about eight pounds. A fully laden bee hive, in a good year, may weigh as much as a cubic meter of freshly fallen snow, two baby elephants, 30 full-grown Dachshunds, five toilets, or one-four-hundredth of the Space Shuttle.

Chimpanzees have been observed using tools to raid bee nests, but some in the Congo Basin are especially good at it. The use of hollow dipsticks to pull honey from a nest is fairly common. But Congo chimps have used clubs to pound on hives and sticks to lever open sealed nests. Congo chimps also rotate sticks to drill into nests and use strips of bark to scoop honey. They use leafy twigs to whisk or swat bees off themselves. They've also used sticks to dig up colonies in the ground. In that these skills seem to be regional, these technologies may be traditions passed on by communities. Traditions imply culture and even history—elements of humanity which may not be restricted to humans.

As of 2013, propolis is mentioned in 2,884 patents. The first patented use was in 1904. Incidence soared at the turn of the 21st century. China filed the most patents, followed by Japan, Korea, and Russia. About six percent of patents involving propolis are for dental treatments.

Brazil exported 91,979 pounds of propolis in 2012, with Japan its biggest buyer. Presumably most of it was the product of Africanized "killer bees," though that would make no difference in the quality of the product.

Marie Therese Bourgeois Chouteau, known as "la Mere de St. Louis" and said to be the first white woman to settle in Missouri, is reputed to have had the first honey bees brought to the territory. As the story goes, someone brought her a gift of a comb of honey from Illinois. She'd never known of the stuff, so she sent a trustworthy black man to find out the secret of it. He returned to report that it came from "a kind of fly." He brought back a box of the strange flies for her to raise. She became Missouri's first beekeeper.

Smoke pacifies bees by threatening an imminent danger of fire. The bees gorge on honey with the expectation of needing to fly it away to safety. Their full bellies make them a little sluggish and less aggressive. The smoke also masks the pheromones that bees release to alert their compatriots to danger.

According to the Food and Agriculture Organization of the U.N., the world is known to have produced 1,663,798 tons of honey in 2013. (An unknown additional quantity was produced in countries that did not report production.) China produced 450,300 tons of honey. The next biggest producers were Turkey (94,694 tons), Argentina (80,000 tons) and Ukraine (73,713 tons). The United States produced 67,812 tons. The Americas as a whole produced only 20 percent of the world's honey that year. Afghanistan produced 2,000 tons—not bad, considering.

To make a beard of bees, grab a queen from a hive and clip her to a man's beard. In short order, all the bees will leave the hive to come join her, draping themselves around her. Since they are not defending a hive at that point, they are nonaggressive. Still, removing the beard of bees can be a bit tricky. The queen must be located in the draping, writhing wad, unclipped without losing her, and returned to the hive, where her family will soon join her and see that she gets back to work.

In 2012, a dozen French beekeepers around the town of Ribeauville became understandably concerned when they found their bees producing honey in a variety of bright colors. They traced the color to a biogas plant that turned organic materials, including industrial waste, into methane. The plant, 2.5 miles away, was processing M&Ms, the little melt-in-your-mouth-not-in-your-hand candies from Mars company. Bees were eating the crunchy shells and bringing them home. While it might seem like a perfect opportunity to produce tutti-frutti honey candy, the contents were too questionable, so the honey had to be discarded.

Ethiopia has two million households that practice beekeeping as their primary livelihood. No single ethnic groupin Ehtiopia does not practice beekeeping. The nation produces the most honey of any African nation and ranks ninth in the world. It ranks third in the world in production of beeswax, after China and Mexico. Still, per-hive production is low, just 11-17 lbs. per year, perhaps because 90 percent of colonies are in "traditional" hives, tubes that do not use frames. Langstroth hives produce an average of over 72 lbs. per year. Eighty-five percent of the honey produced in Ethiopia is used to brew *tej*, a honey wine.

The USDA reports that over half of the honey sold in the U.S. is imported. In 2014 the country imported more than $547 million worth of honey. "Honey laundering" makes it difficult or impossible to determine where a given jar of honey comes from. Since sources are impossible to identify, much (an unknowable amount) of the imported honey is contaminated with sugars, heavy metals, or antibiotics.

Frequently Asked Questions

Q: Do bees have knees?

A: Bees have six jointed legs but no kneecaps, which basically means no knees.

Q: Can bees see color?

A: Bees can see better at the blue end of the spectrum, including ultraviolet light, which flowers tend to reflect. But bees can't see the color at the red end of the spectrum. They know a violet's violet but never suspect a rose is red. Sugar, they are sure, is sweet.

Q: How far can a honey bee fly?

A: No farther than necessary, but a really hungry honey bee can fly five miles to food.

Q: How high can a honey bee fly?

A: No higher than necessary to get over an obstacle. But a desperate drone on a mating flight will fly up over 250 feet for a shot at the queen. If successful, regardless of height, he will be dead before he hits the ground, his endophallus remaining with the queen.

Q: What should I do if I'm being chased by a swarm of bees?

A: The best thing to do is wake up. The bees will instantly vanish. In real life, a swarm of bees does not chase anyone. If you are being pestered by a lot of bees, you are probably near a hive. Walk away, slapping yourself as you go. If it's an actual swarm—a mass of thousands of bees flying in formation or hanging in a wad on a branch—they are in no mood to sting. They are looking for a home. Temporarily homeless, they have no home to defend and therefore no reason to sting. If you wait long enough, the swarm will go away. *Do not kill the swarm.* If you know a beekeeper, he or she will probably be very happy to come get the bees.

Q: Suppose there's a hive of honey bees living in the ground of my yard or making a nest under the eave of my house...what should I do?

A: Honey bees don't live in the ground or under eaves. If they're in the ground, they are probably yellow jackets. If they are under an eave in a papery nest, they are wasps. Neither yellow jackets nor wasps honey, and they sting without a lot of provocation. You'd best get rid of them. If they really are honey bees, call a beekeeper.

Q: What are the advantages of local honey?

A: There is a theory that local honey helps prevent allergies. This is scientifically unproven, but there are many anecdotal cases of people claiming beneficial effects. A good reason to buy local honey is that small-scale beekeepers respect their honey and their bees. They aren't likely to ruin the honey by boiling it or micro-filtering it. They probably don't add sugars to stretch it.

Most honeys sold on an industrial scale have been boiled (to prevent it from crystallizing) or micro-filtered, which removes most of the elements that make honey honey. This is why "supermarket honey" tastes different from real, untreated honey. Another good reason to buy local honey is that beekeepers help bees survive, which helps the pollination of local plants.

Q: How can I become a highly respected member of my community?

A: Become a beekeeper. The best way to start is to find a beekeepers association. A quick search of the Internet or social media will probably turn up a few contacts. You'll also need a good book or two.

Q: What do I need to get started in beekeeping? How much does it cost?

A: You need a complete hive with frames for the bees to build comb on. That costs about $150. You will also need a package of bees. A package is a box with screens on two sides. They usually come with a queen in a small cage inside the package. Depending on where you live, a 3-lb. package costs around $75-$125. Prepare to start your beehive in the spring. A search of the Internet will turn up many companies that sell beekeeping equipment and others that sell packages of bees that can be ordered by mail or from a local distributor. In eastern Connecticut, that would be Stonewall Apiary in Hanover. (See ct-honey.com.) Stonewall Apiary ships honey and equipment but not bees, which have to be picked up on specific dates.

Q: Where's a good place for a beehive?

A: Outdoors. Shade would be nice in a place of brutal sun. Under a linden tree would be heaven to bees. Don't worry about the bees bothering people. Worry about people bothering the bees. Note that you will need to be able to prevent vegetation from blocking the entrance.

Installing Bee Packages

A bee package consists of three pounds of bees in a box with screen on two sides. You want to install those bees as soon as you get them. You can see the bees in there, eager to get out and get back to normal life. You can also see a can in there, hanging from the top. It's full of sugar water from which the bees have been sipping through little holes in the bottom. Beside the can hangs the queen cage, a little box the size of a clumsy carpenter's thumb.

(If you have received a queen only, without a package, to replace an old queen, the instructions are basically the same. Just make sure there is no queen in the hive or the new queen and the resident queen will end up fighting until one of the two is dead. If there's still an old queen in the hive, find her, thank her for her service, then behead her and leave her body outside the hive near the entrance so her loyal subjects get the message.)

The queen is in a cage because she is not the natural, original queen of the bees she is with. The bees in the package still see her as an intruder. If she weren't in a cage, they'd kill her. The complication of installing a package of bees is the process of not releasing the queen until she's accepted as one of the gang. Here's how:

1. Take the package to a hive that is all set up and ready to go, including a feeder with sugar water. A pollen patty would be good, too. This hive should be just a single brood chamber, or, better, a

nuc (short for "nucleus," a small hive with only five frames). A nuc's smaller size makes it easier for a small swarm to keep itself warm. Remove the top from the hive or nuc. Remove the inner cover. Remove a frame from the middle of the set of frames. Ideally, this frame will have comb on it. (Beg or buy a few frames with comb from another beekeeper. It will help a lot because the queen will immediately have somewhere to lay eggs.) In the upper part of the comb, in the corner that will be at the back of the hive, carve out a vertical space big enough for a queen cage, about an inch wide and three inches long. If the frame has no comb, see below.

2. Now it's time to get the queen cage out of the package. Pry up the flat piece of wood at the top of the package. See the can. See the silvery disk next to it. From that disk hangs the queen cage. If you pull it up, bees will start flowing up through the hole, each and every one of them in a bad mood. If you fail to prevent that, you'll be in a bad mood, too. So give the package a solid thump on the ground or the top of the hive. The bees will fall to the bottom of the box in a mass of confusion. This will give you a few seconds to pull up the queen cage and quickly set the flat piece of wood back over the hole before bees come flying out.

3. Look at that queen! Isn't she beautiful? She's long, slender and tan, like a girl from Ipanema with six legs, diaphanous wings, and a spermatheca ready to go. Look at her wiggle in there with her comfort maids. If the queen isn't wiggling, you've got yourself a dead queen and a real problem. Call a beekeeper or the jerk who sold you the bees. You need a queen, and quick.

4. There are two ends to the queen cage, each with a short tunnel capped with a tiny cork. You can't see the cork on one side because of the silvery disk that is nailed over it. Pull that disk off. Now you can see how one tunnel is packed with a white candy. The idea is, the queen and her attendants are going to start eating her way through that tunnel while the bees outside start eating their way in. By the time they meet, the queen and the bees will have been in the hive long enough to become friends. The drones, of course, will be going absolutely nuts. So pull the cork out of the candy tunnel. Leave the other cork in place! It's an emergency exit. We'll get to that.

5. Nestle that queen cage into the place you carved in the comb. Best to put the candy tunnel facing up. This is so that if a bee dies inside the cage, her body doesn't block the tunnel. Set the cage so that the screened part faces the inside of the hive. This is so the bees can see and tend to their queen. Carefully set the frame back in place in the hive. Give the bees a pollen patty to help them produce comb. Put the inner cover on.

6. Now's the part where you might get stung. Once again, thump the package on the ground (not on the hive) so all the bees tumble down again. Now you've got a few seconds to pull that can out of its hole. This can be tricky. You'll need your hive tool or knife blade and some fingernails to pull it up far enough to get your ungloved fingers around it. Pull it up. Slap the wooden top over the hole. Did you get stung? Well, too bad. You're a beekeeper. What were you expecting? Utter the curse of your choice, pull the stinger out, and move on.

7. Now to let the bees go into the hive. Thump them down to the bottom of the package. Remove the wooden top and lay the box upside

down on the inner cover so that the feeding–can hole is over the inner cover hole. Now the bees' only way out is into the hive, which is surely where they will go. It might take them an hour or two to make the move, but they'll like it in there. It smells good, there's some sugar water, it's nice and dark, and there's a queen who ain't bad lookin' even if she still smells a little funny. Why go anywhere else?

8. Go get something to sit on and a beer, unless you're a Mormon, many of whom are beekeepers, and for good reasons. They and other teetotalers might appreciate a lemonade at this wonderful moment. Have a seat near the front of the hive. Drink your chosen beverage. You deserve it. You're a beekeeper, and you've just done the world a favor.

9. Before dark, put the hive cover back on. Leave that hive alone for three days. After that, puff a bit of smoke in the entrance and gently, furtively, pull off the top and inner cover. Check to see if the queen got out. If she didn't, pop the cork from the emergency exit and put the cage back. If she's out, you can assume she's doing her business. Remove the empty queen cage and close up the hive. Go read a book about beekeeping and see what you have to do next.

A Cat Caboodle

A Long Whiskered History

A Biblical Dearth of Felines

The Bible mentions all sorts of animals, from camels to cankerworms, moles to mules, pelicans to porcupines, whales, weasels, wolves, vipers, adders, asps, satyrs, unicorns, griffins, lamia, sea monsters, pyargs, plungers, lammergeyers, mouflons, and sciniphs, but there's just one mention of a cat (other than lions, leopards and such), and biblical scholars aren't even sure it actually refers to a cat. The Common English Bible and a few other versions have a Book of Baruch or a Letter of Jeremiah, verse 21 of which says "Bats, swallows, birds, and cats land on their bodies and heads." It is referring to the bodies and heads of idols, which Jews are being advised not to worship as gods because these animals disrespect (or possibly defecate on) them. But some analysts of the Bible suspect that it isn't really referring to cats at all, that something got lost in the translation of a document that no one has actually seen. No one knows the old Hebrew word for "cat," so it's hard to know how to translate it.

One explanation for the lack of cats in the Bible is that the Jews never had any, possibly didn't even know about them, that they used some kind of weasel to control mice. But the Jews spent a lot of time in Egypt, which is famous for its worship of cats. Maybe the Egyptian worship of cats caused the Jews, who believed in Yahweh and nobody but, to shun cats as they did golden calves and other idols.

Is "Domestic Cat" an Oxymoron?

Five kinds of wild cat (*Felis silvestris*) roamed the Old World thousands of years ago. Only one of them, *Felis silvestris lybica*, succumbed to the temptations of domestication. All domesticated cats descend from this subspecies.

But pet cats have a tendency to take a walk on the wild side. They head into the woods and mate with wild subspecies. Their descendants often end up back on somebody's couch. So genetically, house cats aren't that much different from the wild cats of neolithic times.[1]

The Cats of Yore

Scientists aren't sure how cats became domesticated pets rather than wild animals. The best guess is that domestication began around the time people began farming grains. Stored grain attracted rodents, and rodents attracted cats. The cats were probably encouraged to stay. Before long, somebody fell in love with a kitten—who can resist?—and the next thing you know, our furry feline friends are draped over the top of television sets and coughing up hairballs on a Persian rug.

Actually, they probably started coughing up hairballs on Cyprian rugs some 9,500 years ago. At around that time, somebody was buried with a beloved cat. We suspect it was beloved because its skeleton was found surrounded by carved sea shells just a couple of feet from the person.

But that was Cyprus. The story was different in China. Some 5,000 years ago, people were throwing dead cats in the local garbage pit. Archeological analysis determined that these cats had been eating rodents. But they had also been eating grains, which might indicate that they were being fed human food. If so, maybe they were pets, maybe just bred for food or fur. The presence of cat remains in a garbage pit seems to indicate an early stage of domestication.

Cats were domesticated in Egypt and China at around the same time. One big question scientists are trying to answer is whether domesticated Egyptian cats were taken to China along ancient trade routes, or whether the Chinese also domesticated a wild subspecies. When DNA testing revealed that the Chinese cats were of the leopard cat family, scientists started leaning toward a supposition that there may be two separate domestications.[2]

Little Mummies

In ancient Egypt, killing a cat was a crime punishable by death.

Back then, cats were mummified, and embalmed mice were placed with them in their tombs. In one ancient city, over 300,000 cat mummies were found. Many of them were stripped of their wrappings and sold to farmers in England and the U.S. to be ground up and used as fertilizer.[3]

Sacred cats turned out to be a problem at the battle of Pelusium in 525 BCE. Pelusium was the last stronghold of the Pharaohs before the Egyptian capital, Memphis. Thanks to an Egyptian traitor, the Persian general Cambyses II knew that the Egyptians worshiped cats and would not under any circumstances harm one. So he got a bunch of cats and had his army carry them or drive them before them as they went into battle. The Egyptians, afraid of hurting the cats, could not shoot arrows at the invaders. Pelusium fell, as did Memphis. The Pharaoh was captured, Cambyses took the throne, and the mighty Egyptian empire became Persian. Because of cats.

How the World Once Was

The Middle Ages was a crazy—arguably lousy—time to be alive, especially if you were a cat. During the Festival of Saint John, cats were burned alive in town squares, sometimes in bags, sometimes suspended from poles, sometimes burned at a stake. In a mock ceremony, a garrison of riflemen would shoot off a salute as the cats yowled in the flames. In Saint Chamond, it was fun to light a cat on fire and chase it down the streets. Pre-Lenten Carnaval time was bad for cats, too. In Burgundy, drunken louts incorporated cats into their crude music, tearing flesh from a cat as if playing a musical instrument. Germans had similar fun. They called it *Katzenmusik*.[4]

In 1484 Pope Innocent VIII issued a papal bull granting local officials the right to punish witches (male and female) as they felt necessary. He also declared cats evil, leading to their widespread slaughter. The absence of cats is reputed to have allowed the rat population to increase, leading to a bubonic plague, but there were no major outbreaks in the century following Innocent's declaration.

Cats Ahoy!

From ancient times to modern, ships have kept a cat aboard. In fact, the spread of domesticated cats from ancient Egypt to elsewhere generally followed shipping routes.[5] By the 8th century, even Viking ships were carrying cats on their voyages of plunder and invasion.[6]

The so-called "ship's cat" was such an essential part of a ship's equipment that the cat's presence was no more notable than the presence of a mop. But a few ship logs have noted that a ship had to put in to shore to get a new cat because the ship's cat had died.

The ship's cat had several jobs. Primary was the control of rats. In the absence of a cat, rats would eat cargo, food supplies, ropes, furled sails, and even the wood the ship was made of. Even today, rats on a ship will chew at electrical wiring. Rats also carried the fleas that carried the bacterium of the bubonic plague. The British navy required the presence of a cat aboard every ship until 1975.[7]

A cat was also a comfort. Its soft fur, its calming purr, and its willingness to share affection were much appreciated by a crew long at sea. No wonder cats became the subject of superstitions. Wives of sailors often kept a black cat at home, believing its magical powers could protect a ship at sea. If a cat appeared on deck and approached a sailor, it meant good luck. If the cat came only part way and turned around, bad luck was in the offing. If a cat licked its fur against the grain, it predicted hail. If a cat fell overboard, it would summon a storm. And God save the ship if somebody actually threw the cat overboard.

There may be some truth to the claim that friskiness or a rubbing of the ears foretold wind. Cats' sensitive inner ears may be able to detect changes in barometric pressure, and experience with fearful thunderstorms may teach them that a drop in pressure indicates the approach of meteorological trouble. It was good to know.[8]

Famous Ship's Cats

Blackie served on the *HMS Prince of Wales*. When the ship carried Prime Minister Winston Churchill to Newfoundland in 1941 to negotiate U.S. assistance in the war with Germany, Blackie was there. As Churchill was disembarking, Blackie stepped forward. Churchill stooped to give him a good-bye pat. Later, when the ship was sunk by Japanese warplanes in the Pacific, Blackie survived and made it to Singapore, where he disappeared.[9]

Chibbley was rescued from an animal shelter before serving on the tall ship *Picton Castle*. She circumnavigated the world five times, sailing some 180,000 miles before expiring in 2011.

Emmy, an orange tabby, worked on *RMS Empress of Ireland*, a Canadian passenger ship which, after its ninety-sixth voyage, was nicknamed "Canada's Titanic." Emmy was on board for many voyages, but as the *Empress* was leaving Quebec City on her ninety-sixth voyage, Emmy jumped ship, leaving her kittens behind. Crew brought her back, but again she fled. The ship left without her, but before it left the St. Lawrence River, it struck a freighter and sank within 14 minutes, taking 1,012 passengers and a litter of kittens to their deaths.[10]

Convoy, so named after his many Atlantic crossings with military escorts, was listed as a sailor and slept in a custom-made hammock. He and 87 other crew members died in 1942 when *HMS Hermione* was torpedoed by a German U-boat.

Jenny was transferred from the *Olympic* to the *Titanic* for the latter's maiden voyage. She had a litter of kittens before the ship left. The furry little family met the same fate as John Jacob Astor IV, Benjamin Guggenheim, and 1,501 other people.

Mrs. Chippy, a male, tiger-striped tabby, was aboard Earnest Shackleton's *Endurance*. Mrs. Chippy was so named because the ship's carpenter, Harry "Chippy" McNish, had brought him aboard. It was only later that they discovered Mrs. Chippy wasn't a female. But Chippy loved him nonetheless. The cat was admired for his ability to walk along inch-wide railings even during rough seas. When the *Endurance* was trapped and crushed in Antarctic ice, the crew had to prepare for a long, hard journey. So Shackleton had five sled dogs and Mrs. Chippy shot.[11] Though angry over the fate of his tabby pal, Chippy built the boats that took the crew to safety. The New Zealand Antarctic Society put a bronze statue of Mrs. Chippy on Chippy's previously unmarked grave.[12] In 2011 Mrs. Chippy appeared on a postage stamp issued by South Georgia and The Sandwich Islands. He is also the subject of an opera, *Shackleton's Cat.*

Oscar was the ship's cat on the German battleship *Bismarck* until it was sunk in 1941, killing all but 116 of over 2,200 crew members, or 117, counting Oscar. The *HMS Cossack* found Oscar floating on a plank and rescued him along with 114 other Germans. Oscar went on to serve on escort missions in the Mediterranean and North Atlantic. A few months after Oscar was rescued, a German submarine torpedoed the *Cossack*, killing 159 crewmen. Oscar and other survivors were transferred to the *HMS Legion* before the *Cossack* sank west of Gibraltar. From there, Oscar, now known to all as "Unsinkable Sam," was assigned to the aircraft carrier *HMS Ark Royal*. A year later, the *Ark Royal* was sunk by another U-boat. All but one of the crew survived, and Sam was found floating on a plank in a mood that was described as "angry." Sam was transferred to the *Lightning* and then to the *Legion*, which had rescued the survivors of the *Cossack*. Sam was back in the United Kingdom before the *Lightning* and *Legion* were sunk in subsequent attacks. Sam died in Belfast in 1955. (There is some controversy over whether any of this actually happened, but a portrait of Sam hangs in the National Maritime Museum in Greenwich.)[13]

The Dickin Medal

In 1943, Maria Dickin, founder of the People's Dispensary for Sick Animals, instituted The Dickin Medal. It was awarded to animals for acts of bravery or devotion in the line of military duty. Dickin Medals have been awarded to 32 pigeons, 29 dogs, three horses, but just one cat.

The sole feline medalist was Simon, who had been discovered in the dockyards of Hong Kong in 1948. A sympathetic sailor snuck him aboard the frigate *HMS Amethyst*. Simon befriended the crew and commander and was happily ridding the ship of mice as it went up the Yangtze River toward Nanking. Along the way, a communist gun battery fired on the ship. A shell went through the commander's cabin, killing the commander and badly wounding Simon. Though medical staff did not expect Simon to survive, they treated him for burns and removed four pieces of shrapnel. Simon, being a cat, survived. During his recovery, the ship was overrun with rats as it lay at anchor. Once up, Simon got back to work and soon dispensed with the vermin. His strength and persistence boosted the morale of his shipmates. He was awarded not just the Dickin Medal but the Blue Cross and the Amethyst campaign medal. Returning to England, he was put in mandatory quarantine, where he contracted a virus. He died on November 28, 1949 and was buried with full honors at a well attended funeral.[14]

Cats in the Trenches

An estimated 500,000 British cats were deployed to the trenches of World War I to control rats that were eating supplies, spreading disease, and even chewing on dead and wounded soldiers. Terriers were also recruited and to some extent were more efficient than cats. While cats tended to play with their catch and then take time to eat it, terriers would kill one and then move on to the next. The dogs were also more capable of dealing with the really big rats.

The Fate of Medieval Furballs

Zooarcheologists studying a medieval site in Spain found 899 cat bones. This is not unusual for a site of those times, which were estimated as "the end of the 10th century A.D. and the beginning of the 11th century A.D." Though that phrase makes little sense, the bones themselves revealed something interesting and sad. The cats had apparently been skinned, probably for their fur.[16] In the economy and morality of those moments between centuries, cats were no more significant than weasels or mink.

Rutherford's Siamese

Siam was the first Siamese Cat to reach the United States of America. The female cat was a gift from the American Consul in Bangkok to Lucy Hayes, the wife of the American President, Rutherford B. Hayes, in 1878. This required a two-month trip in a Wells Fargo crate, first by ship to Hong Kong and thence to San Francisco. From there the cat had to cross the continental United States by land.

Mrs. Hayes named the mahogany-colored cat Miss Pussy. Miss Pussy had the run of the White House and became fast friends with the presidential daughter, Fanny. Siam had a regal way of entering a room, so Mrs. Hayes renamed her Siam, the name of the country of her origin, where the breed was a royal pet, not to mention an official guard of Buddhist temples.

In the autumn of 1879, just a few months after arriving in Washington, Siam, took ill. White House staff tried to feed her fish, chicken, duck, cream, and oysters, but Siam only got worse. Dr. J. H. Baxter, the president's personal physician, was called in. He prescribed beef tea and milk every three hours. Siam showed no improvement. The doctor took Siam home for personal care. There Nellie McCrary, daughter of the Secretary of War, visited the patient. She sent a note to her friend Fanny, saying, "[Dr. Baxter] thinks she will die and I do to (sic)."

Five days later, the presidential cat expired. Siam's body was delivered to the Secretary of Agriculture to be taxidermically preserved. In all likelihood Siam did get properly stuffed, but, much in the way of cats, he has disappeared. He's not in the Rutherford B. Hayes Museum. He's not in the Smithsonian. Where could he be?[15]

Felis Municipalis

New York City's City Hall has had many feline residents. The most famous was Tammany. Mayor Jimmy Walker found Tammany on the streets of the Lower East Side around 1930. City Hall had a rat problem (not to mention a Tammany problem, that is, the Tammany Society that ran the corrupt Democratic machine that controlled city politics), so Mayor Walker brought the cat home.

Tammany had all the rats he could eat, but to ensure a balanced diet, the municipal budget had a line item for calf livers for the City Hall exterminator.

Tammany did a good job. He was reputed to be so tough that no rat of any size could escape his claws. New York loved tough then as much as now, so Tammany became quite the celebrity. His habit of hanging out in the reporters' room facilitated his publicity. He was often photographed sleeping on desks, prowling the halls, and strolling into public meetings.

When Fiorello LaGuardia became the city's 99th mayor, he pushed for "anti-Tammany" reform. But that applied to politics, not cats. A front page headline in the New York Sun declared "City Hall Cat's Job Saved Under LaGuardia."

LaGuardia also ran on a budget-cutting platform, so he felt compelled to do away with the city-funded cat food. The mayor also promised a "fusion" of political parties and allowed a cat by the name of Fusion to take up residence on Tammany's turf.

One dark and stormy night, Fusion disappeared without a trace.

Then one day the Commissioner of Public Buildings, Edward Markham, said the cat had to go. Deputy Mayor Henry Hastings Curran put his foot down. In a letter typed by Tammany himself (in case you don't believe it, there's a photograph of him at the typewriter in the reporters' room), Curran predicted a major battle if the ASPCA tried to evict Tammany. "The carnage will be cheerful, instantaneous, and complete," Curran said. "Let them come!"

Though a veteran of World War I, Markham apparently lost the battle with Tammany. Within a year, Markham fled to Chicago.

On April 10, 1939, Tammany was found suffering great pain in a City Hall phone booth. He was taken to an animal hospital under police escort. He was found to be suffering from bladder stones. He died the next morning and was buried on a country estate in Scarborough-on-Hudson.[17]

Felis Mafiosis

Also in the Where-but-New-York section is a story reported in the *New York Sun* in 1911 and 1914. Apparently there was something of a butcher battle going on not far from the Brooklyn Bridge. First, in 1911, a homemade bomb went off in front of a Jewish butcher shop on James St. The Italians of a butcher shop across the street were suspected. In 1914, a cop walking past a butcher shop at the same address heard a strange and horrifying noise coming from inside the shop. Recalling the 1911 incident, he rallied other cops to come investigate.

The cops couldn't get in, but they were able to heft a skinny young man through a narrow transom window. He was immediately assaulted by 25 cats who were attacking each other while trying to consume all the meat in the shop. As the Sun reported, "The cats were of all sizes and colors. They had been hungry, but they were no longer. They had eaten every scrap of meat in the market—chicken and beef and everything else, and were fighting over the bones."

Though wounded enough to need hospitalization, the boy managed to open the door. Only with great effort and courage were the police and several civilians able to dispatch the cats, who ran off with meat in their mouths. Also evicted were two resident mousers who had been taught not to eat meat unless they killed it themselves. The police theorized that a rival butcher had inserted the cats through the transom in order to ruin the business.

With classic New York tabloid alliteration, the Evening World reported the incident as if it had witnessed it all: "The first cat pushed through the transom was pounced on by the faithful felines on watch. They grabbed him and sought to shove him in the sausage grinder. But then it began to rain cats. The guardians of the garbage made short shrift of the tame tabbies of the butcher shop."[18]

Meanwhile in Brooklyn

On Sept 21, 1879, the New York Times reported a cat in a little shanty at the corner of 15*th* St. and 3*rd* Ave. in Brooklyn who had hatched three broods of baby chicks. It was sitting on a fourth brood when discovered by an officer of the Sanitary Squad.[19]

Also in Brooklyn, in 1902, the organist at the Episcopal Church of the Transfiguration wondered what was wrong when his organ began emitting a horrible, haunting screech during a service. It sounded like something risen from hell. Then it stopped. But later, during the sermon, the demonic caterwaul broke forth again. It wasn't until the following Sunday that the faithful discovered the Maltese cat and her litter of kittens, the mother deeply concerned about the pipe tunes, though not concerned enough to evacuate.[20]

From the Aug. 4, 1902 issue of the *New York Times*:

COVERED CAT WITH CRABS

Panic in Women's Cabin of Ferryboat Followed Man's Prank.

Animal Frantic with Pain Made Wild Effort to Escape and Caused Passengers to Faint—Tormentor Arrested.

A man who had been crabbing yesterday came over on the 2 o'clock trip of the ferryboat Texas of the Broadway (Brooklyn) Twenty-third Street ferry line. He put a crab on each ear of a cat, one on each foot, three on the cat's tail, and stuck some more on the cat's sides. Then he let the animal go in the womens' cabin. One of the wildest scenes ever witnessed on a ferryboat took place. There was a panic in midstream. Women fainted as the cat and crabs frantically crawled over them, and the shrieking was terrific. The excitement lasted until the boat landed, when it was resumed again by half a hundred women excitedly pointing out a man who gave the name of George Ceiss, twenty-nine years old, of 20 Woodbine Street, Brooklyn, who is said to have put the crabs on the animal. He was arrested.

Louis Kraft of 208 East Twenty-first Street and his wife owned the cat. He was a large striped animal, with a fine head, and one that Kraft called a "prize cat." He had refused $100 for the cat, he said, and was taking him as a present to his sister in the Bronx. They held him in their laps by turns, partly covering him up.

Ceiss was with two or three friends who had been crabbing with him. They had a net, some poles, and a big basket, in which the day's catch was being carried home. Though it was a crowded boat, and the women's cabin was filled with women and children and some men out for the holiday, Ceiss and his friends, with the basket, sat down in the women's cabin, near Kraft and his wife.

Soon the men spied the cat. Ceiss began to talk to Kraft about the animal. He admired him, and Kraft talked about the cat's good looks, and readily handed him over to Ceiss, who got the cat off his guard by scratching the animal's head, and he opened the basket with the other hand.

In a jiffy Ceiss had a crab out, and the instant he held it close to one ear of the cat, the crab grabbed it with the claw in a bulldog grip. The cat howled, and everybody became curious. In another instant Ceiss had picked up another crab and held it to the cat's other ear, and the crab nipped it and held on.

There was another howl from the cat.

[...]ss only a few seconds to haul [...]r crab, and let each one nip [...] each leg, then three on the [...]n two or three more on the

[...]t!" shouted Ceiss, as he threw [...] on the floor of the cabin, to [...]f the crowd.

[...] the world ever went it like [...]ith a bound he tried to free [...] the agonizing nips of the [...]ing across the cabin at a window. He struck it ght was open. He struck it woman's head. She shrieked from excitement. The cat [...]dness of pain, and its wails [...]se of a convulsive child. It [...]n[...] at the sides of the cabin. It jumps across the cabin's [...]st the sides, and on the seats, [...]rst few minutes was on some [...]or head quite as often as on eats.

[...]was in a panic. There were women and children and [...]n. Another woman faint[...]on the floor. Some wo[...]rush out with children, holding [...]the hand or skirt, and some seats, believing in their ex[...]this was the best thing to do. and down the cabin, bumping [...]ther, and some sat still and [...]k after shriek. The basket [...] other crabs came out to in[...]ey crawled here and there, a [...]pped on. All the worse was [...]nto the cabin of people from [...] what was doing.

[...]le the cat was making wild [...]stance and height only pos[...]made wild by a dozen crabs [...]m. The way the crabs stuck ears and legs and tail was None was shaken off, even [...]turmoil and the innumerable made.

[...] ferryboat was nearing its [...]ip the cat escaped from the [...]c crabs still clinging to him. [...]d by men who sought to re[...]t the cat did not know that, of their way till a man cor[...]d seized him by the neck. A [...]same thing for the man, only [...]er, and the man dropped the [...]urse and smashed the crab [...]de of the boat.

[...] knew how cornered the cat [...]t his foot on him. When the [...]oosened the cat was weak [...]ht and pain, and he bled a

[...]'erryboat reached its slip and [...]e opened, Ceiss and his friends [...]ape hurriedly. But women [...]e boat and up to Policeman [...] East Twenty-second Street [...]res of women pointed Ceiss [...]ounced him, and Braun put [...]rest on a charge of cruelty to [...]lisorderly conduct. Ceiss and [...]rabs were taken to the East [...]d Street Station. The Society [...]ntion of Cruelty to Animals and they took charge of cat

Cat Studies

When Cats Hit the Bottle

University of Chicago researchers J.H. Masserman and K.S. Yum taught some cats to dispense themselves some food by pawing a switch. When they hit the switch, food fell into a food box. The experimenters then divided the cats into two groups. The lucky group was allowed to continue dispensing and eating food from the food box. But the others were subjected to blasts of air or electric shock when they tried to get the food they had successfully dispensed. These unlucky cats became afraid to go near the food box and the food in it. The hungrier they got, the more they wanted it, but they were afraid to go for it. The necessity and impossibility drove them crazy. They became neurotic.

The experimenters then gave all the cats doses of alcohol, and they all got delightfully drunk. (Not Masserman and Yum, just the cats.) They got playful but a bit uncoordinated. They wanted food, and even the neurotic cats explored the food box. But none of them could remember how to work the switch.

Next the experimenters set out two dishes of milk. One dish was pure milk, the other milk with booze. The non-neurotic cats went for the pure milk; the crazy ones headed straight for the bar. All the cats continued to fearlessly probe the food box for food. After two weeks, however, the neurotic cats lost their fear of the box and stopped drinking the milk cocktail! Apparently they'd really been using the booze to lessen their fear or, conversely, increase their courage. Once there was nothing to fear, their dependence ceased.[24]

Playing and Preying

Do cats hunt for pleasure or food? An experiment let hungry cats and well fed cats hunt for prey. The conclusions were only a little surprising.

• Both hungry and fed cats hunted, chased, played with, killed, and ate their prey.

• The hungry cats played with the prey less and got right down to eating.

• The fed cats ate only three mice. Then they simply killed without eating.

• The hungry cats killed and ate as many as 12 mice. But after the tenth, they slowed down.

• After 15 kills, both cohorts of cats slowed down and stopped chasing, at which point the mice actually started intimidating the cats. One mouse was so bold as to bite a cat's paw, the cat yowled and ran away.[25]

Nine Is Not Enough

A study of 994 dead cats in the Saskatoon region of rural Saskatchewan, Canada, found that 79 of the cats had died prematurely, in the following proportions.[26]

General cause of death	Number of cases	% of total
Trauma	31	39.2
Heart Disease	16	20.3
Intestinal disease	6	7.6
Respiratory disease	5	6.3
Urinary tract disease	4	5.1
Feline leukemia virus	3	3.8
Meningoencephalitis	1	1.3
Hepatic necrosis	1	1.3
Sepsis	1	1.3
Non-trauma hemorrhage	1	1.3
Undetermined	10	12.7

True Love

In the millenniums during which cats have cohabited with humans, the latter have wondered one crucial question: Does my cat really love me, or is it just out for the food?

Animal researchers at Oregon State University and psychology researchers at Monmouth University wondered the same thing, so they teamed up to perform an experiment. They got 50 cats—25 raised as pets, 25 adopted from shelters, all of them residents of Oregon. Of the 50, five freaked out and couldn't participate.

The experimenters presented the cats individually with four choices, or, in psych-speak, stimuli:

1. Food (tuna, chicken meat, and chicken-flavored soft cat food)
2. Human interaction (opportunities to be petted)
3. Tempting scents (catnip, gerbil, a cloth rubbed with an unknown cat's scent glands)
4. A toy (movement toy, feather toy, mouse toy)

Here are some of the results:

- There was a lot of individual variation.
- When presented with the food choices, 22 went for the tuna, only four for the chicken meat, and just one for the chicken-flavored stuff.
- Presented with scents, 22 went for the catnip, only 6 for the gerbil, which was equally popular with the gland scent.
- Half of the 38 cats who responded to anything at all (six didn't) preferred the human interaction. Fourteen cats preferred food, four a toy or food, and one preferred a scent.
- Obviously some cats just fake their love of humans. Some have other interests.
- Results did not take into consideration any previous experiences of the cats.

- Results were about the same for shelter and pet cats. Other experiments found significant results between shelter dogs and pet dogs when presented with food. The shelter experience apparently has no effect on cat preferences.[27]

Pawedness

People tend to be left-handed or right-handed. What about cats? Can they be left-pawed or right-pawed? And what difference does it make?

Yes they can be, and it makes a difference.

Researchers tested "pawedness" by building a two-level feeding maze tower. Cats had to work hard to get at a treat by reaching up into a tray. The researchers noted how often each cat used each paw to reach for the food.[28]

Some cats were right-pawed, others were, well, southpaws, and some were ambilateral, using both paws equally.

Big deal, right? Well, yes. Because the researchers also rated each cat for a) friendliness toward humans, and b) human perceptions of friendliness, obedience, affection, and aggression.

The findings:

• Right-pawed and left-pawed cats were equally friendly, but ambilateral cats were significantly less friendly.

• Right-pawed cats were *perceived* as more playful.

• Stronger paw preference correlated with more friendliness.

• Stronger paw preference correlated with stronger perceived friendliness.

Fake Cat News

Was there really a study that found that your cat wants to kill you?

No. But for some reason in the summer of 2016, a host of online publications tried to shock their readers with that misinformation. They claimed to have gotten it from a University of Edinburgh study that compared the personality traits of various types of felines, from lions to domestic cats. Nothing indicated that domesticated cats had any tendency or desire to do ill to their owners. At most the study found some similarities between lions and house cats, but not an inclination to kill people.[29]

A cat behavior consultant commented that people might suspect cats of murderous thoughts because it's so hard to read a cat's face. But, the consultant noted, after thousands of years of people living with cats, if they really wanted to kill people, wouldn't they have done it by now?

EXTRA! EXTRA!
Science Detects Existence of Personality in Cats!

Not so long ago, misguided scientists concluded or at least presumed that animals did not have personalities, not even if they were called animalities or something.

Recently, however, a group of researchers applied principal axis factor analysis to measure owner perceptions of personality in their cats. The owners had to note which of 52 personality traits applied to their cats. All of the cats were from South Australia or New Zealand. From their answers, the researchers determined that the domestic cat has five ("the Feline Five") identifiable personality traits: Neuroticism, Extroversion, Dominance, Impulsiveness, and Agreeableness.

The researchers expressed hope that defining personality traits might someday facilitate the matching up of cats and humans. The researchers noted that humane shelters in Australia receive some 53,000 cats a year, a third of them destined to soon be returned to their maker. In the United States, half of 3.4 million animal shelter cats are put to death. A better understanding of cat (not to mention human) personality might help avoid this situation.[30]

Felinology

Taxonomy of the Domestic Cat

Kingdom: *Animalia*

Subkingdom: *Bilateria*

Infrakingdom: *Deuterostomia*

Phylum: *Chordata*

Subphylum: *Gnathostomata*

Superclass: *Tetrapoda*

Class: *Mammalia*

Subclass: *Theria*

Infraclass: *Eutheria*

Order: *Carnivora*

Suborder: *Feliformia*

Family: *Felidae*

Subfamily: *Felinae*

Genus: *Felis*

Species: *Felis silvestris*

Subspecies: *Felis silvestris catus (a.k.a. F. s. catus, or Felis catus)*

So *Felis silvestris catus* is your domestic cat, the slouch on the couch, the purring pillow, the only feline species most people have ever seen. It doesn't matter whether it's a Siamese, angora, or mutt, it's a *Felis silvestris catus*.

Felis comes from the Latin *felix*, whence the name of the famous cartoon character, Felix the Cat. Felix can mean lucky, happy, successful, or even fruit-bearing. No known subspecies of *Felis silvestris catus* has been known to bear fruit (ticks and fleas aren't fruit), but lying around in the sun all day waiting for your next meal to be served can be considered a successful situation. And lucky. And, in some way, happy. *Felis catus* means "happy cat." It's a *Felis catus* even if it's stuck outside in a sleet storm.

There are three genera of unhappy cat, that is to say, undomesticated cats—cats without couches, cats who have never known a lap. The *Felidae Pantera* are the "greater cats"—your lions and tigers and such. *Felidae Acinonyx* are the cheetahs. *Felidae Smilodon* were the saber-toothed tigers who roamed the earth until just 12,000 years ago.

These various genera share a few characteristics. They are all carnivores. They all have retractable claws. They all look like cats. And they are the only animals on earth that can purr. (Whether the extinct *Felidae Smilodon* could purr is not known for sure. Any Cro-magnons close enough to hear a purr probably didn't live long enough to tell others.)

The difference between the greater cats and lesser cats isn't in their size. It's in their throats. The lesser cats have small bones that support their larynx. The larynx of greater cats is mostly cartilage, which is more flexible than bone. This flexibility means a more flexible throat. A flexible throat allows a cat to roar. Lions and tigers can roar. The best a lesser cat can come up with is a blood-curdling caterwaul.

Cat-Scratch Disease

Cat-Scratch Disease (CSD), brought to fame by the Ted Nugent song "Cat Scratch Fever," is indeed transmitted to humans from cats, though not necessarily so. It's actually the common cat flea, (Ctenocephalides felis) that carries the Bartontella henselae bacterium, carrying it from cat to cat. The bacterium can enter a cat's bloodstream and saliva. Typical infection of a human occurs from the saliva or from a scratch that becomes infected with flea feces. Tick bites can also infect humans. Symptoms include headache, chills, and pain in muscles, joints, belly, and back. In most cases, the infection resolves itself without treatment, but in 5 to 14 percent of cases, it can lead to serious complications of the liver, spleen, eyes, and central nervous sytem.[31]

The Cat's Vibrissae

Those long, straight hairs coming out of a cat's face are vibrissae to veterinarians, whiskers to everyone else. The average cat has about 24 of them—four rows of three whiskers on each side of the snout. They are twice as thick as other cat hairs, and they are rooted 3 times as deep. Their roots connect to the nervous system. Among the things cat whiskers can sense are air pressure, air movement, and touch. Whiskers are an advantage in the hunt, in passing through tight spaces, and in the dark. But their span and sensitivity are a disadvantage when a cat has to stick its face into a narrow food dish. The pressure on the vibrissae doesn't hurt, but it's a distraction from degustation.

In darkness, when a cat can't see its prey, the vibrissae extend around the mouth like a basket. This enables the cat to detect the precise location of close-in prey and bite them precisely.[32]

Nine Lives + Six Senses

Psi-trailing is the apparent ability of some pets to travel great distances to be reunited with a mate or a beloved "master." (We use the word "apparent" because it isn't certain that it ever happens. We say "some" because most pets never exhibit this inexplicable ability. We put "masters" in quotes because in the case of cats, it's questionable who has mastered whom.)

Take the case of Pooh, a two-year-old tomcat who walked 200 miles from Newnan, Georgia to Wellford, South Carolina when its companion animals moved and left him behind. Then there's Chat Beau, a tom twice the age of Pooh who hiked 300 miles from Lafayette, Louisiana to Texarkana when his folks moved away. And how to explain the Persian Smoky who spent twelve months traversing 417 miles from Tulsa to Memphis. But Smoky was a tenderfoot compared to Sugar, who followed her family 1,500 miles from Anderson, California to Gage, Oklahoma.

These psi-trailing superstars showed no signs of fraud or fiction. Well, probably not. A pair of researchers with Duke University's Parapsychology Laboratory—J.B. Rhine and Sara Feather—looked into some 500 cases of supposed psi-trailing by animals. To qualify as possibly real, the incidents had to meet 4 qualifications:

1. Was the arriving animal accurately identified by some physical or behavioral trait?

2. Was there evidence of arduous travel?

3. Were there supporting witnesses?

4. Does the reported incident seem to be honest, not a hoax?

These were not incidents of cats being taken somewhere and then finding their way back. There may be scientific explanation for that. But in these cases, the animals were not retracing their routes. Out of the

500 incidents, Rhine and Feather found eight dogs, 22 cats, and four birds who qualified.

Skeptics tend to claim that people often have a psychological need to see their lost pets again. In that cats of a given breed look kind of the same, it's easy for people to forget certain details and, emotional necessity, see a random cat as their old pal. In the cases of Pooh, Smoky, Chat Beau, and Sugar, the owners were quite certain it was their cat, and all of the cats looked like they'd walked a long way. Whether the claims were fraudulent, of course, cannot be known for sure.

If the cases are true, one interesting question is why so few pets exhibit psi-trailing capability.

Researcher Rhine was quite convinced that these cases were real. And he wrote something very interesting in a letter. He said, "How deeply moving these performances are; what they tell us of the bonds of affection that so controlled the animals' lives through hardship and long periods of wandering in the wilds. Not food, not sex, not fear—just plain love, isn't it?"[33]

Independent Claws

A cat's front claws are sharper than its back paws because the ones in the back ones touch the ground as the cat walks. Each steps blunts them a bit. The front claws are normally tucked inside the paws. It would not be correct to say the front claws are retracted. They aren't. They're just in there. When the cat needs the claws, it *pro*tracts them.

Cats sharpen their front claws by scratching them on trees or the best upholstered furniture they can find. They sharpen the back claws by chewing on them.

Though the back claws are duller, they are also thicker and stronger. The cat will use only its front claws (and mouth) to catch and kill a mouse. For a larger animal, the cat will grip the victim with its front claws while eviscerating it with the back claws.

Of course the back claws are also used for climbing up trees. But because of the curve of front claws and back, climbing down the tree is more difficult. If the cat tried to climb down head first, like a squirrel, it could lose its grip and fall. The alternative is to go down backwards, which is not natural to any cat or other quadruped. Fearful of the process, cats tend to hang out on a branch and complain, hoping the fire department will come get them. Left there long enough, they will eventually, awkwardly, figure out how to climb down. There are no known cases of cats dying of old age in trees.

How Cats Do It

More Than a Throaty Rumble

The low rumble of a cat's purr—27 Hz—is close to the lowest note on a piano, an A of 27.5 Hz. (Hz stands for Hertz, a measurement of sound vibration. One Hertz would be one vibration per second. The human ear can detect 20—16,000 Hz, that lower end being just a little lower than a purr.)

But Dr. Karen McComb, a University of Sussex (UK) professor, determined that a purr—a pushy purr of a cat wanting food—can include a high-pitched meow. That higher note, barely perceptible, is at a frequency similar to that of a human infant's cry. Humans instinctively react to the sound without being aware they hear it. Dr. McComb used acoustic analysis to measure the frequency and level of the low-pitch/high-pitch purr, then had ten cat owners listen to recordings and rank the purrs according to perceived urgency. The higher the level of the high-pitch, the more the purr sounded urgent.[34] How cats came to mimic the cry of a baby is anybody's guess.

How They Lap it Up

Cats make the lapping of water or milk look easy. But what they're doing involves the use of lingual dexterity to use inertia to overcome gravity.

A cat's lap is different from a dog's. For one thing, it's a lot quieter, and not just because dogs are dogs. It's quieter because dog and cat tongues do different things. A dog dips its tongue into the water, curls it into a scoop, and lifts the liquid up to the mouth. A cat's tongue, on the other hand, never penetrates the liquid it is drinking. The tip of the tongue merely touches the surface without penetrating it. Only the tip of the tongue, which is smooth, not rough like the rest of the tongue, touches the liquid. It then lifts upward very quickly, pulling up a column of liquid. This column actually detaches from the surface of the liquid as the upper part of it is pulled into the mouth. The tongue then forms a scoop and dumps the liquid back onto the rough part of the tongue. The rough part of the tongue holds the liquid, preventing it from succumbing to gravity. After three to 17 laps, the cat swallows.

This process, so quick and precise, requires a great deal of lingual dexterity. Each lapping cycle is too quick for the naked eye to capture. Scientists had to use high speed imaging to see what was happening.

Neither cats nor cat owners need concern themselves with this. It's the scientists who are most interested. They want to see how the cat's lapping skills might be applied to "soft robotics," that is, a robot's use of something cushy and flexible to, say, pick up a cupcake. Thus once again cats are proving their usefulness in the world.[35]

Oscar the Uncanny Cat

According to an article in the *New England Journal of Medicine*, a nursing home therapy cat named Oscar was known for identifying and curling up with elderly people who were about to die.[36]

Oscar, one of several therapy cats (and parakeets, dogs, and bunnies) at Steere House Nursing and Rehabilitation Center in Providence, RI, was not known as a friendly cat. He tended to avoid people and hiss at strangers. But he had an uncanny ability to perceive imminent death. More than 50 times he crept into rooms and slept next to terminally ill patients who died within the next two hours. Oscar was so consistent that when staff found him in bed with a patient, they immediately informed family so that they could come in for a last good-bye. Oscar was still making his rounds in 2017.[37]

What does it take to be a professional therapy cat?

Just being a cat is not enough. A therapy cat is either naturally capable of helping or trained to help humans with medical problems. Unlike mere "companion animals," therapy cats are typically deployed by a handler or medical professional to alleviate a specific medical problem. They are often employed at nursing homes, retirement homes, hospices, mental institutions, and even prisons and public schools.

Temperament is a key quality of therapy cats. They must be "people cats" who are comfortable with being touched, stroked, hugged, and cuddled. They must demonstrate a propensity for friendliness, patience, confidence, and, above all, gentleness in all human interactions. Fear and skittishness are disqualifications. Sharpening claws on a patient's legs, however affectionate, is cause for dismissal.

Therapy cats have been proven to:

- lower blood pressure
- decrease anxiety and induce calm
- lessen depression and apathy
- inspire purpose and a reason to live
- pacify violent tendencies
- nurture empathy and compassion
- increase alertness in the elderly[38]

Biophilia

E.O. Wilson offered a hypothesis to explain the effectiveness of animal therapy. He called it biophilia. He suggested that humans have an inborn tendency to appreciate coexistence with animals. This instinctual compassion evolved from ancient times when the presence of calm, passive, nonthreatening animals—be they dogs, frogs, or birds—indicated a safe environment. Once domesticated, cats, then as now renowned for being alert for trouble, probably served as creatures of early warning. Yes, they were watchcats. Today, the hypothesis goes, if your cat is calm, all is calm. You can relax, let your guard down, and feel better about life.

How Hairballs Happen

The regurgitation of a hairball ranks high among a cat's specialized skills. Other animals can develop hairballs, or trichobezoars, in their gastrointestinal system, but only cats are capable of delivering them onto carpets and upholstery as a normal part of their day.

A hairball is a mass of swallowed hair that forms in the stomach. Not as spherical as the word implies, hairballs tend to come into daylight as elongated cylinders. Hair may be the predominate element, but the package can include other items from the stomach.

Felines are prone to hairballs because they groom themselves by licking their fur, inevitably ingesting some of it. Hair doesn't digest very well, so it tends to remain in the stomach. Rabbits groom the same way, but they lack the ability to regurgitate. A stomach full of hair will cause a rabbit to stop eating, so eventually the rabbit dies. People (especially young women) suffering from trichophagia—the eating of hair— can develop hairballs, too. Sometimes they do what a cat does, albeit not normally on furniture, and sometimes they don't. If they don't, they may need surgery. A young female in Chicago had to have a 9.9 lb. hairball surgically removed from her stomach.[39]

CAT ODDITIES

The catgut once used as strings in tennis rackets and musical instruments does not come from cats. Catgut actually comes from sheep, hogs, and horses.

The word *caterwaul* apparently comes from a Middle Dutch word, *cater*, "tomcat" and a Middle English word, *waul*, "yowl," which itself apparently comes from an Old English word, **wrag*, meaning "angry," probably because that's what an angry person sounds like—a mad cat.

According to the American Pet Products Association, in 2017, 47.1 million U.S. households had a total of 94.2 million cats. (More households had dogs—60.2 percent but they had a total of only 89.7 million dogs.) Cat owners spent an annual average of $245 on cat surgery, $182 on other vet visits, $235 on cat food, $56 on cat treats, $164 on cat kennels, $46 on cat vitamins, $30 on grooming, and $30 on toys. Total sales of pet food in 2017 was estimated at $29.69 billion, compared with $7 billion for baby food for 22.9 million infants and toddlers).[40]

Guinness Cares about Cats

The most prolific cat was a tabby named Dusty, of Bonham, Texas born in 1935. Dusty gave birth to 420 kittens.

The largest litter of a domestic cat was 19, born to a Burmese-Siamese in UK.

The heaviest cat was an Australian named Himmy, who tipped the scales at 46 lb, 15 1/2 oz when it died in 1986 at the age of 10 years, 4 months. Please note, however, that Guinness is no longer keeping records on overweight cats because too many people were trying to fatten their cats to record levels, which is considered abusive.

The cat with the longest whiskers was Missi, a Maine coon cat living in Finland, whose whiskers were 7.5 inches long.

The oldest cat ever was Creme Puff, of Austin, Texas, who lived to be 38 years and 3 days old.

The cat capable of performing the most tricks was Didga, of Tweed Heads, New South Wales, Australia. On command, Didga performed 24 tricks, including jumping, spinning around, rolling over, and riding a skateboard.

(continued)

The cat getting the most views on YouTube was Maru, whose name means "round" in Japanese. 340,280,203 people watched his rotundity getting stuck in various places.

The most productive mouser was a longhaired tortoiseshell cat named Towser who worked at Glenturrent Distillery in Scotland. Guinness auditors estimated the total by observing Tower's production over the course of a few days. Each day Towser lined up several dead mice, averaging three per day for a theoretical total of 28,899 during her lifetime. She died in 1987 at the age of 21. Her paw prints can be seen on the label of Fairlie's Light Highland Liquer.[41]

The people with the most cats were Jack and Donna Wright, of Kingston, Ontario. In 2010 they had 689 cats.

The cheetah is the fastest cat, exceeding most state speed limits when racing along at 70 mph.

Don't Forget

Change a Pet's Life Day—January 24

World Cat Day—February 17

Love Your Pet Day—February 20

Nyan Nyan Nyan Day in Japan—February 22

World Cat Day in Russia—March 1

World Stray Animals Day—April 4

National Pet Day—April 11

Hug Your Cat Day—June 4

World Pet Memorial Day—Last Sunday in June

International Cat Day—August 8

International Homeless Animls Day—August 16

National Black Cat Appreciation Day—August 17

National Pet Memorial Day—second Sunday in September

National Feral Cat Day—October 16

National Black Cat Day in UK—October 27

National Cat Day in the United States—October 29

National Black Cat Day in the United States—November 17

Phrases Involving Cats

"Cat got your tongue?" The origin is unclear, but it is apparently an expression that children used in 1880 and years before. It is also conjectured that it dates back to ancient Egyptian times when blasphemers got their tongues cut off and the tongues were then fed to cats. It is not something that came from the naval days when sailors were whipped with a cat o' nine tails for, among other things, refusing to give a proper answer.

"Let the cat out of the bag." The origin is not clear. It may come from the cat o'nine tails used for punishment on British naval vessels because the cat was stored in a red sack. It might also be related to the proverbial warning about "buying a pig in a poke," a poke being a sack. The supposed pig might actually be a cat. There is no documented evidence that either is true.

"More than one way to skin a cat." The earliest documented use was in a short story by Seba Smith in 1840, in which was written "There are more ways to skin a cat, so there are more ways than one of digging for money." In 1855, the novel *Westward Ho!* said, "There are more ways of killing a cat than choking it with cream." It has also been conjectured that it referred not to a cat but a catfish. In 1889 the phrase appeared in Mark Twain's *A Connecticut Yankee in King Arthur's Court*: "She was wise, subtle, and knew more than one way to skin a cat."

"Raining cats and dogs." Maybe from the Greek phrase "cata doxa," meaning "contrary to experience or belief." If it rained "cata doxa," it was raining harder than could be believed. It might also be from the results of heavy rains in 17th-18th century England, when a heavy rain would wash street debris into piles, including dead animals. There is no certainty about any of this.

"As much chance as a wax cat in Hell." Right in there with snowballs.

"As nervous as a cat in a room full of rocking chairs." You can imagine!

"The cat's meow." Something that's just as fine as can be. Originated with American cartoonist Thomas Dorgan.

"Dead cat bounce." A financial market in recovery, much like a cat bouncing back from yet another brush with death.

"Keep no more cats than will catch mice." This refers to useless people.

"Let sleeping cats lie." Needless to say, a French expression.

"Not enough room to swing a cat" This goes back to the old English naval days, a reference to the cat o' nine tails. The area below the main deck was blessedly cramped, so no one would be whipped there. Not enough room.

"Look what the cat dragged in!" A friendly insult, based on the fact that cats never, ever drag something pleasant into the house.

"Wanton kittens make sober cats." Sometimes those most crazy in youth grow up to be especially serious and well behaved.

"A cat can look at a king." That is, even a cat has certain basic rights, especially if they don't hurt anybody.

Cat Advice

If you have a cat and want to have another cat, it will be easiest to introduce a female kitten. An elderly cat that is alone, however, should not be bothered with another cat. Let it rest in peace. Bringing a new cat into a household is always very stressful for all the cats concerned.

If you have to break up a cat fight use a broom to separate them.

Only a mother cat should pick a cat up by the scruff of the neck.

Brushing your cat daily will reduce the frequency of hairballs.

Many things should never pass the palate of a cat. Chocolate, Tylenol, avocado, cannabis, poinsettia, lily-of-the-valley, and morning glory are all poisonous and sometimes deadly to cats.

Proverbs

You can throw a cat however you wish, it always lands on its feet.

Yiddish

An old cat likes young mice.

Greek

After dark, all cats are leopards.

Native American

In the dark, all cats and all girls are beautiful.

Hungarian

A cat always knows whose meat it eats.

Russian

A cat with gloves catches no mice.

Greek

A house without a dog, a cat, and a child is a house without joy or laughter.

Scottish

You should not call a cat to settle the argument of two birds.

Indian

It is better to be in a cat's mouth than a lawyer's hands.

Spanish

In the long run, even a dog will compromise with a cat.

Hungarian

The kind man feeds his cat before sitting down to dinner.

Hebrew

A borrowed cat catches no mice.

Japanese

The dog for the man, the cat for the woman.

English

All dogs are male; all cats are female.

Unknown

The cat who frightens mice away is as good as the cat who eats them.

German

It takes a good many mice to kill a cat.

Unknown

Cats in Conversation

What greater gift than the love of a cat?

Charles Dickens

Artists like cats; soldiers like dogs.

Desmond Morris

Those who play with cats must expect to be scratched.

Miguel de Cervantes

If a dog jumps in your lap, it is because he is fond of you, but if a cat does the same thing, it is because your lap is warmer.

A.N. Whitehead

Cats are connoisseurs of comfort.

James Herriot

Of all God's creatures, there is only one that cannot be made slave of the lash. That one is the cat. If man could be crossed with the cat it would improve the man, but it would deteriorate the cat.

Mark Twain

You see, wire telegraph is a kind of a very, very long cat. You pull his tail in New York and his head is meowing in Los Angeles. Do you understand this? And radio operates exactly the same way: you send signals here, they receive them there. The only difference is that there is no cat.

Albert Einstein

A countryman between two lawyers is like a fish between two cats.

Benjamin Franklin

Cats will outsmart dogs every time.

John Grogan

Meow means woof in cat.

George Carlin

That's the great secret of creativity. You treat ideas like cats: you make them follow you.

Ray Bradbury

I have lived with several Zen masters—all of them cats.

Eckhart Tolle

There is not a single case on record of a cat who died in his bed.

François Copée (1842-1908)

A cat has absolute emotional honesty.

Ernest Hemingway

A kitten is in the animal world what a rosebud is in a garden.

Robert Southey

Cat: one hell of a nice animal, often mistaken for a meatloaf.

B. Kliban

Cats are intended to teach us that not everything in nature has a function.

Garrison Keillor

No cat purrs unless someone is around to listen.

Elizabeth Marshall Thomas

Bathsheba:

To whom none ever said scat,

No worthier cat

Ever sat on a mat

Or caught a rat:

Requies-cat.

John Greenleaf Whittier

Epitaph for a Good Mouser

Take, Lord, this soul of furred unblemished worth,

The sum of all I loved and caught on earth.

Quick was my holy purpose and my cause.

I die into the mercy of thy claws.

Anne Stevenson

The Owl and the Pussy-cat

The Owl and the Pussy-cat went to sea
In a beautiful pea-green boat,
They took some honey, and plenty of money.
Wrapped up in a five-pound note.
The Owl looked up to the stars above,
And sang to a small guitar,
'O lovely Pussy! O Pussy, my love,
What a beautiful Pussy you are,
You are
You are!
What a beautiful Pussy you are!'
Pussy said to the Owl, "You elegant fowl!
How charmingly sweet you sing!
O let us be married! Too long we have tarried:
But what shall we do for a ring?"
They sailed away, for a year and a day,
To the land where the Bong-tree grows
And there in a wood a Piggy-wig stood
With a ring at the end of his nose,
His nose,
His nose,
With a ring at the end of his nose.

'Dear Pig, are you willing to sell for one shilling
Your ring?' Said the Piggy, 'I will.'
So they took it away, and were married next day
By the Turkey who lives on the hill.
They dined on mince, and slices of quince,
Which they ate with a runcible spoon;
And hand in hand, on the edge of the sand,
They danced by the light of the moon,
The moon,
The moon,
They danced by the light of the moon.

Edward Lear

Superstitions

Dreaming of a white cat means good luck.

American superstition

To see a white cat on the road is lucky.

American superstition

It is bad luck to see a white cat at night.

American superstition

If a cat washes behind its ears, it will rain.

English superstition

A strange black cat on your porch brings prosperity.

Scottish superstition

A cat sneezing is a good omen for everyone who hears it.

Italian superstition

A cat sleeping with all four paws tucked under means cold weather ahead.

English superstition

When moving to a new home, always put the cat through the window instead of the door, so that it will not leave.

American superstition

When you see a one-eyed cat, spit on your thumb, stamp it in the palm of your hand, and make a wish. The wish will come true.

American superstition

In the Netherlands, cats were not allowed in rooms where private family discussions were going on. The Dutch believed that cats would definitely spread gossips around the town.

Dutch superstition

To reverse the bad luck curse of a black cat crossing your path, first walk in a circle, then go backward across the spot where it happened and count to 13.

American superstition

In 1944, researcher Mildred Moelk analyzed the sounds that come out of a cat's mouth. She called the most basic vocalization a "murmur" produced with a closed mouth. It starts with something like an *m* followed by an exhalation that is something like an *h*. Then there's a little trill, something like an *r*, and finally a fading of the breath, kind of like an *n*. In other words, the basic cat word is *mhrn*. It is used to greet someone, call a kitten, ask for something, or even, apparently, when the final *n* sounds like an *ng* (the ending of "rung"), to say "thank you."[42]

Whisker Fatigue

Cat whiskers are like antennae sticking out the sides of a cat's face. They are like antennae because their purpose is to receive information. Like sensitive instruments, they receive information about food, danger, and environment. Day and night, a cat's whiskers receive information.

That's why "whisker fatigue" can be a problem. Whisker fatigue occurs when a cat's food lies at the bottom of a narrow bowl. When the cat leans in, the whiskers are pushed back. This doesn't necessarily hurt, but it's a ton of information the cat doesn't need, and the poor pussy gets annoyed.

Symptom of whisker fatigue: Cat batting food out of the bowl, then eating it off the floor.

The cure: A bowl somewhat wider than the whiskers, ideally not of plastic, which can harbor germs, but stainless steel. A dinner plate would also work.[43]

Think this is silly? Get two cat bowls—one narrow, one not. Put food in each. See which the cat prefers. Give the other one to a dog.

Just say "No"!

Medical marijuana has been proven to make people with certain illnesses feel better. In fact, even people without illnesses often feel better.

But what about cats?

ALERT: THC, the psycho-active ingredient in the cannabis plant is toxic to non-human animals. Many a cat and dog have been taken to the vet by disappointed people who have found their indoor plant chewed up or their special brownie snatched from the counter. Do not let pets eat your pot.

However, there is an ingredient in industrial hemp that seems to relieve pain and anxiety in pets. Industrial hemp looks like but is crucially different from the stuff of bongs. It has a cannabinoid called CBD, which has negligible amounts of THC. Smoking or eating it won't get you or your pet high, but it is known to alleviate certain symptoms.

In some states, CBD products are available for cats. There are oil drops, pills, gel caps, and something in the tradition of Tater Tots. CBD has been known to ease the pain of cancer, the fear of fireworks, and the stiffness of arthritis. It can sooth the itch of skin problems, and prevent seizures.

The Food & Drug Administration has not approved of CBD products for pets, but that doesn't mean they aren't available. In states where veterinarians cannot prescribe CBD, cat owners have been known to fake symptoms in themselves (insomnia's an easy one) to get medications for their furry, ailing friends.

Danger: *Often there are no approved doses for animals.* Guesswork can be dangerous. Get a veterinarian's advice before trying CBD, and keep pot plants and special brownies out of the reach of cats![44]

On Fur

Here's something you don't need to know: It takes 24 cats to make a cat fur coat. If you don't have that many cats, you can make cat fur gloves, hats, shoes, blankets, or stuffed toys. There's an international market for these things. But it's illegal to make, import, or export a cat fur in the United States, European Union, Australia, and other civilized nations—except Switzerland, which allows cat fur blankets, which are supposedly a remedy for rheumatism. China, which has no animal welfare laws, is not among the civilized nations.[45]

On Litter

Have you ever lain awake in bed at night and wondered how much Americans spend on cat litter each year? Well now you can go back to sleep. The answer is "about $2 billion." That's roughly the cost of a no-frills nuclear submarine.

The term "Kitty Litter" was the brand name of one of the first commercial litters, the first to use a clay called Fuller's earth instead of sand. It was conceived of and marketed by a guy named Edward Lowe, son of Lulu. To get people used to paying for Kitty Litter rather than just using sand, he gave the stuff away until people got used to using it. Then sand just wasn't good enough.

Modern conventional non-clumping cat litter is the same thing as the oil absorbent that is used to soak up oil spills. Clumping litter is made from bentonite rather than Fuller's earth. Both are natural materials, but they require strip mining, which causes severe damage to the environment. Some two million tons of cat litter—the weight of 125 no-frills nuclear submarines—is dumped in American landfills each year.

Biodegradable cat litter, made of a variety of plant materials—everything from pine pellets to orange peels—is more expensive than clay-based litter, but, once enriched with animal waste, it can be composted, then used to grow things, such as catnip.

What's a Tidy Clump Worth to You?

Somehow it figures that the miracle of clumping cat litter has a downside. A bad one, the one called cancer.

Clumping litter contains an added ingredient, silica gel. It's extra absorbent, but of course every upside has a downside. In this case, the downside is cancer and a multitude of other health problems—in cats as well as people.

Cats are especially endangered. They walk in it, then kick up dust. Then they lick it off their paws. It's in their fur all day. It clumps up in their digestive track, leading to all sorts of problems.

The silica dust wafts around the house. People breath it in. Since 1997, the International Agency for Research on Cancer has classified silica as a human carcinogen. Silica also causes silicosis, a deadly lung disease. In 2013, 46,000 people died of it.[46] How many had indoor cats? Nobody knows.

Cats with Class

The International Progressive Cat Breeders Alliance recognizes 73 breeds. The International Cat Association recognizes 58. The Cat Fanciers' Association recognizes 44, and the Fédération Internationale Féline recognizes 43.

Among the breeds recognized by at least one of these organizations are:

Aegean, Arabian Mau, Australian Mist, Balinese, Bambino, Birman, Bombay, Brazilian Shorthair, Burmilla, Chantilly-Tiffany, Chartreux, Cheetoh, Cymric, Cyprus, Devon Rex, Dragon Li, Egyptian Mau, Foldex, Havana Brown, Kurilian Bobtail, Khao Manee, Korat, Korn Ja, Laperm, Lykoi, Mekong Delta, Minskin, Munchkin, Negelung, Napoleon, Norwegian Forest Cat, Ojos Azules, Perfold, Peterbald, Pixie-Bob, Raas, Ragamuffin, Ragdoll, Sam Sawet, Selkirk Rex, Serrade Petit, Singapura, Sokoke, Sphynx, Suphalak, Thai Lilac, Tokinese, Toyget, and Ukrainian Levkoy.

Odds and Ends

Cats do not think that they are little people. They think that people are big cats. This influences their behavior in many ways.

Most cats have no eyelashes. But they have 26 teeth.

Cats lack a true collarbone. Because of this lack, a cat can generally squeeze its body through any space it can get its head through. You may have seen a cat testing the size of an opening by careful measurement with the head. You may have noticed cats' tendency to get stuck in tight places. It's because they have no collarbone.

Unlike humans and dogs, cats do not suffer a lot from loneliness. It is a mistake to project our social feelings onto our cats. Cats are social to a degree, but they are far more concerned with territorial issues than we can even imagine.

Like birds, cats have a homing ability that uses its biological clock, the angle of the sun, and the Earth's magnetic field. A cat taken far from its home can return to it. But if a cat's owners move far from its home, the cat can't usually find them.

Besides smelling with their nose, cats can smell with an additional organ called the Jacobson's organ, located in the upper surface of the mouth. When you see a cat wrinkle its muzzle, lower its chin and let its tongue hang out, it is opening a channel to the Jacobson's organ.[47]

Cats can land on their feet because they have a flexible spine. They can twist around better than most other mammals.

Most deaf cats do not meow.

Multi-colored male cats are very rare. For every 3,000 tortoiseshell or calico cats born, only one will be male.

Cats can see in the dark six times better than humans. But if there's enough light, humans can see objects 200 feet away clearly, but cats can see clearly for only about 20 ft. Humans see more color, too. Cats apparently see the world as shades of blue and gray.[48]

A third of American cat owners think their cat can read their mind.[49]

Why do cats never have smelly armpits? Because they sweat only through their paws.

Why do a cat's back paws smell like Fritos? Maybe it has something to do with sweat. The more poignant question: Why do Fritos smell like a cat's back paws?

Cats respond to women more than men because women have higher-pitched voices.

A group of cats is called a *clowder*. The word came about in the 19th century, probably a dialect variation of the word *clutter*.

A male cat is a tom. A female cat is a queen or a molly.

The color of a cat's coat often indicates personality. And often it doesn't.

A cat's nose pattern is as unique to it as fingerprints are to a human. Look around the Internet and you can find companies that will help you make a silver model of a cat's nose. The process begins by pressing special molding material onto the nose to make a print. The company then fills it with silver to duplicate the nose.

Some of the foods that cats should not eat: chocolate, garlic, grapes, green tomatoes, onions, raisins, raw potatoes. Milk might make your cat fart. Aspirin and Tylenol might make your cat die.[50]

Some Cat Museums

Cats Museum
Lloret de Mar, Spain — lloret-de-mar-stuff.com/cat-museum

The Lucky Cat Museum
Cincinnati, OH — clockworkvoices.com/neko

American Museum of the House Cat
Sylva, North Carolina — catman2.org/the-american-museum-of-the-house-cat

Moscow Cat Museum
Moscow, Russia — moscowcatmuseum.com/eng

The Cat Museum
Minsk, Belarus — catmuseum.by/index_en

De Kattenkabinet/The Cat Cabinet
Amsterdam, Netherlands—kattenkabinet.nl

Feline Historical Museum
Alliance, OH — felinehistoricalfoundation.org

Cats Museum
Kotor, Montenegro — catsmuseum.org

The Cat Museum—
Singapore — thecatmuseum.com.sg

Cat Museum of San Francisco
catmuseumsf.org

Happy Hunting

It turns out cats are picky about their prey.

Predators can be classified as specialists, if they prey on a narrow range of species, or generalists, if they hunt multiple types. But within each group, such factors as sex, age, size, and personality type may determine individual preferences for prey.

Researchers detected apparent hunting preferences in pet cats. Owners were asked what kind of prey their cats dragged in. Twenty-six cats brought at least ten prey home. The researchers observed considerable variation in each individuals prey prefs. Eight cats specialized in small birds, five preferred lizards, four nailed black rats, three managed to down large birds, and six showing up with a variety of types.

The researchers also observed the actual hunts and calculated success rates. Fifteen of the cats were very efficient. Four of them were 83-100 percent successful in their attacks on rats. One ballsy individual managed to kill 94 percent of rabbits it attacked. Cats would hunt hard for their preferred prey even if the prey was scarce and other prey were available.

Conclusion: Cats are individuals who exhibit individualized behavior, at least with regard to killing things.[21]

Male and female cats are polygynandrous—that is, they are anything but monogamous. They have various mates throughout the year.

Male cats do not get involved in rearing kittens. But sometimes one female will care for another female's kittens while their mother is off hunting.

Male cats are much more serious about territory, but the size of it depends on habitat. A farm cat may claim and defend 150 acres, while a female farm cat will be satisfied with a tenth of that. A city cat will claim much less, often overlapping with other males' territories, resulting in a lot of fights over a lot more females.[51]

It is mathematically possible for a pair of loving cats to produce 420,000 kittens in seven years.[52]

The Norse goddess Freya is believed to have used cats to pull her chariot.

CATS AND DOGS

Dogs like sweets, but cats generally don't. They lack the gene that would let them taste sweetness. This is one reason why dogs are more likely to get sick (or dead) from chocolate toxicosis.[53]

A dog can make about ten sounds at most. A cat can make a hundred.[55]

When cats and dogs are confronted with a problem they can't solve, dogs will tend to look to humans for help. Cats will keep trying on their own.

Humans have about five million scent receptors in their noses. Cats have 45 to 80 million.[56] A dog has more than 220 million. This does not mean they smell good. It means they smell well.[57]

Dogs and Cats in Space

Dog ventured into outer space long before cat.

Between 1951 and 1952, Soviet rockets carried nine dogs into space on several flights. Some were sent in pairs. The first pair survived. The second pair did not. Three of the canine astronauts made the trip twice. One dog, Bobnik, missed her dubious opportunity by escaping before her scheduled flight. Whether she made it to and over the Berlin Wall is not known.

The Russian street mutt Laika was launched on November 3, 1957 aboard the Sputnik 2. (Americans nicknamed her Muttnik.) The first living being to orbit the earth, she was supposed to live six days before her oxygen depleted. However, in 2002 it was revealed that she had died from overheating in the first few hours.

The French cat Félicette, a black-and-white female stray found on the streets of Paris, was launched on October 18, 1963. She and 13 other cats had been trained for the mission in high-G centrifuges and compression chambers. Her rocket was a Véronique. Unlike Laika's trip around the planet, her trip was suborbital, lasting only 15 minutes, reaching a height of just under 100 miles before her capsule parachuted safely to earth.

Four days later, another *astrochat* was launched, but due to technical difficulties, the courageous cat never again walked the earth.[58]

Ever wonder why dogs defend their territory but cats don't? Both are hunters and can be very vicious. But cats are better built for fleeing. They can sprint faster and climb up a tree. Dogs, who long ago lived in packs, have found they're better off if they stand (with their friends) and defend their turf rather than run and try to climb a tree.

Ever wonder why cats are stealthier than dogs? It seems to be because cats are better sprinters. They can move fast but only for short distances. They have to get as close to their prey as possible. Dogs are better built for the long haul. They can hound their prey for a long time, so rather than sneak up on their prey, they wear them down.

Dogs and cats love meat. But cats are obligate carnivores. They have to eat meat. Dogs can live without it. But get some advice before you put your dog on a vegan diet. He'll need protein. He'll have to eat a lot of beans which can only lead to trouble.

According to John Bradshaw, a cat researcher at the University of Bristol and author of *Cat Sense*, dogs understand that they are different from people. They behave differently with people than with other dogs. Cats, on the other hand, generally behave the same way around people as they do with other cats.[59] Anyone who has owned two or more cats, however, knows that isn't necessarily true. The relationships are different.

When dogs chase prey, their heads bob up and down. Cats keep their heads level, their eyes on the business at hand.[54]

How Cats Say "Get Meow da Here!"

A study of the behavior of dogs and cats in animal shelters detected different means of appealing to potential adopters.

The study found that dogs who raised their eyebrows a lot were more likely to be adopted. A dog that raised its eyebrows 20 times while meeting a human was twice as likely to be adopted. A lot of tail wagging, oddly enough, resulted in more time behind bars. Apparently the tendency to use the eyes to appeal to humans is a trait that goes way back to the early days of the domestication of wolves. Raised eyebrows increased the likelihood of being taken into human circles. The consequent safety and dependable food supply resulted in more puppies born with that trait. Dogs were unconsciously bred to look cute and acceptable by manipulating their faces.

Another study found that cats made no such use of their facial muscles. The study mapped out all the muscles in cat faces so that scientists could measure their expressions as potential adopters looked them over. There was no correlation between cat facial expressions and the rate of adoption. (A cat's expression is the same whether, in the words of comedian Paula Poundstone, it sees a moth or an ax-murderer.) But cats who frequently rubbed their bodies on furniture and objects in their pens were 30 percent more likely to be adopted.

One theory accounting for this difference is that dogs, who were domesticated before cats, were taken in for companionship and had more time to evolve traits appealing to people. Cats were first domesticated not to warm laps but to kill vermin. Endearing expressions had nothing to do with it.[23]

Belling Cats with Colors

Domestic cats are the biggest anthropogenic—i.e., created by mankind—threat to songbirds in North America.

Nobody but a cat likes to see a songbird die. Colorful collars may help minimize the slaughter. The theory is that it's easier for a bird to spot bright colors than fur roughly the color of dirt or dead leaves.

Researchers tested the collars. Cats with collars killed 19 times fewer birds in the spring and 3.4 times fewer in the fall. The brand of the tested collar was Birdsbesafe.

Cats in Trouble

Furicane Ernest

As if having a few extra toes weren't enough of a problem, the descendants of Ernest Hemingway's cats had to ride out Hurricane Irma, one of the worst in Atlantic history.

The 54 polydactyl cats (not all necessarily descended from the great writer's white pet) still live in or around Hemingway's famous Key West house. They somehow sensed that approach of the storm, probably by detecting the drop of air pressure. Ten of their staff remained at the house during the storm despite pleas by Hemingway's granddaughter, Mariel Hemingway, to put the cats in a car and get to safety on the mainland. Maybe it was concern for the house, which is today a museum, maybe concern about the complexity of herding 54 cats into a car, but the loyal staff let all the cats into the house and stayed behind to care for house and cats. Everyone survived unscathed. The rest of Key West did not fare as well, with more than 30 people dying and most houses destroyed.[60]

Don't Let This Happen to You

Every year some 40,000 people in the United States are bitten by cats seriously enough to report it.[61]

Don't Let This Happen to Your Cat

Florida Senator Ken Myer's cat Andy fell 16 stories and lived to tell the tale. This is probably a world record.[62]

Cat Caca Coffee, Anyone?

The most expensive coffee in the world, Kopi Luwak, comes from an Indonesian luwak wildcat. The cat eats the coffee beans off trees and processes them through its digestive system. The beans are collected from the cat's dung, then washed, roasted, and sold for about $500 for a one-pound bag.[64]

The Tale of the Rally Cat

Every boy has had this fantasy...at least the beginning of it. It's a home game for the home team, in this case the St. Louis Cardinals. The other team, a local rival, in this case, the Royals from nearby Kansas City.

It's the bottom of the sixth. The home team's down four to five. Two outs. *Bases loaded with Cardinals.* You step up to the plate. (In this case, you are Yadier Molina.) Nervous? Yes. Things have not been going well for you. You're 2 for 5 against this pitcher. A pop fly or a weak grounder will end the hitting streak, the inning, and, in all likelihood, the dreams of a hundred thousand fans.

Enter the cat. From out of nowhere, the little tiger dashes down the third base line and out into right field. The crowd goes nuts. This isn't the first cat to bust into a Cardinals game. It happened in Anaheim, too, before St. Louis whipped the Angels. And then there was the time a squirrel dashed across home plate in a playoff game against the Phillies in 2011. The Cardinals went on to win that game and the subsequent World Series. But is this cat the return of a winning spirit or the cat from hell, sent in on a mission to mess with Molina's head?

From out of nowhere dashes grounds crew guy Lucas Hackmann. Incredibly, he manages to catch up with the cat and grab it. But the cat doesn't want to stay grabbed. It bites Hackmann at least twice on the way off the field.

Back to baseball. Molina takes a swing at the next pitch. It's a hit. The ball flies high into the blue sky of St. Louis, out over right field, farther and farther...and into the stands. It isn't just a home run. It's a grand slam.

End of game? No. For this is America, and there's a cat involved. Groundskeeper Hackmann, just in from the field, sets the cat down to lick his wounds. Cardinals fan Korie Harris picks up the cat. Even though she doesn't notice the grand slam, she remembers the batter and names the cat Yodie. As Harris tries to leave the stadium, a guard stops her. She does what anyone would do in such a situation. She lies. She says it's her cat. The guard believes that Korie has actually brought her cat to a baseball game. And on her way she goes.

But Yodie (not its real name) gets loose. Before long, it's found by an organization that rescues feral cats, St. Louis Cat Outreach (STLCO). The cat goes into mandatory quarantine. The Cardinals declare that the "Rally Cat" belongs to the team. It's going to be a locker room mascot, an in-house good luck totem, kind of like the Red Sox beards, except that it bites and needs a regular supply of kitty litter. But STLCO says not so fast. They wouldn't wish locker room life on a dog. The cat needs a loving home with a couch and everything, "a serendipitous match" with "some chemistry."

Now it's no longer just any cat. It's a cat with a lawyer. Negotiations proceed. For the Cardinals, this isn't just a question of love and luck. It's money. They remember the Rally Squirrel T-shirts of 2011, which raked in $210,000 for the Cardinal Glennon Children's Foundation (named after not the team but the Archbishop of St. Louis, John J. Glennon). Vicious insults are exchanged on social media. "Nobody likes a bully in the litter box," the STLCO lawyer said. The team PR man finally says the Cardinals "don't want to be engaged in a cat fight."

As the season drew to a close, the Rally Cat was still being fattened up for adoption. Meanwhile, a September Rally Cat Appreciation Day was scheduled complete with Rally Cat T-shirts for fans of Cardinals and cats.[63]

The Cat House of Latvia

It's not every day you see a cat used as a tool of insult—unless you live in Riga, the capital of Latvia. There stands the famous Cat House, built by a wealthy tradesman in 1909. The five-story building was built in medieval style but with art nouveau touches. At the peak of two turrets are two copper statues of cats, each in an angry, arched-back position with tail raised as if in preparation for a big-time bowel movement. Their rear ends both face the same direction.

At whom the insult is aimed is a matter of controversy among Rigans. Some say the cats are aimed at the House of the great Guild, a trade organization that denied him membership. Others say they aim at City Hall, where the building's owner had some kind of dispute with the City Council. The City Hall of the day was destroyed in World War II, but the Cat House and cats and the insult still remain.[65]

Incendiary Cats

Cat bombs. Just what the world needs.

A few have reached the concept and even experimental level of development. Fortunately—for cats as well as other living things—cat bombs have never been deployed.

One of the earliest ideas, dreamed up around 1430, was an incendiary bomb that would be carried to the enemy on the back of a cat. It was called a "rocket pack," though it wasn't meant to make the cat fly. Instructions went something like this:

"Create a small sack like a fire-arrow...if you would like to get at a town or castle, get a cat from that place. Bind the sack to the back of the cat, ignite it, let it glow well, and then let the cat go so that it runs to the nearest castle or town, and out of fear it thinks to hide itself in the hay or straw of a barn, which will be ignited."[66]

When Feline Eyes Are Shining

Cat eyes are amazing in the daylight and in the dark. By day they look like glass marbles, sometimes blue, sometimes gold or copper-colored, sometimes green. By night they shine with unearthly brilliance.

The night shine is known as *chatoyan*. The same word is used to describe gems that reflect light because of the way they're cut. The word comes from a French word based on the word *chat*.

A thousand years ago, people suspected that the nighttime glow was actually coming from the fires of hell. This was one reason why cats were considered evil.

A cat with gold or copperish eyes glow yellow-green or blue-green in the dark. A blue-eyed cat's eyes glow red. The glow occurs only immediately after light hits the eyes in the dark, while the pupils are still wide open for better vision in the dark (or rather, what seems to humans to be dark. Cats can't see in total darkness). The light hits reflective cells on the retina at the back of the eyeball. These cells contain a lot of zinc. The cells reflect any light that was not absorbed during the first passage through the eye. This allows the cat to see in low-light situations.[67]

Your Tax Dollars at Work

The Central Intelligence Agency almost got its middle name revoked after the agency's innovative attempt to enlist a patriotic cat to the service of his country. This was back in the 1960s, when counter-Soviet espionage was most urgent. The CIA needed to know what its nuclear adversary was up to.

The top-secret plan: Surgically implant listening devices into a cat, code-named "Acoustic Kitty."

A former CIA officer described the gruesome process. "They slit the cat open, put batteries in him, wired him up," the officer said. "The tail was used as an antenna. They made a monstrosity."

Then they tried to train the cat—whose real name remains a government secret—to hang out on window sills, under park benches, and near embassy garbage cans, picking up and transmitting conversations.

To the surprise of the intelligence agency, training a cat proved difficult.

"They tested him and tested him," the CIA agent said. "They found he would walk off the job when he got hungry, so they put another wire in to override that."

Five years (a mighty long time for a cat) and $10 million (a mighty lot of money for a cat) later, they took the secret agent out for a trial run.

"They took [a specially equipped van] out to a park and put him out of the van," the CIA man said, "and a taxi comes and runs over him. There they were, sitting in the van with all those dials, and the cat was dead."[68]

A heavily redacted CIA report, released in 2001, said, "Our final examination of trained cats...for...use in the...convinced us that the program would not lend itself in a practical sense to our highly specialized needs...."[69]

The Cat That Was a Mule

Some clever—but not quite clever enough—prisoners in a prison in Brazil, attempted to use a cat to smuggle a cell phone, saws, batteries, and drills into the prison.

Guards caught the cat, which was loaded down like a pack mule. The prison's more than 250 inmates were all suspects, though officials were not able to identify any individuals linked to the escape attempt.[70]

Some Idiot's Idea for a Cat Bomb

According to the Internet, the following is true.

Back during World War II, before the CIA got its name, the Office of Strategic Services got a brilliant idea to solve a complicated problem.

The problem: How to get a moving bomb dropped from a moving plane to hit a moving target, in this case, an enemy ship.

The solution: Strap the bomb to a cat.

Why a cat: Because a) cats know how to land on their feet, and b) cats hate water. Dropped from a plane several thousand feet in the air, the bomb-laden furball would attempt to get into a feet-first toward-the-ship position. That attempt would somehow guide the bomb toward the ship.

How the cat would actually guide the bomb was going to take a lot of experimentation, one cat per shot, each cat terminally precluded from learning how to do it right a second time. According to an animated illustration on youtube.com, the cat was inside a capsule with a window and a bomb. Strings attached to the cat's paws guided the bomb as the cat tried to land on its feet on the ship.

Under the urgency of war, the OSS skipped over technical concerns and went ahead and outfitted a courageous volunteer cat with a bomb and dropped it from a plane. The bomb missed the target. The OSS said that the cat had passed out at some point during its breathtaking—one can only imagine—descent and thus was unable to complete its mission. How the OSS detected the cat's lack of consciousness is another mystery in this story, which, though terrible, is just too interesting to ignore. Whatever the answer to these mysteries, there were no further attempts to use a cat to guide a bomb. One cat, and they were done.

Litter, Litter, Litter, and Litter

What do roadside trash and a stretcher for wounded soldiers have in common with a bunch of kittens and a shallow box reserved for the defacatory needs of America's favorite household pet? They all involve the word *litter*.

But why? What else do they have in common?

All four uses of the word come from a French word brought to England by William the Conqueror and his French hordes. The French *litere*, referred to a portable bed, bier, or bedding material, such as straw. The word eventually became the modern French *lit*, for bed. Over time the English word evolved to *litter*, referring to an animal's bedding, and then to the animals offspring, and then to scattered debris resembling straw on a barn floor.

So: the litter on the side of the road is disorderly debris. The litter for the soldier is a portable bed. The litter where the cat takes a dump serves the purpose of straw on a stall floor, and the litter to which a cat gives birth is an animal's offspring.

Why Caboodle

So what does *caboodle* have to do with *kitten*? Nothing. In the middle of the 19th century, caboodle referred to a crowd, a pack, a company, a bunch, a lot. Then the phrase "kit and caboodle" came along to mean *kit and cargo*. *Kit* referred to a number of things that were seen as a single whole, such as a cargo or, for that matter, a kit. So *kit and caboodle* simply meant *everything and everybody, the whole bunch*. From caboodle we get the word *oodles*. Same idea. (*Kitten* derives from the Middle English *kitoun*, which comes from the Old French word *chitoun*, which became *chaton*, the diminutive of *chat*, meaning *cat*. Nothing to do with caboodles.)[82]

So what's a "kitten caboodle"? It's either a joke and pun on *kit and caboodle* or just somebody who doesn't understand the original phrase.

So what's a "Cat Caboodle"? It isn't a caboodle that belongs to a cat. It's caboodle of or about cats, such as the one you're holding in your hands.

If Your Cat Bounces...

Chocolate is deadly to both dogs and cats. The minimal lethal dose for a cat is unknown, but two ounces of milk chocolate can be enough to do away with a dog. The utter lack of finickiness in dogs predisposes them to consume a deadly dose.

Symptoms of chocolate toxicosis: vomiting, diarrhea, loss of body control, rapid heartbeat, rapid breathing, high blood pressure, weakness, cardiac arrhythmia, tremors, seizures, coma, and death (from cardiac or respiratory failure). An intoxicated cat dropped just a few inches to its feet will seem to bounce.

The cure: Induce vomiting within 4 hours of consumption. If you can get the cat to swallow activated charcoal, that might work, but stand back! Better yet, rush to the vet.[71]

Do cats have nine lives?

The idea of multiple lives for cats is found all over the world, though the numbers vary. The myth comes from the cat's readiness to flee danger, to land on its feet when falling (they've been known to survive falls of over 150 feet), and to be able to twist itself into (and out of) tight spaces.

Cats in many countries are said to have nine lives, but cats in Italy, Germany, Greece, Brazil and some Spanish-speaking countries get only seven lives. In Turkish and Arabic regions, six is the limit.

A Downside to Cats

Cats often carry a parasite called Toxoplasma gondii. And they're not alone. An estimated 60 million people carry the little buggers, too. Few develop obvious symptoms, but people with compromised immune systems—the elderly, HIV patients, infants, pregnant women—can develop blindness, flu-like symptoms. The pregnant can have miscarriages or fetal development disorder. Some people go so far as to die.[72]

Cleaning cat litter is a common way of picking up the parasite. Children can get it from contaminated sand in a sandbox. You can also get it from undercooked pork and unpasteurized goat milk. A fetus can get it from a mother.

Recent research out of Johns Hopkins University School of Medicine has found a possible link between the parasite and mental illnesses such as schizophrenia and bipolar disorder. Three studies found a connection.

"Cat ownership in childhood has now been reported in three studies to be significantly more common in families in which the child is later diagnosed with schizophrenia or another serious mental illness," the authors of the study said.

A study published in *Acta Psychiatrica Scandinavica* found that people with the parasite are twice as likely to develop schizophrenia.

The experts' advice: Keep your cats indoors, and if you have kids with a sandbox, keep it covered when not in use.[73]

When Cats Get High

What is it with catnip? That's a good question. Scientists have determined that the active ingredient in the *Nepeta cataria* plant is nepetalactone. A cat can detect as little as one part nepetalactone per billion parts of air.

Cats go ape when they smell catnip. When they find it growing, they roll around in it, get the oil on their fur, lick it off, then roll around some more. When they find a catnip-filled toy, they toss it around, claw it, clutch it, have a lot of fun with it.

Leopards? Cougars? Lynxes? Lions? They love the stuff, too. Tigers? Not so much. It depends on the tiger.[74]

An experiment with various plants found that nearly all domestic cats responded to some kind of olfactory stimulant. Almost 80 percent responded to silver vine, and about 50 percent to Tatarian honeysuckle. Catnip? One in three domestic cats couldn't care less.[75]

How about people? Desperate marijuana smokers have been known to try smoking catnip, but all it does is make them feel not just desperate but stupid. However, an experiment conducted by two Marquette University researchers found that when people smoked tobacco that had been sprayed with catnip oil, they hallucinated as if on lysergic acid diethylamide (LSD). In that trans,cis nepetalactone is molecularly similar to LSD, it is possible that when cats are flipping out over catnip, chasing phantom butterflies, they may be tripping like hippies.[76]

Who Gets the Cat?

The American Academy of Matrimonial Lawyers found that in 2014, 88 percent of pet custody contentions in divorces were over who gets the dog. Only five percent of the arguments were over cats.[77]

Increasingly judges are taking the pet's interest into consideration. For other kinds of assets, such as a piece of furniture, a judge might consider a person's attachment to a given item. In the case of a pet, judges may consider the pet's attachment to a given owner.[78]

The Cat of the Future

Tired of cleaning a litter box? Hasbro—yes, the maker of Nerf balls, Monopoly, Play-doh and a host of action figures—makes a robotic cat. It's a reasonable facsimile of the real thing except that it doesn't shed hair, shred furniture, heave up hairballs or leave indelible odors in the basement. And at $99.99, it costs less than the annual upkeep of a pet with a pulse. "No litter box. Just love." is the slogan for Hasbro's Joy For All Companion Pets.

The battery-operated cats are in use in nursing homes. Hebrew Home in New York City has deployed dozens of them in their Memory Unit, which cares for dementia and Alzheimer patients.[79]

The "cats" have built-in sensors that respond to motion and touch. The fur feels real, and the movements are much like those of a live animal. Sounds mimic the real thing. Petting the cat's cheek causes it to nuzzle its head into the hand. Pet its back, and it will emit a VibraPurr™. Pet it enough and it will roll over on its back for a belly rub. If you do it right (or forget to do it), it will close its eyes for a snooze until touched again.[80]

In a crucial oversight, Hasbro neglected to install a heater. The robocats come with instructions:

To start your cat for the first time, turn it over and find the opening on its underside. Pull the opening apart to reveal the power switch. Pull bottom rear leg for full access to the switch. Flip the switch from OFF to ON. Turn cat over and place it on lap or flat surface.

"Cat care: Wipe dirt off immediately. Do not use detergent or stain removers. To remove stains, simply wipe with a slightly damp cloth. Do not immerse in water. To avoid tripping, never put your cat on the floor.

Troubleshooting: If your cat stops working, try switching it off and then back on again. If that doesn't work, follow the directions to replace the batteries. For additional assistance, call 1-800-255-5516.

Available in orange tabby, creamy white, and silver. Four C batteries included.

When Cats Vocalize

You may never have taken the Ainsworth Strange Situation Test (SST), but 20 cats have, as did their "owners." In fact, they not only took that test but took another that had been specially adapted for cats. It was a great day, a test of a test involving cats in strange situations.[81]

Researchers observed the cat's behavior toward an owner and a stranger in a strange situation. They used non-parametric analyses. They observed that the only difference in behavior toward the owner and the stranger was a tendency to "vocalize"—or "meow"— more when the owner was there. Other than that, the cats showed no more attachment to either human.

Conclusion: The cat-human bond does not make a cat feel more secure. On the other hand, does a cat make a human feel more secure? The study did not say.

Notes on Incarceration

Preliminary Thoughts

These brief notes on incarceration do not purport or pretend to be a thorough examination of the history or current state of imprisonment. They touch all too lightly, too briefly, on only a few of imprisonment's many serious problems. Its only purpose is to give the reader a sampling of the information that is available.

A lot of information is available. Innumerable studies identify innumerable problems with the current use of prisons as a form of punishment and personal improvement. Recidivism rates indicate clearly and undeniably that imprisonment fails to make society safer. As a deterrent, prisons are minimally, if indeterminately, effective. As a form of mandatory "correction," they fail miserably. They aggravate violence, destroy families, drain public funds, cause poverty, hurt children, and accomplish little more than temporarily isolating a criminal from society and giving a few people the satisfaction of revenge.

Some of those innumerable studies explore solutions. Some are just ideas, others actual programs proven to work. Shorter sentences, fewer sentences, more family visits, working with animals, religious conversion, art programs, college courses, meditation, shorter and less demanding paroles, more responsibility, restorative justice, less youth incarceration, even doing away with prisons altogether—there is so much that could be done, yet social, political, and economic pressures too often prevent change. The ever-popular "tough on crime" approach rarely recognizes the possibility that inducing a former criminal to go straight is more productive than making a criminal suffer.

Some of these notes, of course, aren't identifying a problem or offering a solution. They're just giving the reader an inside look at the inside life, that other world where so many people live.

Prisons are a real problem, a sad, painful, tragedy affecting, at the moment, over two million people in the United States, with millions more in the pipeline of racism, poverty, poor education, and erosion of generally accepted social values. The gravity of the problem and the existence of solutions led to the notes in this section.

In that each topic is presented in just a few paragraphs, the author hopes that interested reader will refer to the documents cited in footnotes. Many of these references are available on web sites, and they tend to have footnotes of their own, tempting the reader from casual reading into deeper research.

But neither reading nor research is enough. Something—a lot of things—need to be done. Solutions exist. They are known. What is not known is why the solutions are enacted only sporadically, if at all, a moral and political negligence that seems almost criminal.

Prison Life

Meet & Greet

Welcome to your new home! It may not be as spacious as you like, but at least you'll have someone to talk to.

You may not be escorted to your cell. A guard will give you a cell number and point the way. If you can't find your cell, find someone who looks like you and ask where to go.

The first thing you have to do is meet your new roomie. This will be a big moment for both of you, and perhaps a bit awkward. The thing to do upon arrival is knock on the door. If there's someone inside, introduce yourself thus: "My name's Bob. They told me to bunk here."

If no one's there, go in, but don't touch anything. Don't lie on a bunk. Just wait. Stand up to introduce yourself.

Your cell mate may need some time to clean off the bunk that will be yours. It's a good time to break a little ice. Ask for advice. Where do I put my stuff? When do we eat? What's the rule on leaving and coming back? Don't ask any personal questions. Presume the best. Be nice—polite but not weak.

Read Up to Survive

Know someone going to prison? There are books on how to go about being a prisoner and surviving imprisonment. Some titles:

Behind Bars: Surviving Prison, Jeffrey Ian Ross, Alpha, 2002.
Prison Survival Guide: Words of Wisdom and Encouragement from an Inmate, Russell Ferguson, Rosedog Books, 2016.
How to Do Time: What to Expect and How to Survive When Going to Prison, Jamonz M. Ross and Taleana K. Ross, 2017.
How to Survive in Prison: A Guide for Prisoners, their Families and Supporters, Createspace, 2017.
How to Survive Prison for the First Time Inmate: Take a Look at a Dangerous Society within our Society, Createspace, 2009.
How to Survive Prison, Andrew V. Kudin, Amazon Digital, 2012.
First Timers Guide on How to Survive in New York State Prison, Kemp McCoy, Trafford, 2013.
Inmate to Convict: A Guide to Prison Survival and the Art of Penitentiary Warfare, Brian Anderson, Amazon Digital, 2016.
Federal Prison Handbook: the Definitive Guide to Surviving the Federal Bureau of Prison, Christopher Zoukis, Middle St. Pub. 2017.

Any Questions?

Federal Prison: A Comprehensive Survival Guide, by Jonathan Richards, purports to answer some good questions. Here are some of them.

Will I be assaulted? What will the other inmates think of me? Will I be extorted? Will I be strip-searched? Will I be given a body cavity search? What will a normal day be like? How will I pass the time? Will I be able to exercise? What will I eat? Will I be locked in a cell? What will the sleeping arrangements be like? Will I have to shower in front of other men? Will I have to go to the bathroom in front of other men? Can I bring anything with me? Which one of the hundreds of federal prisons out there will I be sent to? What about my medications? Will I be locked up with murderers and rapists? What if I get sick? Will everyone know the details of my crime? What will happen to my business? How soon and how often can I have visitors? What will the prison look like? Who will I eat with in the chow hall? What about gangs in federal prisons? Will I need money in prison? If so, how much? Will I be forced to work? If so, what kind of job will I get? Can I use the bathroom at any time day or night? Will I be able to access the Internet or send email? What about listening to music?

Prison Literature

Some of the world's greatest writers have done time. In fact, some have done time for being great writers. Inevitably, some of the world's greatest literature—philosophy, fiction, memoir, commentary—has been either composed in or inspired by prison.

- Marco Polo wrote about his travels to China while imprisoned in Genoa.

- Miguel de Cervantes, captured by Barbary pirates, spent five years as a galley slave.

- Sir Walter Raleigh wrote his *History of the World, Volume 1* while held in the Tower of London.

- John Bunyan, arrested for unapproved preaching, wrote *The Pilgrim's Progress* in prison.

- Martin Luther translated the *New Testament* into German and wrote many polemical works while he hid from authorities at Wartburg Castle.

- Marquis de Sade wrote several novellas, volumes of essays, and plays during an 11-year term in the Bastille.

- Napoleon Bonaparte wrote his memoir while held at St. Helena island.

- Fyodor Dostoevsky was inspired to write *The House of the Dead* while serving four years of hard labor in Siberia.

- Oscar Wilde wrote his essay "De Profundis" while in jail for "unnatural acts" with other men.

- e.e. cummings wrote *The Enormous Room* in a French prison during World War I.

- Adolf Hitler wrote *Mein Kampf* while in prison.

- O. Henry wrote 14 stories while doing time for embezzlement.

- Iranian Mahmoud Dowlatabadi wrote *Missing Soluch* in his head while in prison for writing things that revolutionaries read.

- Albert Speer wrote *Inside the Third Reich* and *Spandau: The Secret Diaries* while at Spandau prison.

- Nawal El Saadawi, "The Simone de Beauvoir of the Arab world" wrote *Memoirs from the Women's Prison* while under arrest for publishing a feminist magazine.

- Martin Luther King wrote "Letter from the Birmingham Jail" during one of his 29 arrests.

- Wally Lamb helped several female prisoners write autobiographical essays in *Couldn't Keep It to Myself* and *I'll Fly Away*.

Other imprisoned writers include Chris Abani, Nelson Algren, Precious Bedell, Boethius, Ernest Booth, Kathy Boudin, Vera Figner Antonio Gramsci, Jean Genet, Hugo Grotius, George Lester Jackson, Robert Lowell, Donald Lowrie, Lady Constance Lytton, Caesarina Kona Makhoere, Danny Martin, Patricia McConnel, Raimundo Montecuccoli, Kate Richards O'Hare, Madame Roland, Béatrice Saubin, Ken Saro-Wisa, Agnes Smedley, Ngugi wa Thiongo, Pramoedya Ananta Toer, Jim Tully, and Krystyna Wituska.

In Nigeria

In January of 2017, Nigeria had 47,229 people in prison while waiting for trial. That's from a total prison population of 67,586. According to the vice president of Nigeria, Prof. Yemi Osinbajo, their average wait was about three years.[1]

Three years is a long time in a Nigerian prison. According to the U.S. "Country Reports on Human Rights Practices for 2015," "Prison and detention center conditions remain harsh and life-threatening. Prisoners and detainees, the majority of whom had not been tried, were reportedly subjected to extra-judicial execution, torture, gross overcrowding, food and water shortages, inadequate medical treatment, deliberate and incidental exposure to heat and sun, and infrastructure deficiencies that led to wholly inadequate sanitary conditions that could result in death. Guards and prison officials reportedly extorted inmates or levied fees on them to pay for food, prison maintenance, and release from prison. Female inmates in some cases faced the threat of rape."[2]

No Saint for San Quentin

San Quentin is not named after St. Quentin, a Roman missionary who was arrested for his preaching, manacled, and tortured and then was to be transported and put on trial, except he escaped, then captured, tortured, beheaded, and thrown in a swamp, where his body was later found thanks to his "odor of sanctity." The Quentin of California fame was a Miwok Indian who was captured on what was later known as Point Quentin, where a prison was built in 1852.

Groups and Programs at San Quentin

There's no reason to be bored while doing time at San Quentin. Here are some of the organizations and programs that prisons can use to improve themselves and prepare for a return to outside society.

- AA -- Alcoholics Anonymous
- Alliance for CHANGE -- self-development
- ARC -- addiction recovery counseling
- CenterForce -- peer health counseling
- Change is Possible -- self-development
- CRI -- California Reentry Institute
- Developing a Positive Attitude -- self-development
- Green Life -- environmentally healthy living
- GRIP -- Guiding Rage Into Power
- IMPACT -- enabling positive choices
- Kairos -- spiritual retreat program
- Kid CAT -- lifers convicted as juveniles
- MOMAS -- fostering business and financial literacy
- NA -- Narcotics Anonymous
- No More Tears -- violence prevention

- Non-Violent Communications -- (self-explanatory)
- Over-Comers -- Christian Narcotics Anonymous
- Project REACH -- peer tutoring
- RE Choices -- youth mentoring
- Richmond Project -- issues in the city of Richmond
- San Quentin News (newspaper)
- S.Q. TRUST -- responsibility for self, family, and community
- SQUIRES -- youth mentoring
- The Last Mile -- business and technical literacy
- The Work -- self-development
- Vietnam Veterans -- addressing veterans' issues
- Violence Prevention
- VOEG -- victim-offender restorative justice
- Yoga

Keeping Women Busy

The programs and treatments at York Correctional Institution in Niantic, Conn., include 12-Step recovery programs, day job assignments, trauma recovery, alternatives to violence, anger management, artists in residence, book club, books for babies, Bible studies, Protestant and Catholic choir, Catholic retreats (Kairos, Emmaus, Legion of Mary, Life in the Spirit), literacy, English as a second language, public service projects, Habitat for Humanity, Warm the Baby/Warm the Elderly crocheting, Daybreak Protestant programs, puppy training, exercise classes, Good Works re-entry mentoring, greenhouse work (planting, garden design, etc.), grief and loss recovery, trauma healing for abused women, GED, how to be happy, certified nurse's aide, Islamic studies, Performance Project, childbirth support, library, life skills, Microsoft software, Miracle of Melody, Motivation and Self-Mastery, Overeaters Anonymous, parenting, pre-natal and post-partum education, Project Rap, Quinnipiac University, Weslyan University, and Trinity College for-credit courses, self-esteem, Seven Challenges, sex offender treatment, Sisters Standing Strong, Storybook Project, stress management, textile shop, certified cosmetology and barbering training, culinary arts, adult basic education, business education, computer education, hospitality operations technology, smoking cessation, women's wellness, creative writing, and yoga, and many others.[3]

The News from San Quentin

From the January 2018 edition of *San Quentin News*[4]:

YOUTH OFFENDER MIX TAPE CAPTURES
GENERATIONAL TRAUMA OF INCARCERATION

Daniel Gutierrez, 21, says with regret that prison has been the norm in his family. "Everyone has been to jail except my mom."

When I got to San Quentin, I ended up three cells down from where my grandfather was once housed. In the county jail I was in the same dorm my father was once in. I was even on the same (prison) yard with my uncle," said Gutierrez.

A musician, Gutierrez said he shares a parallel life with his grandfather, Jose Moreno, who has been out of prison two decades. He even reflected on that relationship in a rap song, "The Same Prison as My Grandfather," on a San Quentin Youth Offender mix-tape project. Gutierrez uses the song for therapeutic relief and guidance for his future....

Drugs and Drones, Eagles, and Death Rays

The extent of the use of drugs and alcohol in prisons around the world is largely unknown, but it is estimated that a third of the world's prisoners have managed to ingest drugs during their time behind bars. Many inject drugs for the first time while locked up.[5]

England has seen a sharp rise in the use of drones to drop drugs and other contraband into prison yards. The government called it "a significant new and evolving threat."[6] The Chief Prison Inspectorate for England and Wales reported that drones were a reason for high levels of drug use in certain prisons.

In July 2016, a man received the first prison sentence for using a drone to fly contraband into prisons.[7]

But England has a plan. Actually, it's a Dutch idea, and it seems to be working. Police in Netherlands have been using trained eagles to hunt and intercept illegal drones.[8] The French have been doing the same. In early 2017, the French military also began to use trained eagles to bring down drones.[9]

But the Brits aren't putting all their eagle eggs in one basket. If eagles can't do the trick, there may be other ways to skin the cat. The alternatives include a bazooka that fires a net,[10] a net-carrying interceptor drone being used by police in Japan,[11] and an anti-drone death ray.[12]

Half a Million Kids

Feel like having your soul crushed for an hour and a half? Watch the documentary film "Kids Behind Bars—Real Stories." It tells the stories of a few of the half a million children who are in prisons around the world, from England to Mongolia. It's on YouTube.com.[13]

Other documentaries on YouTube include

- "Lockdown Prison: Kids Behind Bars"
- "The Hardest Kids Prison"
- "Prison: Kids Behind Bars, why are children in prison?"
- "Life in Prisons: Kids Serve LIFE in Prison"
- "Teenagers Serving Life in Prison"
- "America's Youngest Sex Offenders"
- "Kid Criminals"
- "Babies Behind Bars"

Don't Get Busted in Brazil

Brazil has one of the ugliest prison situations in the world. There may be places with worse prisons, but Brazil ranks fourth in number of prisons with close to 650,000 people behind bars, 42 percent of them just waiting for trial.[14] The conditions are horrific. Prisoners are 30 times more likely to contract tuberculosis. Cells hold many times more than they were built for. A Minister of Justice called the nation's prisons "medieval dungeons."[15] Brazil has the fourth largest prisonpopulation in the world.

The Curado prison complex in Recife, state of Pernambuco, holds some 7,000 prisoners in a facility built for 1,800. A reporter found 60 prisoners in a cell built for six. Cells are left unlocked because prisoners would suffocate if packed in at the same time. Guards cannot enter cell blocks, so keys are entrusted to powerful inmates. Conditions are so filthy that leprosy is a problem.[16]

In 2016, during riots at two juvenile facilities in Pernambuco, 11 teens lost their lives and 11 others were injured. One of the dead had been attacked while in handcuffs in solitary confinement. A few days later, an uprising at the Caruau facility in São Paulo left seven teens dead, one of them decapitated.[17]

Gangs control the prisons more than guards do, and their conflicts result in mass killings, beheadings, mutilated bodies, and sometimes mass escapes.[18] An uprising and gang-versus-gang battle in a prison in Manaus resulted in 56 deaths and more than 130 escapes. President Michel Temer called it a "dreadful accident."[19]

All Is Not Bad in Brazil

Brazil is finding success in a very innovative program called the Association for the Protection and Assistance to Convicts (APAC). At APAC prisons, prisoners are given respect and responsibility...and keys to their cells and even the main gate of the prison. Inmates wear their own clothes, prepare their own food, and, believe it or not, provide their own security. There are no guards or weapons. The inmates govern themselves.

And there's no violence. Inmates don't even want to escape. They are in the last years of their sentences, and their ultimate freedom depends on good behavior. Good behavior includes a strict routine of work and study. Some prisoners can leave the prison to do volunteer work for the community, reconstructing the social pact they broke by committing a crime.

The inmates are not called prisoners but *recuperados*, that is, people in recovery. Conditions are much better than in other prisons. The population is limited to avoid crowding. Consequently, recidivism is lower, and so is the cost of operating the prison.

Similar programs are operating in Costa Rica, Chile, and Ecuador.

APAC prisons work. They cost less and actually produce better citizens rather than better criminals. Why aren't there more? For one thing, the program depends on support by the Italian AVSI Foundation. For another, Brazilian politicians tend to put self-interest over concerns for country and people. For another, political will is always hard to sustain when the general population is boiling with anger over criminal violence. For another, communities resist the idea of hosting a prison where, under certain conditions, inmates are allowed to walk out the front gate.[20]

Why aren't there APAC prisons in the United States? Same reasons.

Wild Horses Scared Inside

There does seem to be something about the outside of a horse that is good for the inside of a man.

Winston Churchill

Several states are having success with prisons involved with farming, especially the care of animals. Arizona, Colorado, Florida, Kansas, Louisiana, Nevada, Texas, Virginia, and Wyoming have programs involving horses.[21] Some of the programs involve the domestication and training of wild horses, a process known as "gentling." Generally the gentled horses are sold off for adoption. The inmates who are with them are well aware of the similarity of the men's and horses' situation: once wild, now fenced in, eventually to get out. One inmate said, "I look at them like us: I helped the horse become a better person so he can make parole."[22]

An article about the program at the maximum-security prison in Florence, CO, said this:

The horses were just trying to survive. They acted mean and aggressive, but in reality they were scared to death, just like the men. For the first time in the lives of these men, they were shown the undeniable truth about who they were.

They had learned and believed that being tough and vicious was their only hope of survival. But now — just like these beautiful, wild, violent, and unpredictable animals — the men could see that their motive had also been fear. And maybe, just like the horses, they too could change.

Behind their violence, the mustangs were deeply afraid. The inmates identified with that. They saw themselves. They began to feel compassion, an emotion they had probably never known or felt before. They felt it for the horses, they felt it for each other, and they felt it for themselves.

The inmates were trying to gentle the horses, but in truth the horses were gentling the inmates.[23]

Tablets for Prisoners

In early 2018 the New York State's Department of Corrections announced that each of the state's 50,300 inmates would be receiving a free tablet computer.

The tablets were to be provided free of charge by a company called JPay, which manufactures the tablets and installs them with free educational materials and books. However, the prisoners would have to pay for any additional downloads, such as apps, games, books, and music. There would also be a charge of 35 cents to send or receive email.

All revenues would go to JPay. There would be no expense to taxpayers.[24] The DoC said that the purposes of the program were to promote education and safety and help families communicate.[25] Prisons are said to be calmer when prisoners are zoned out with tablets, and more communication with families reduces recidivism.

Maybe Education Works

Bard College's Bard Prison Initiative has been offering college level courses to inmate students in New York State prisons since 2001. The program has been an unquestionable success. Hundreds of inmate students have earned degrees. Only four percent of those who take courses, and 2.5 percent of those who graduate, commit a crime and return to prison after their release. These graduates are not people who normally pursue and earn college degrees. They tend to come from poor communities with limited educational resources. The majority were first arrested when they were children, and few arrived with high school diplomas. But when presented with an opportunity to improve themselves, they take it. In fact, they compete with each other for limited slots in the program. At some of the New York prisons, more than ten percent of the inmates are taking courses.

Now a dozen other colleges are emulating the program at other prisons. The Bard initiative has been reported in the New York Times and the *New York Review of Books*. The *60 Minutes* television program brought the story to millions of people. The program received even more publicity when the Eastern New York Correctional Facility debate team defeated a team from Harvard.[26]

Unfair Education?

Higher education in prisons is proven to work, and the success of the Bard Prison Initiative is no secret. Ex-prisoners become responsible, taxpaying citizens rather than go back to a life of crime. So why aren't all prisons offering college courses and degrees?

Money is certainly one reason. The inmates don't have much of it. Legislators, unable to see that college courses cost less than post-release crime and recidivism, see no reason to educate criminals. Even New York legislators turned down a proposal from Governor Cuomo to dedicate $1 million to finance college education behind bars. Colleges can't easily afford to dedicate professors and materials to a program, so they depend on donations.

But it isn't just the money. The issue has been swept up in a "get tough on crime" controversy, and many feel it isn't fair to educate prisoners when many taxpayers can't afford to go to college.

One of the New York legislators said the governor's proposal was "a slap in the face of honest taxpayers."

A Republican senator from Texas said it was unfair for felons to benefit from Pell grants when low-income students were denied them.

President Clinton signed a crime bill preventing prisoners from using federal funds for college courses, stating, "This bill puts government on the side of those who abide by the law, not those who break it, on the side of the victims, not their attackers."

A college professor whose daughter was murdered, said, "This does not make sense to me. What is the point?"

It's an old argument, that vengeance is sweeter than actually solving a problem.[27]

Like Little Prisons Where Everyone Can See

Stocks—a hinged device used to restrain a prisoner's ankles and wrists—have been in use since biblical times, but it was in colonial America that stocks had very much the same purpose as prisons: to prevent flight, to punish, and to deter.

The prevention from flight was generally to hold the accused until trial. The punishment was not just physical pain but public humiliation. The two combined to deter others from similar crimes.

In the New Testament, the Book of Acts refers to Paul and Silas, disciples of Jesus who "advocated customs unlawful for Romans," were stripped, beaten with rods, thrown into prison, and then locked into stocks in an inner cell.

Statute of Labourers 1351 required that every town maintain a set of stocks for "unruly artisans."

In colonial times, people locked in stocks could be humiliated, beaten, paddled, whipped, spat upon, smacked with trash, doused with the contents of chamber pots, even tickled by any passerby with such an urge.

A Captain Kemble was sentenced to several hours in the stocks for kissing his wife in public on the sabbath. That he was returning from three years at sea was no excuse.

In Puritan Boston, Edward Palmer was sentenced to an hour in the stocks for the crime of charging too much for the stocks that he had just built.

Being sentenced to stocks is still legal in the United States. In 1989, a town in Arkansas passed a curfew law that would condemn an offender's parents to time in the stocks, though the ordinance was removed because the town did not have or want to pay for stocks. In 2004, the U.S. Court of Appeals upheld public humiliation as a reasonable punishment with the objective of rehabilitation. (No stocks were involved, but a mail thief had to wear a sandwich board stating "I stole mail; this is my punishment."[28]

Resistance to the PIC

An organization called Critical Resistance is aiming at the complete abolition of prisons. While the organization doesn't claim to have a plan or model for doing so, it has identified a problem—prisons as a result and cause of problems—and is working on a viable solution. Here's a statement from their website, criticalresistance.org:

> The prison industrial complex (PIC) is a term we use to describe the overlapping interests of government and industry that use surveillance, policing, and imprisonment as solutions to economic, social and political problems.
>
> Through its reach and impact, the prison industrial complex helps and maintains the authority of people who get their power through racial, economic and other privileges. There are many ways this power is collected and maintained through the PIC, including creating mass media images that keep alive stereotypes of people of color, poor people, queer people, immigrants, youth, and other oppressed communities as criminal, delinquent, or deviant. This power is also maintained by earning huge profits for private companies that deal with prisons and police forces; helping earn political gains for "tough on crime" politicians; increasing

the influence of prison guard and police unions; and eliminating social and political dissent by oppressed communities that make demands for self-determination and reorganization of power in the US.

PIC abolition is a political vision with the goal of eliminating imprisonment, policing, and surveillance and creating lasting alternatives to punishment and imprisonment.

From where we are now, sometimes we can't really imagine what abolition is going to look like. Abolition isn't just about getting rid of buildings full of cages. It's also about undoing the society we live in because the PIC both feeds on and maintains oppression and inequalities through punishment, violence, and controls millions of people. Because the PIC is not an isolated system, abolition is a broad strategy. An abolitionist vision means that we must build models today that can represent how we want to live in the future. It means developing practical strategies for taking small steps that move us toward making our dreams real and that lead us all to believe that things really could be different. It means living this vision in our daily lives.

Abolition is both a practical organizing tool and a long-term goal.

A free book on the topic is available at http://criticalresistance.org/resources/abolitionist-tools/

History

Île du Diable

Devil's Island was one part of a prison system established by France in French Guiana and on three islands off its coast. Previously, prisoners had been kept on hulks and in prison camps. When Napoleon III took power in 1851, he saw a way to increase the French population in Guiana, which was failing as a colony. He'd increase the population with prisoners and use them for labor. Those who survived their sentence—a small minority—would be required to remain in the colony. It was called "forced residency."

Most of the prisoners were petty criminals. A few were political prisoners guilty of criticizing the government. Captain Alfred Dreyfus, framed as a traitor, was the most famous, sentenced in 1895. Political prisoners and the worst of violent criminals were assigned to Devil's Island. Living conditions were not compatible with life. Prisoners there had a certain freedom to roam since the island was surrounded by shark-infested waters. Escape was virtually impossible.

A few managed to escape. Anarchist Clément Duval attempted escape over 20 times in 16 years before succeeding and making his way to New York City. Four other managed to reach St. Thomas, Virgin Islands. René Belbenoît escaped and wrote two memoirs: Hell on Trial and Fifteen Years among the Living Dead.

Henri Charrière wrote *Papillon*, a bestseller about his escape from Devil's Island. It was later discovered that he'd never been to Devil's Island, that he'd escaped from a mainland prison camp. He based his tale on Clément Duval's escape, but it was mostly fiction.

France didn't stop sending prisoners to the prison complex until 1938, though the prison didn't really close until 1953. Of the estimated 70,000 prisoners who had spent time in the prison complex, only some 2,000 ever saw France again. The last prisoner on Devil's Island when the prison closed refused to leave. He was still there in 1958. Nobody knows his name or what happened to him.[29]

Easy In, Easy Out

Jack Sheppard (1702-1724) knew how to put the "escape" in "escapade." Before he finished his apprenticeship as a carpenter, he was tempted into a life of crime, not to mention an adventurous relationship with a prostitute much larger than his diminutive self.

At the age of six, little Jack was sold off to a workhouse to learn the trade of making cane-chairs. Over the next 14 years he worked his way up to an apprenticeship in carpentry. But by the age of 20 he'd had enough of the honest life of de facto indentured slavery. He started hanging out at a tavern populated by local thieves. There he fell in love with a prostitute. Her name was Elizabeth Lyon, though everyone knew her as Edgworth Bess. Jack began his criminal career with shoplifting and petty burglary. He had no legal problems until Elizabeth got arrested and thrown into prison. Jack broke in, freed her, and the two of them got away.

A while later, he and his brother committed a burglary. The brother got caught, and since it was his second arrest, he faced possible execution. The only way out was to rat out his brother Jack. When Jack got tempted into a game of skittles at a tavern, somebody fetched the local constable. Jack got arrested and locked in the upper floor of a building. He escaped through the ceiling and lowered himself to the ground with knotted bedclothes.

Within a month he got arrested for picking a pocket. When Bess came to visit him in the local slammer, she got locked up, too. They got transferred to a real prison. Within a day they filed through some window bars and again used bedclothes to lower themselves to the ground. This second escape ensured their working-class heroism.

Two months later a colleague in crime got Bess drunk in a tavern. She revealed where Jack could be found. He was arrested and sentenced to death for his thievery. Five days before his execution date, Bess distracted a guard long enough for Jack to remove an interior window bar and squeeze out. Disguised in women's clothing, he slipped out of the prison and got away.

Too cocky to leave town, he was arrested a few days later. He was put in handcuffs and leg irons in a "strong room," but he soon picked the lock of the handcuffs and, still in leg irons, made his way up a chimney, onto the roof, then through six barred doors to get into the chapel and from there onto the roof of a neighboring house, then down through the house (without awakening anyone) and into the street.

Within two weeks he was captured. This time he was chained to a 300-pound block in a cell under constant observation. He was soon relieved of a pocket knife he was planning to use to cut his gallows rope. An estimated 200,000 people accompanied his trip to the gallows. Due to his light weight, his hanging failed to break his neck, so he was left strangling for 15 minutes. The crowd, fearing he would be dissected—a common fate of the executed— closed in on his body, preventing an attempt by friends to whisk him off to a doctor.[30]

Controlling Society Like a Prison

In the late 18th century, English philosopher Jeremy Bentham published an idea for a new kind of prison. It was new in both physical and psychological senses. He called it The Panopticon.

The name derives from a mythological Greek giant named Panoptes. Panoptes was so called because he could see (*-optes*) everything (*pan*). He had 100 eyes and thus was considered the perfect watchman. But one day Panoptes fell asleep and closed all his eyes. Along came the god of messages, Hermes, who bashed his head in.

Bentham's Panopticon prison was designed in a circle with cells around the outside and guards in the center. The guards, or even just one guard, could at any moment observe any prisoner. They could not, however, observe all the prisoners all the time. The prisoners would never know whether they were being observed. Louvered blinders would allow the guards to see the prisoners without the prisoners seeing the guards.

Bentham claimed that the Panopticon would not only save money but reform prisoners. It would save money by minimizing the need for guards. It would reform prisoners by inducing them to behave themselves all the time, not just when they saw a guard nearby. Theoretically, they would take that self-control with them when released.

No such prison has ever been built, though the theory has been applied in prisons and in public venues. People under the eyes of video surveillance cameras never know whether they are being watched. Cameras deployed in certain English cities actually have loudspeakers so distant observers can give information—or orders—to the public. The dystopian rulers in George Orwell's 1984 had cameras installed in all homes and other places. With draconian punishment for misbehavior, citizens would never take a chance that they were not under observation.

The theory of panopticism, therefore, has the potential to shift from control of prisons to control of society, rendering both not much different from each other.[31]

Prisons as Social Failures

Q: Are there really architects opposed to the common, quasi-panopticon design of prisons?

A: Yes, for this is America, home of an organization called Architects/Designers/Planners for Social Change (ADPSR —adpsr. org). Here is part of the ADPSR's position on the issue, based on Discipline and Punish: The Birth of the Prison by French philosopher Michel Foucault.[32]

> Foucault believed that disciplinary systems, and prisons in particular (with the Panopticon as the ideal type) were social failures. He considered that the way disciplinary systems crush individuality and individual freedom is antithetical to positive social goals such as rehabilitation and peaceful coexistence. He also saw the inherent cruelty of prison buildings for what they are - spaces where state agents, dedicated to maintaining state power, exact revenge and enforce discipline on those who fail to abide by the system. Given the overwhelming failure of prisons to reduce crime, and the endless catalogue of abuses committed within prisons, ADPSR agrees with Foucault. It is time for architects to find new means of building a just society, and new buildings for a better set of institutions. The disciplinary model of the prison/Panopticon is a failure.

The Cat Mule

Some clever—but not quite clever enough—prisoners in a prison in Brazil, attempted to use a cat to smuggle a cell phone, saws, batteries, and drills into the prison.

Guards caught the cat, which was loaded down like a pack mule. The prison's more than 250 inmates were all suspects, though officials were not able to identify any individuals linked to the escape attempt.[33]

Patron Saints

Maximilian Kolbe is the patron saint of prisoners. He was a Franciscan friar in Poland when the Germans invaded in 1939. He was arrested briefly, then allowed to return to his monastery. When the Germans caught the monastery publishing anti-Nazi materials, they shut it down and arrested five friars. On May 28, 1941, Kolbe was transferred to the Auschwitz prison camp, where he was designated Prisoner #16670.

In July of that year, three prisoners escaped. To discourage any further escapes, the German picked ten men to be starved to death in an underground bunker. When one of the men pleaded that he had a wife and children, Kolbe volunteered to take his place. Two weeks later, Kolbe was the only man alive. Impatient and in need of the bunker for other purposes, the Germans gave Kolbe a lethal injection of carbolic acid. Kolbe raised his arm to facilitate the execution. He was canonized by the Pope John Paul II, a Pole himself.

Guards have three patron saints in the Catholic ranks.

Peter of Alcantara, a friar in Spain who could pray himself into ecstasy and even levitation. In 1562 he died on his knees while in prayer. He was known for sleeping very little, and when he slept, he slept sitting up. Thanks to his late-night vigilance, he was designated patron saint of night watchmen.

Adrian of Nicomedia is patron saint of soldiers, butchers, and guards. Until 306 A.D. he was a typical Roman pagan working as bodyguard for the emperor. He was present when 22 Christians were put on trial and subsequently imprisoned and subjected to horrific torture. Adrian (a.k.a. Hadrian) asked one of the prisoners how he could withstand such torture. The prisoner quoted Corinthians: "Eye hath not seen, nor ear heard, neither have entered into the heart of man, the things which God hath prepared for them that love him"

Adrian was so impressed that he converted on the spot. He was then imprisoned himself. After repeatedly refusing to renounce his Christianity, he was tortured to death, the last part of which involved smashing his arms and legs on an anvil. His body was supposed to be burned out of existence, but a storm arose, quenched the fire and, for good measure, killed several guards with lightning. Adrian's wife, Natalia, managed to retrieve one of his hands. She took it home and then to Constantinople.[34]

Big Leaks at Leavenworth

In 1910, Frank Grigware, a prisoner at Leavenworth held for train robbery, and five other prisoners hijacked a supply locomotive on prison grounds and used it to smash through a gate. The other five were soon recaptured, but Grigware made his way to Canada, where in 1916 he was elected mayor of Spirit River, Alberta.[35]

Basil "The Owl" Banghart escaped from Leavenworth three times. In his long career as a criminal, he was involved in or allegedly involved in car theft, robbery, mail truck armed robbery, a hoax kidnapping, racketeering, tossing a bomb into a bar, brewing wine in a prison, escape not only from Leavenworth but a federal building and a local jail, and—get this—failing to inform the Selective Service of his change of address.[36]

Convict Leases

The 13th Amendment to the U.S. Constitution—the same that does away with slavery, explicitly allows involuntary servitude as punishment for a crime. After the Civil War, states in the south commonly leased out prisoners to private companies, effectively a continuation of slave labor. In 1898, 73 percent of Alabama's state revenues were generated by leased prisoners.[37]

The profitability of such leases motivated states to arrest and convict more blacks. In Nashville, for example, 33 percent of prisoners were African-American when the war ended in 1865. Four years later, it was 64 percent.[38] A contract with the Georgia and Alabama Railroad specified "one hundred able-bodied and healthy Negro convicts" in exchange for $2,500.[39] In Tallahassee, a young man from North Dakota, Martin Tabert, was arrested for vagrancy and leased to the Putnam Lumber Company, where he was flogged to death by the flogging boss, an incident that led to the end of convict leasing in Florida in 1923. Alabama stopped in 1928, and North Carolina ended a similar practice in 1933.[40]

Why

• California downsized its prison population by 23 percent between 2006 and 2012. During that period, the national average saw a decline of just one percent.

• During these periods of "decarceration," violent crime decreased in those states far more than in the rest of the country. Between 1999 and 2012, New York's and New Jersey's violent crime rate fell by 31 percent and 30 percent respectively. The national average was a decrease of 26 percent. Between 2006 and 2012, California's violent crime rate dropped by 21 percent, slightly more than the national decline of 19 percent.

• Numbers were similar for property crime, though California's rate declined by 13 percent, a little less than the national average of 15 percent.

The study found "no reason why a reduction of 25 percent should be considered the maximum that might be achieved." It pointed out that even if every state managed such reductions in prison population, the United States would still have an incarceration rate three to six times higher than those of most industrialized nations.[41]

Population Explosion

According to the Institute for Criminal Policy Research, prison populations have been increasing rapidly all over the world, but not everywhere.[42]

- Total prison population in 2017 was about 10 million.

- From 2000 to 2015, the prison population of Oceania increased by 59 percent.

- In that period, the U.S. prison population increased by 41 percent.

- In that period, the Asian prison population increased by 29 percent.

- In that period, African prison population increased by 15 percent.

- In that period, the European prison population decreased by 21 percent.

- Much of the decline in Europe was due to a drastic reduction in Russia, where numbers fell from about one million in 2000 to 640,000 in 2015.

- Brazil's prison population increased 20-fold from about 30,000 in 1973 to 600,000 in 2017.

- The number of prisoners in England and Wales increased from 40,000 in 1975 (a rate of 81 per 100,000 people) to 87,000 in 2012 (a rate of 153 per 100,000.)
- The U.S. prison population peaked in 2008 at over 2.3 million, accounting for a full fifth of the world's prisoners.
- The prisoner rates (prisoners per 100,000 people) were highest in the U.S. (666 per) and Thailand (428).
- Prisoner rates were lowest in Netherlands (61) and India (33).

The ICPR report listed several reasons the over-use of incarceration is counter-productive. It found that over-use:

- leads to crowded, inhumane, degrading conditions,
- worsened rehabilitation outcomes,
- disproportionately harmed the poor and marginalized, whose families can least afford the absence of a wage-earner or parent,
- reduces the prison system's capacity to deal with the few who really need to be isolated from society,
- increases the risks to prisoners, prison staff, and the general population,
- imposes enormous costs on public funds, and
- impedes economic development.

Some Findings

• Prison education reduces recidivism more than boot camps, "shock" incarceration, or vocational training.[43]

• Prison education reduces recidivism by 29 percent.[44]

• Only six percent of corrections spending goes to prison programs (of which education is just one).[45]

• Fifteen prison systems account for 89 percent of the nation's prisoners taking postsecondary classes and awarded 96 percent of college degrees.[46]

• Lack of funding is the most common barrier to enrolling prisoners in college courses.[47]

• A $1 million investment in incarceration will prevent about 350 crimes. The same investment in prison education will prevent more than 600 crimes.[48]

• Post-secondary prison education increases societal productivity, increases tax revenues, and decreases reliance on government support.[49]

• Changes in behavior can be attributed to improved cognitive capacity and to the prisoner feeling human again by engaging in an activity as commonplace as going to classes.[50]

• Post-secondary education in prisons can break down racial barriers that are a major cause of disciplinary problems.[51]

254

• Children of the women enrolled in the Bedford Hills College Program expressed pride in their mothers' academic achievements, were inspired to take their own education more seriously and were more motivated to attend college themselves.[52]

High Rent Districts

How much does it cost to incarcerate in various prisons?

The average cost of incarceration for Federal inmates in Fiscal Year 2015 was $31,977.65 ($87.61 per day). The average annual cost to confine an inmate in a Residential Re-entry Center for Fiscal Year 2015 was $26,082.90 ($71.46 per day).[53]

The average cost of incarceration in a state prison averages about $33,849 per year. The most expensive prisons, per capita incarcerata, were New York ($69,355), California ($64,642), Connecticut ($62,159), New Jersey ($61,603), and Rhode Island (($58,564)[54].

The average annual cost of holding an inmate in a New York City jail in 2017 was about $143,130 per year. In 2017, total cost of the city's jails hit a record at $1.36 billion.[55]

The Real Cost

A commonly cited figure for the cost of incarceration is $80 billion, but that is only the cost of operating corrections facilities. A study conducted at Washington University measured 23 different associated costs and came up with an aggregate burden of about $1 trillion—11 times more than the commonly reported cost. More than half of the aggregate cost is borne by families, children, and community members who had committed no crime. Among the costs outside of government "corrections" budgets are:

- Foregone wages of prisoners ($33,066 each, average, in 2014 dollars)
- Reduced lifetime earnings due to incarceration record (10-40 percent)
- Cost of injuries suffered in prison
- Higher mortality rate for released prisoners (3.5 times higher than average)
- Increased infant mortality (40% higher for children of prisoners)
- Increased criminality of children of prisoners ($130.6 billion)
- Visitation, eviction, and moving costs
- Family debt caused by incarceration
- Adverse health effects on families (depression, PTSD, suicide)
- Effect on children's education level and subsequent lifetime

wages ($30 billion)

- Children rendered homeless by parental imprisonment ($14,400 each, excluding cost of psychological harm)

- Homelessness of released prisoners (25-50% of homeless people)

- Decreased property values around prisons

- Criminogenic nature of prisons (crime born of prison experience, $285.8 billion)

- Divorce (rates are tripled, totaling $17.7 billion)

The study also found the $80 billion figure to be low because it didn't represent pension obligations, health care benefits for staff, and health care provided to inmates. The more accurate figure is $91.1 billion.

The study did not figure in the benefits of incarceration, such as crime avoided by deterrence and incapacitation.[56]

Clink, Inc.

Governments often contract a private-sector company to run its corrections programs. In some cases, a company owns the prison. In others, it administers a prison owned by a government. In either case, these corporations have a vested interested in a high prison population.

In 2016, the nation's largest imprisonment company, the Corrections Corporation of America (CCA), changed its name to CoreCivic. The change was an apparent attempt to shed the bad image it acquired when an inspector general found substandard living conditions, inadequate medical care, and higher rates of violence at 14 prisons run by the CCA and other companies. The company explained that it was transforming itself from corrections and detention to "a wider range of government solutions."

At the time of the name-change, the CCA was housing some 70,000 prisoners in more than 70 prisons or jails.[57] It owned 50 of the facilities. In 2015, the company reaped a profit of more than $3,300 per prisoner. Part of its profit is made possible by "occupancy guarantees" that require the government to provide a certain number of prisoners. At one facility, the government is obliged to maintain an occupancy of 96 percent. Long sentences, mandatory sentences, stringent laws, and recidivism are means of guaranteeing a supply of prisoners.

The biggest investors in CCA in 2016 were the Vanguard Group, Blackrock, FMR, New South Capital management, Prudential Financial, and Bank of New York Mellon Corp.[58] Meanwhile, Pershing Square Capital Management, Systematic Financial Management, General Electric, Columbia University, and many other investors divested themselves of all CCA stock and in many cases all private prison company stock.[59]

Four Justifications for Imprisonment, None Good

Rehabilitation

Theory: The experience of incarceration will teach criminals a lesson. Upon release, they will be law-abiding citizens.

Reality: Incarceration alone does not improve the character or attitude of criminals.

Deterrence

Theory: Severe punishment, such as long prison sentences, will scare potential criminals away from criminal acts.

Reality: Studies show that high incarceration rates increase crime or have no measurable effect. Crime apparently increases because prisons tend to a) educate prisoners in the art of criminality, b) create anti-social attitudes, c) break up communities, d) break up families, e) prevent released prisoners from finding work.[60]

Incapacitation

Theory: Criminals cannot commit crimes while they are prison.

Reality: Prisons are incubators of crime. Criminals continue criminal activity while in prison. Upon release, they are more likely to commit crimes.

Retribution

Theory: Prison is a form of vengeance. Victims and society are pleased to see perpetrators suffer what they deserve.

Reality: Vengeance—"pay-back"—does not create some kind of balance, nor does it negate the effects of the crime, nor does it deter criminals from criminal acts in the future. To the contrary, it leaves them angered and...seeking revenge! Future crimes are more likely and more severe. Ultimately, vengeance through incarceration causes communities to suffer.[61]

Highest and Lowest Rates of Incarceration

According to the most recent data available for each country, these are the nations with the highest and lowest rates of prison populations, that is, prisoners per 100,000 population, according to World Prison Brief.[62]

Rank	Nation	Rate per 100,000
1.	Seychelles	738
2.	USA	666
3.	El Salvador	598
4.	Turkmenistan	583
7.	Cuba	510
15.	Russia	419
26.	Brazil	322
37.	Iran	287
133.	China	118
203.	Japan	45
222. (lowest)	Guinea Bissau	10

Federal Prison Industries

Federal Prison Industries, also known as UNICOR, is a corporation owned by the U.S. government. It was established in 1934 to give federal prisoners an opportunity to learn a trade and make a little money. By federal law, all able-bodied federal prisoners who are not a security risk are required to work for either their prison or at a UNICOR factory. In 2016, some 17,900 prisoners worked at 66 UNICOR factory operations in 52 prisons, earning between 23 cents and $1.15 per hour. UNICOR produces more than 100 products, most of which are sold to federal agencies. Prisoners with court-ordered restitution obligations must use at least half of their earnings for those debts. U.S. manufacturers can use UNICOR to manufacture products if the company is repatriating operations from overseas, in which case costs are set at those of offshore sites.[63]

Some Stats to Think About

Some national statistics for the United States.[64]

- One percent of released killers kill a second time, and 99 percent don't.
- Over 70 percent of released robbers and burglars commit the same crime again.[65]
- 85 percent of prisoners are involved in drugs, but only 11 percent receive treatment.
- Among 16-24 year olds, high school dropouts are six times more likely to be imprisoned.
- Dropouts in that group are 63 times more likely to be imprisoned than people who earned a Bachelor's degree.
- Participation in a prison education program reduces recidivism by 63 percent.

Mass Incarceration Explained?

A report from The Sentencing Project, written by three university professors, found that in 2016, an estimated 6.1 million Americans were not eligible to vote due to a felony conviction. That's up from 1.17 million in 1976, 3.34 million in 1996, and 5.85 million in 2010. [66]

Other key findings:

• Approximately 2.5 percent of the total U.S. voting age population—one in every 40 adults—is disenfranchised due to a felony conviction.

• Individuals who have completed their sentences in the twelve states that disenfranchise people post-sentence make up over 50 percent of the entire disenfranchised population, totaling almost 3.1 million people.

• In six states (AL, FL, KY, MS, TN and VA), the rate is more than seven percent of adults.

• Florida—that crucial state that determines presidential elections—accounts for 1.5 million, about 27 percent of the disenfranchised in America.

• One in 13 African-Americans is disenfranchised, four times the number of non-African-Americans.

• In 1980, only nine states disenfranchised more than five percent of their African-American population. In 2016, 23 states did so.

• In FL, KY, TN, and VA, more than 20 percent of African-Americans are disenfranchised.

• Maine and Vermont are the only states that have no restrictions on felons voting. Even prisoners can vote.

• The total number of disenfranchised citizens tripled since roughly the beginning of the civil rights movement. In 1960, it was 1,762,582. In 2016 it hit 6,106,327.

• A "significant majority" of Americans favor voting rights for people on probation or parole or otherwise completing their sentence. If those rights were restored to all released prisoners, 77 percent of the disenfranchised would be able to vote. That's 4,701,871 people.

Trouble in Jersey

New Jersey has prison problems, and serious reform may be the only solution.[67]

- In 2017, New Jersey had some 41,000 people in federal, state, or local prisons and jails.

- The ratio of black to white prisoners was 12.2:1, more than twice the national average of 5:1.

- The state spends over $1 billion on "corrections" each year.

- In 2017, incarceration cost an average of $53,681 per prisoner per year. (Tuition at Princeton is $43,450. At Rutgers, it's $14, 238.)

- Parole costs an average of $6,349, about a tenth the cost of incarceration.

- Over half of released prisoners are arrested again within three years.

- 37.2 percent of released prisoners do not have a high school diploma.

- 92.3 percent have no college education.

- At least a third and possibly half of individuals with medical conditions are not treated while incarcerated.

268

- 41 percent "max out," serving their entire sentence, almost twice the 22 percent national average.

- In 2003, New Jersey had the highest proportion of drug offenders in the country.

- Not counting arrest and court costs, In 2017 the state spent $182,051,328 to incarcerate people who had been released from prison in 2011 and re-incarcerated by 2014—enough to educate 9,265 children for a year.

- New Jersey loses about $71,218,455 in taxes each year due to people in prison rather than working.

- Over half of New Jersey prisoners have a chronic medical condition.

Banned Books

The Texas Department of Criminal Justice bans some 10,000 books from its prison system.[68] Among the prohibited titles: *A Charlie Brown Christmas (pop-up edition)*, *The Color Purple*, *Memoirs of a Geisha*, *A Time to Kill*, *To Kill a Mockingbird*, *MapQuest Road Atlas*, *The Daily Show with Jon Steward Presents America: A Citizen's Guide to Democracy Inaction*, *Women Behind Bars: The Crisis of Women in the U.S. Prison System*, *Where's Waldo*, *Game of Thrones*, *Uncle Tom's Cabin*, *Freakonomics*, *Brokeback Mountain*, *Big Sur*, Dante's *Inferno*, *All the Dave Barry You Could Ever Want*, *The Boys of Summer*, the 1908 Sears, Roebuck catalog, and many titles by such authors as Jenna bush, Noam Chomsky, John Gisham, Langston Hughes, Philip Roth, Salman Rushdie, Studs Terkel, and Sojourner Truth.

Among the 248,000 books allowed: *Lolita, Mein Kampf,* and David Duke's *My Awakening*.

In 2018 the Department began a review of banned and permitted titles.

Damage Control

A Better Place to Spend a Dollar

Long prison sentences may feel good to angry victims of crime, but they don't make anyone any safer, at least not for long. A ten-year penalty isn't twice as effective at preventing crime as a five-year penalty. People of criminal tendency are notoriously poor at thinking long-term. They also presume that they aren't going to get caught. Consequences in the immediate future are well within their vision. The certainty of punishment deters them far more than the severity of the punishment. A dollar spent on policing and other crime prevention efforts is 20 percent more effective than a dollar spent on imprisonment.[69]

Criminals as Artists

From *Art Therapy: An Introduction to the Use of Art as a Therapeutic Technique,* chapter titled "Art Therapy in Prisons," by Joyce Laing, edited by Tessa Daily.

...Surprisingly, of all the professionals—the doctors, the social workers, the psychologists, or the teachers—who work in a supportive role with the prisoners, it is the artist who may have the closest personality traits. For it seems there may be underlying links in the drive of certain offenders and that of the creative artist.

While labeled as deviants, many offenders are inventive, ingenious, quick-witted and have great vitality. It may be that the creative aspects of the criminal have, for reasons of background experience or psychological make-up, been misdirected towards destructive ends. If the art therapist can channel these talents in a positive, creative direction, the offender will experience a new perception of the self and where he belongs in society. Over the weeks in which the art work is being produced, step by step, an alteration in his previous thinking pattern will take place. The more he becomes engrossed in art, the less likely will he be content to see himself just as a criminal who is destroying his own potential prospects and the lives of his family, as well as being a menace to everyone else. Art opens so many doors in life.

Where Prisoners Are
Treated Like Adults

When you think about it, inmates are treated like children. They are relieved of all responsibility. They have "parents" watching them constantly. They are told what to do. If they don't obey, they are punished. They are not trusted with sharp objects. Their food is prepared for them. And after a certain number of years, they are declared "grown up" and, for better or worse, released to the world.

Too often it's for the worse. They soon fail at adulthood. A high percentage—the numbers vary widely according to jurisdiction—end up back in prison. There they return to a life free of responsibility and decision.

Norway has figured out that forcing extreme childhood on prisoners doesn't work. At Bastoy prison, inmates are expected to make their own decisions, think ahead, take responsibility, control their impulses, and enjoy the benefits of work. If they want food, they have to make it. If they want better food, they have to tend to crops. If they want to lie on the beach, they have to clean the beach. If they want to make furniture, they have to go cut down a tree. They

274

are entrusted with tools that could easily be made into weapons, everything from hammers to chain saws.

And if they want to escape, they can. There are no walls or razor wire. But who would want to escape from what's been called "the world's nicest prison"?

Completing a sentence at Bastoy (inmates have to earn the right to be transferred there) may not give a crime victim the full pleasure of vengeance, but it results in a better person who is far less likely to commit another crime. They leave Bastoy with a marketable skill and a track record of self-control and responsibility. Only 20 percent are back in the can within two years, half the rate of the United States. Result: a safer community.

As Norway sees it, the issue is a mutually exclusive set of choices: What is the purpose of imprisonment—public safety or revenge? Until someone thinks of some other purpose, public safety is the most beneficial for society.[70]

Solitary

Solitary confinement was originally an idea of Quakers who saw it as a merciful alternative to public whippings. Isolation was less obviously painful, and it gave inmates a chance to meditate on their wrongdoing. But it didn't take long for the Quakers to see the detrimental effects. In 1826, Alex de Tocqueville observed them, too, when a New York prison tried putting all prisoners in solitary. He wrote, "This experiment, of which the favorable results had been anticipated, proved fatal for the majority of prisoners. It devours the victims incessantly and unmercifully; it does not reform, it kills."[71]

Solitary confinement can provoke so many physical and psychiatric problems that it is considered a form of torture.

Due to lack of exercise, it can cause high blood pressure, migraine headaches, profuse sweating, abdominal pain, neck pain, back pain, muscle stiffness, heart palpitations, weight loss, and changes to brain physiology.

But the most serious and painful consequences are in the mind. After a period of confinement, prisoners experience hallucinations and pseudohallucinations,[72] hypersensitivity to stimuli, aggressive fantasies, overt paranoia, inability to concentrate, lack of impulse control, confusional psychosis, dissociative tendencies, agitation, aimless violence, delusions, irrational anger, social withdrawal, depression, suicidal ideation, feelings of helplessness, self-mutilation, suicide. They start to babble and shriek. They've been known to smear themselves with feces, bang their heads on walls, and scrub at imaginary bugs. A few develop Ganser syndrome, which is characterized by nonsensical talk, echolalia and echopraxia (the imitation someone else's speech behavior, respectively).

Often mentally ill inmates are the ones who end up in solitary confinement. The confinement tends to worsen, not improve, their symptoms.[73]

In one lawsuit (Ruiz v. Johnson) a judge ruled that "Solitary confinement units are virtual incubators of psychoses—seeding illness in otherwise healthy inmates and exacerbating illness in those already suffering from mental infirmities."

Prisoners have been put in solitary not as punishment but for isolation required due to sexual orientation, race, and religion.

Estimates of the number of prisoners in solitary at a given moment range from 20,000 to 80,000. The numbers range widely because of the difficulty of defining "solitary confinement."

The Supreme Court has never taken a position on whether solitary confinement is unconstitutional.

Numbers in the Box

In the US, over 65,000 prisoners were held in prolonged solitary confinement (defined by the Nelson Mandela Rules as more than 15 consecutive days in solitary), with 3,000 held there for over six years (half of these in Texas). A 2016 report on New York State prisons demonstrated a racial bias in the use of solitary confinement, showing that Black and Latino prisoners are disciplined at up to twice the rate of white prisoners and for longer.

While the use of solitary confinement in the U.S. has been decreasing in recent years, there were at least 67,442 inmates in the U.S. locked in their cells for 22 or more hours a day in the fall of 2015, according to a report released by the Association of State Correctional Administrators (ASCA) and Yale Law School.[74]

The report, "Aiming to Reduce Time-in-Cell," gives a significant, albeit incomplete, snapshot of the use of solitary confinement in the U.S., which is an outlier among countries in its use of the widely condemned practice. The census includes federal and state inmates placed in any form of "restricted housing" for at least 22 hours a day for more than 15 consecutive days. It did not include local and county jails, federal immigration detention centers, and juvenile and military detention centers, meaning the number could be higher.

Information for the report was provided by 41 jurisdictions. They reported on length of stay, gender, race, age, and mental illness for a sample population of over 54,000 inmates who had spent time in solitary. Of those, 29 percent spent one to three months in solitary confinement. At the other extreme, 11 percent endured three continuous years or more in isolation. Among all respondents, the share of prisoners in solitary in a given facility ranged from under one percent to more than 28 percent of the general population.[75]

A Blink of Time

Rick Raemisch, the executive director of Colorado Department of Corrections, had himself locked in solitary confinement—or, as they say in Colorado, "ad seg"— for 20 hours. In his words, it was "just a blink" of time compared with the average of 23 months that Colorado prisoners spend in isolation when sent there, and that's a blink to the 20 years that some prisoners spend there. He wrote about the experience in an op-ed in the New York Times.[76]

> First thing you notice is that it's anything but quiet. You're immersed in a drone of garbled noise — other inmates' blaring TVs, distant conversations, shouted arguments. I couldn't make sense of any of it, and was left feeling twitchy and paranoid. I kept waiting for the lights to turn off, to signal the end of the day. But the lights did not shut off. I began to count the small holes carved in the walls. Tiny grooves made by inmates who'd chipped away at the cell as the cell chipped away at them....

The main light in my cell block eventually turned off, and I fell into a fitful sleep, awakening every time a toilet flushed or an officer yanked on the doors to determine they were secure....

"When I finally left my cell at 3 p.m., I felt even more urgency for reform. If we can't eliminate solitary confinement, at least we can strive to greatly reduce its use. Knowing that 97 percent of inmates are ultimately returned to their communities, doing anything less would be both counterproductive and inhumane.

Can Architects Help?

A study of Dutch prisons found that, of five architectural styles, the radial, panopticon format (often in leaky, dungeon-like conditions featuring solitary confinement) was most likely to cause prisoners to feel estranged from guards. Prisoners in more communal, campus-like settings were more likely to have supportive relationships with guards. The good staff-prisoner relationships were seen as important for the manageability and safety in prisons.

On the other hand, a study conducted among males at Texas prisons found that architectural design had no effect on violence in the prison, though nonviolent behavior problems appeared to be lower.

But then, Netherlands and Texas are two very different places, the Dutch and Texans two very different peoples.[77]

In Case You Ever Need to Know

An anonymous blogger who identified himself as X-Con offers these 8 rules for surviving prison.[78]

1. Respect other inmates. Don't call anyone names. Don't cut in line. Don't reach over someone's plate. Don't touch another inmate's stuff. Do not steal.

2. Don't join a gang. In most prisons, you can avoid them. If you do join, you cannot opt out later, and you will have to commit crimes.

3. Do not do drugs or get involved in smuggling.

4. Do not gamble.

5. Do not engage in homosexuality. AIDS is rampant, and jealousy can be deadly.

6. Do not talk to guards at all about anything—not the weather, not the things you've seen.

7. Stay busy with positive activities—exercise, classes, reading, jobs.

8. Get God in your life. Reading the Bible will make you feel better, you'll associate with better people, and it looks good to the parole board.

The Perfect Gift for Someone Who Has Nothing

There aren't many things you can send to a prisoner, but those few things can be deeply meaningful. Each facility has its own rules, and they are probably available online.

1. Letters and Messages.

Many prisons allow prisoners to receive email. Note that these messages are usually reviewed by staff.

Physical mail, especially hand-written, is especially appreciated. The mail is probably reviewed by staff. Do not include staples, paper clips, perfume, cash, or, of course, contraband. Just send sheets of paper, nothing more.

2. Money.

You cannot send cash to an inmate, but facilities usually allow deposits into accounts. There are limits on totals. Inmates can only buy items from the commissary. These include toiletries, snacks, stamps, envelopes, etc.

3. Photos.

Photos bring the outside world into the cell. They can include not just portraits of loved ones but pictures of neighborhoods, pets, and events. There may be limits on quantities and sizes. No frames. No porn. No hidden messages. Write inmate's name and other ID information on the back.

4. Reading Material

Since reading material is considered helpful for rehabilitation, prisons generally allow books and magazines to be sent to prisoners. Often they have to come straight from a publisher or bookstore. Certain topics are prohibited. Paperbacks only.

5. Celebratory Cards

Birthday cards and such are generally allowed, but note: no "singing" cards with electronics, no heavy cardboard stock, no pop-ups, no multiple layers, no suggestive material (not even satire), no glitter, no string or ribbon, no added decorations, no perfume.[79]

Experience Counts

Inmates of the Eastern New York Correctional Facility in Napanoch, NY, have become champion debaters. The debate team has out-argued teams from the University of Vermont, West Point, and Harvard.

The inmate team of three is handicapped with difficulties researching. They have no access to the internet, and written materials need to go through a lengthy approval and inspection process. The prison library doesn't have much to offer.

But the team has a big advantage in experience. They are generally older than the college students, and they've seen a side of life far removed from that of middle- and upper-class students. While facts are essential in a debater's arsenal, subjective experience can also be used.

In the debate with Harvard, the ENYCF team was put in the uncomfortable position of defending the denial of education for undocumented immigrant children. Though personally disagreeing with any denial of education, they made the case that such children, being poor, would go to schools so bad they weren't worth attending.
80

Education vs. Incarceration

In 2015, according to the National Association of State Budget Officers, corrections expenditures for state prisons totaled $56.9 billion, an average of more than a billion dollars per state.

In that year, Louisiana had the highest rate of incarceration—776 prisoners per 100,000 residents. Oklahoma followed close behind, followed by Alabama, Mississippi, Arizona, Arkansas and Texas. Four of those seven states were among the ten states with lowest per-pupil spending on education. Maine had the lowest rate of incarceration, 132 per 100,000, followed by Massachusetts, Minnesota, Rhode Island, Vermont, Utah and New Hampshire. Four of those seven states were among the ten states with the highest per-pupil spending on education, though Utah ranked absolute last in per-pupil spending.[81]

Collateral Punishment

War has its "collateral damage." Imprisonment has its "collateral punishment." According to The Sentencing Project:

- One in 50 children in America has a parent in prison.
- In mid-2007, 809,800 of the nation's 1,518,535 state and federal prisoners were parents of children under the age of 18. Of these parents, 65,600 were mothers.
- Fewer than half the parents were living with their children when they were arrested.
- Incarcerated mothers were three times more likely to have been living in a single-parent household than in a two-parent household. Percentage was about the same for fathers.
- Parents in *federal* prison were more likely to have had two-parent households, but mothers were two and a half times more likely to be in a single-parent household.
- About half of the parents in state prisons were their families' primary financial support.
- Nine percent of parents reported homelessness in the year before arrest.

288

- Mothers were twice as likely to have been homeless.

- Twenty percent of the mothers had a history of physical or sexual abuse.

- Forty-one percent reported a current health problem.

- The prisoners reported having 1,706,600 children, which would be about 2.3 percent of the nation's children.

- Black children were seven and a half times more likely to have a parent in prison.

- Four out of five fathers were black. Five out of ten mothers were white.

- The number of children with a mother in prison increased 131 percent from 1991 to 2007. The number with fathers in prison increased 77 percent. The difference in increase was due to a relative increase in the number of women in prison, up 122 percent.

- About a quarter of the children were under the age of four. A third were under nine. A third would reach the age of 18 before a parent was released from prison.

- Youth whose parents were imprisoned are nearly five times more likely to be imprisoned than children separated from parents for other reasons.[82]

Feasible Reforms

In 2018, Prison Policy Initiative pursued several prison reforms that might make America and various states better places to live.[83]

End Prison Gerrymandering

State governments divide their states into congressional districts according to populations in each district. Some municipalities do the same to allot city council seats. Many states count prisoners as residents wherever they are incarcerated. Thus prisoners count as constituents even though they can't vote. Since a prison houses a large number of people, a district with a prison effectively gives a relatively small number of voters much more political influence. Counting prisoners at their home address would result in more equitable political power. It would also more accurately represent the needs of neighborhoods.

Lower the cost of calls home

Why do calls from prisons often cost more than $1.50 per minute? There is no good reason, and communication between inmate and family would help keep families intact and children less traumatized.

Not letting video calls replace in-person visits

Video calls cost prison systems less than in-person visits, but obviously the impact on families is less positive. The money saved isn't worth the social repercussions.

Allowing letters from home in local jails

Incredibly, sheriffs in 14 states are experimenting with a policy of not allowing prisoners to receive letters from home—a dehumanization of an already dehumanizing situation.

Reducing Pretrial Detention

Many prisoners are held simply because they can't afford bail. One result: more plea bargaining, which results in overcrowding, loss of job, apartment, child custody, and higher costs to taxpayers. There are many alternatives to the detention of people not proven guilty.

The Value of Visits

The Minnesota Dept. of Corrections tracked recidivism among 16,420 offenders who were released between 2003 and 2007. It was looking for a relationship between visits in prison and the likelihood of returning to prison. The study found that inmates who were visited had a 13 percent lower risk of recidivism for felony violations and 25 percent for technical violations. Each visit reduced the risk by 0.1 percent. One visit a month reduced it by 0.9 percent. Prisoners visited close to their release date had a 3.6 percent reduction. With each different individual visitor, the risk rate dropped three percent. Visits by siblings, in-laws, fathers, and clergy all had a positive effect. But one visitor had a negative effect: ex-wives.[84]

Yet Another Bad Idea

Despite the beneficial effects of visits to prisoners, many prisons are trying to replace them with video visits. Prison administrations say video visits improve safety and reduce the cost of having staff arrange prisoners, check in visitors, and oversee visits. Often video and telecom equipment providers will install video systems for free so that they can collect usage fees from families and prisoners. At least one contract between a provider and a facility required that nonprofessional in-person visits be totally banned. In some cases, the prisons benefit from the fees. South Dakota's Minnehaha County Jail reaped $109,400 in video visiting fees in a two-year period.

A study by the Dept. of Justice listed several limitations of video visits. Many of the limitations relate to the poverty that tends to parallel crime and imprisonment.

- Families may lack computers for remote visits.
- Video systems are often of poor audio and video quality.
- The technology may be confusing the families and inmates.
- Illiteracy can hinder setting up a video visiting account.
- Families are less likely to go to a facility if they cannot have

an in-person visit.

• Fee charged for video visits may be onerous or impossible for poor families.

• Poor families may not have a necessary credit card.

The study said, "Video visiting cannot replicate seeing someone in-person, and it is critical for a young child to visit his or her incarcerated parent in person to establish a secure attachment."[85]

The study quoted a family member saying, "We want to see him for real. We want to touch our hands through the window. It makes him feel better. Even just to kiss the window, it makes us feel better."

Rikers

Rikers Island serves as the main jail of the City of New York. Though considered a jail because it's used mostly for short, in-transit stays, by many measures it is larger than most of the world's prisons. Some of the space is actually an asylum for the mentally ill who must be isolated from society.

- The area of the island is 413 acres—four times larger than the original island.
- Ten of New York's 15 corrections facilities are on the island. One of the ten is for women.
- The annual budget is $860 million.
- Staff is larger than many towns, with 9,000 officers and 1,500 other staff.
- Daytime population—staff+inmates—is three times that of Montpelier, VT.
- The facility includes schools, medical clinics, ball fields, chapels, gyms, drug rehab programs, grocery stores, barbershops, a bakery, laundromat, power plant, track, tailor

shop, print shop, bus depot, car wash, and a composting plant.

- Inmate capacity is 15,000. Population in 1991 was 21,688.

- 100,000 people are admitted each year, though 90 percent are soon released or transferred.

- The consistent inmate population is about 10,000, most of whom will be released within a year.

- Only 15 percent have been convicted of a crime. The rest are waiting for bail or trial.

- It has been ranked as one of the worst jails or prisons in the United States.

- In 2015, there were 9,424 assaults reported.

- Lawsuits over illegal strip searches at Rikers have cost New York City over $100 million

- 48 percent of adolescents held at Rikers have been diagnosed with mental health issues.

- In 2012, over 14 percent of adolescents were subjected to solitary confinement for an average of 43 days.[86]

Four Consecutive Prison Terms

Prison hulk—a ship no longer capable of going to sea, converted to use as a prison. As a verb, *to hulk* means to convert a ship to a prison.

Oubliette—a dungeon accessible only from a hatchway in a high ceiling. In some cases the hatch is a trapdoor. Oubliette comes from a French word, *oublier*, which means "forget."

Immurement—imprisonment in a walled-in space with no exits and therefore no hope. Also, in most cases, no food or water, making the practice a combination of imprisonment, torture, and execution. The word comes from Latin, *im*, meaning "in" and *murus*, meaning "wall." Edgar Allan Poe's "The Cask of Amontillado" was about an immurement.

Ergastulum—a prison workhouse in ancient Rome, usually underground, where slaves were chained to work as punishment.

Incarceration College

In 2009, a select group of prisoners at Connecticut's high-security Cheshire Correctional Institution were taking courses offered by the elite Wesleyan University. The 19 students earned their seats through a rigorous application process. Among them were six murderers, two drug dealers, and a kidnapper. Collectively, the 19 expected to serve more than 600 years behind bars, and several had little hope of ever taking their education outside the prison.

The students were motivated by the alternative of losing their place in the classes. The courses were of the same content and standards as the ones taught on the university campus. Admission to Wesleyan is extremely competitive. Tuition, room, and board at the time was $51,000 a year. The program was funded for two years by Bard College's Bard Prison Initiative, but future funding was uncertain. Many people complained that the funds might have been better spent helping victims.

The university was named after John Wesley, an 18th century minister who advocated for prison reform. The program was started by two students who had volunteered in prisons and saw the potential. [87]

Pay-to-Stay

Criminals in California often have the option to upgrade their cell for as little as $25 a night in La Verne or as much as $251 a night in Hermosa Beach. In Monterey Park, $51 will let you serve your time in half-day increments or just on weekends. Upgraded cells may include such frills as single occupancy, computer, refrigerator, phone, television, and other amenities. The upgrade option is especially attractive to sexual offenders who would be dangerously vulnerable among the general prison population. The majority of upgraders were convicted of traffic offenses, such as DUI, but three percent of cases were cases that involved violence or sex crimes. Some of the prisoners come in from other states in order to enjoy the better conditions. The average cost of a stay is $1,756, but some prisoners can afford to spend tens of thousands of dollars for a long sentence. The upgrade option is always at the discretion of a judge.

So if you must commit a crime, make sure it yields enough to afford decent prison conditions.[88]

Does Parole Work?

When New York City decided in 2017 to close its infamous Rikers Island jail complex, the city began releasing as many prisoners as possible. The population of the city's jails fell below 9,000 for the first time in 35 years. At the same time, crime, which had been decreasing, continued to decrease. Just one type of crime rose: parole violations.

New York State was having the same experience. Commitments to prison declined by an amazing 31 percent from 1999 to 2017. Thirteen prisons closed and 6,000 beds were eliminated. The state has been saving $160 million per year. At the same time, the crime rate declined, but re-incarceration for parole violations increased by 21 percent. In 2015, 47 percent of exits from parole were exits into prison for parole violations.

What's interesting is that only 16.3 percent of the recidivism was for crimes other than parole violations. The rest were posing no threat to society.

So one question is, how much could recidivism be reduced by reducing the terms and the length of parole?

And another question is, if recidivism and the monitoring of parole were reduced, might the money saved be better applied to preventing that 16.3 percent from returning to crime?[89]

Justice Is Sweeter Than Revenge

Here's an idea: Instead of using prisons as places of punishment, why not use them as places to repair the harm of crime, bring criminal and victim together, and transform people and communities for the better?

Why not give it a shot? We know that the current use of prisons isn't working. Once released, former prisoners tend to return to the life of crime. The deterrent effect isn't very effective. The term "correction" is generally a joke.

The concept of Restorative Justice offers a different way to use and perhaps avoid or minimize the use of prisons. Rather than focus on counter-productive punishment, it focuses on repairing the harm done by crime. It brings together all stakeholders— offender, victim, and community. It makes amends possible. It assuages victims by inducing offenders to take responsibility for their actions. It helps offenders become safe, constructive members of their community.

The four cornerstones of restorative justice are:

1. Inclusion of all parties,
2. Encountering the other side,
3. Making amends for the harm,
4. Reintegration of all parties to their communities.

Ten Commandments of Restorative Justice

I. You will focus on the harm of crime rather than the rules that have been broken,

II. You will be equally concerned about victims and offenders, involving both in the process of justice,

III. You will work toward the restoration of victims, empowering them and responding to their needs as they see them,

IV. You will support offenders while encouraging them to understand, accept, and carry out their obligations,

V. You will recognize that while obligations may be difficult for offenders, they should not be intended as pain,

VI. You will provide opportunities for dialogue, direct or indirect, between victim and offender as appropriate,

VII. You will find meaningful ways to involve the community and to respond to the community bases of crime,

VIII. You will encourage collaboration and reintegration rather than coercion and isolation,

IX. You will be mindful of the unintended consequences of your actions and programs,

X. You will show respect to all parties—victims, offenders, justice colleagues.[90]

For the Well Appointed Prison

Part of the prison-industrial complex is the companies that supply "detention equipment"—everything from disposable handcuffs to soccer balls. You can get "virtually indestructible" padded cells and padded cell repair kits. You can get a ready-made entry guard tower. You can get anti-shank razors, jumpsuits in orange or stripes, dental floss, belly chains, coffee mugs, humane body wrap, suicide safety blankets, economy bath towels, stainless interviewing chair, miniature "DOC" tactical vest beverage holder, "gotcha" tamper-proof handcuffs, rappelling gloves, *CO's Guide to Understanding Inmates*, a full riot suit, correctional officer wife charm bracelet, exam gloves, "My Heart Belongs to a Correctional Officer" sweater, and CrossBar brand electronic cigarettes.[91]

Cashless Prisons

In Belgium, the "Prison Cloud" program introduced in 2015 is now running in three prisons, involving a cloud-based digital service enabling prisoners to purchase items, watch video on demand, make phone calls and access limited pages on the internet, for example. The Prison Cloud also allows for a centralized electronic file for every prisoner that can be used by all relevant agencies, including medical files. Cashless prisons can be found in many countries from Georgia, to Thailand and Finland.[92]

Women and Children

Why Women Go to Prison

The female prison population has been rising all over the world. While the total number of prisoners has risen 20 percent since 2000, the number of female prisoners has risen by 50 percent. The estimate in 2015 was about 700,000 women and girls being held in 219 national prison systems.

What have women been doing wrong? According to a report from Penal Reform International, a "high number" were charged with or convicted of nonviolent minor offenses generally relating to poverty and "family roles," including property and drug-related offenses.[93]

A 2016 study in Kenya, for example, found that, of 97 women interviewed, 36 percent were being held for illegally brewing and selling alcohol.[94]

In 2014, 80 percent of female prisoners in Ireland had been convicted of nothing more serious than not paying fines.[95]

In England and Wales, 36 percent of women in prison were locked up for not paying a mandatory "television license" fee.

In Sierra Leone, the rate of arrest for women was attributed to the Ebola epidemic, when women were selling goods and food during curfew hours or gathering crowds after a family member had died.[96]

In 2016, over 90 percent of women in prison in Indonesia and Philippines were charged with drug-related offenses. In Thailand in 2013, 83 percent were under similar charges. In Cambodia, many women arrested for drug offenses had been coerced into the crime by their male partners.[97]

In Argentina, Brazil, Costa Rica, and Peru, 60 percent of women prisoners were charged with drug offenses.[98]

The United Nations General Assembly Session on drugs recognized the special vulnerabilities of women and called on nations to address protective and risk factors.

White Women Rising Downward

In the United States in June 2016. African-Americans were imprisoned at more than five times the rate of whites. In five states, the rate was ten times higher.[99]

But the rate was different for female inmates, data from 2015 indicates that the number of imprisoned black women was declining while that of white women increased. Still, in 2014, the rate of imprisonment of black women was more than double that of white women, 109 per 100,000 versus 53. The national average was 65 out of 100,000 women, with wide variation among states. Oklahoma led with 1,423 per, with Rhode Island last at 12. The overall rate of imprisonment increased 50 percent faster for women and than for men between 2000 and 2014. In 2014, 106,232 women were in prison, 109,100 were in jail, 102,825 were on parole, and 966,029 were on probation, a total of about 1.2 million.[100]

Girls (under 18 years of age) were behind bars for "status offenses and technical violations" far more often than boys. These are offenses such as truancy and running away—violations that

More Prisoners = Less Crime?

Can the drop in crime over the last 10 years be linked to the high rate of incarceration during the same period?

The answer almost seems obvious until the question gets complicated. Various factors can affect crime rates and incarceration rates, so it's hard to determine how effectively incarceration deters crime. An economic recession can cause an increase in crime, making it hard to compare one year with another. Economic recoveries in Baltimore and Houston and other places aren't necessarily happen at the same time or to the same extent, so it's hard to compare crime rates in different places. At the same time, state changes in mandatory sentencing affect incarceration. Likewise, the legalization of marijuana or a change in legal attitudes toward addiction and treatment affects incarceration rates.

A study published by The Sentencing Project found that in three key states—California, New York, and New Jersey—crime dropped substantially even as prison populations declined.

• New York and New Jersey led the nation by reducing prison populations by 2 percent between 1999 and 2012. The national average saw an increase of 10 percent.

would not apply to adults. Thirty-four percent of girls were in for such violations, compared with 20 percent of boys. Boys were more likely arrested for crimes involving persons, property, or public order. Boys and girls were about equal for drug offenses, which was the least common offense.

International Law on
Imprisonment of Children

How many children (people under 18) are in prison? Nobody knows.
Many countries don't count them, and it depends on the definition
of "prison." Just as a prison for adults may be euphemized as a
"correctional facility," prisons for children are known by such softer
terms "detention center" or "young offenders institution."

UNICEF estimates a round number of 1,000,000 around the
world. In many cases—again, no one knows how many—prison
conditions are decrepit and abusive, with no possibility of education
or rehabilitation.

As with the imprisonment of adults, the United States leads
the world. In 2011, 60,000 children were imprisoned in juvenile
detention centers. Another 95,000 were locked in adult prisons.

Often the children are imprisoned for offenses that would not be
crimes if committed by adults. In Texas in 2010, Texas imprisoned
over 6,000 children for such "status offenses" as truancy, underage
drinking, running away from home, and curfew violations.

In Saudi Arabia, girls (and adult women) can imprisoned and flogged for such crimes as "seclusion" and "mingling," which include "being in a apartment by herself...or sitting in a place where she is not natural for her to be."

In Israel, children as young as 11 have been arrested, choked, beaten, threatened, and interrogated without parents or lawyers present. They are automatically prosecuted and sentenced by military courts.

Juvenile offenders have been put on death row in Egypt, Iran, Maldives, Pakistan, Saudi Arabia, Sri Lanka, Sudan, Yemen, and Nigeria. Children in 73 countries, including the United States, can receive death sentences.[101]

53,000

On any given day, 53,000 youths are held in some kind of prison. Nearly one in ten is in an adult jail or prison. Of the 48,000 in juvenile facilities, 31 percent are no older than 15. More than 500 are under the age of 12.

Here are nine types of juvenile facilities:

Correctional Facilities

1. Detention Center: Temporary restriction pending court disposition or awaiting placement elsewhere.

2. Long-term secure Facility: Strict confinement but with training, schools, reformatories.

3. Reception/Diagnostic Center: Short-term facility pending assignment to another facility.

Residential

4. Treatment Center: Facility focused on individual treatment for drug abuse, sex offense, mental health, etc.

5 Group Home: Long-term facility where residents are allowed contact with community, school attendance, job, etc.

6. Ranch/Wilderness Camp: Long-term facility for youth who do

not need confinement, with activities on ranch, farm, forestry camp, etc.

7. Shelter: Short-term facility with little physical restriction, typically for runaways and homeless youth.

8. Boot Camp: Secure facility with military-style physical and mental training, with strict rules and drilling to break youth resistance to improvement and cooperation.

9. Other: Alternative schools, independent living, etc.

In 2015, at least 30,714 youths were held in detention centers, long-term secure facilities, or reception centers. Two out of three were held in the most restrictive facilities—the juvenile equivalent of jails and prisons, 4,656 of them in facilities for adults.

Over 4,000 of those in detention centers were there for low-level "technical violations" or "status offenses such" as probation violations, which are not considered law violations for adults. Almost half of all youths held for status offenses are locked up for over 90 days.

The Prison Policy Initiative (which provided all the above information) calculates that one in three youths under detention—17,000 people—could be released without endangering the public. Another 6,000 are being held without being tried or found guilty of delinquent.[102]

Mothers' Duress

The Great American Incarceration[103] that began in the 1980s landed a lot of mothers in prison—65,000 of them by 2010. Because of women's traditional importance to family life and household health, the imprisonment of a mother impacts society in several ways. Children end up with alternative caregivers, often landing in different families, schools, and towns. Households often lose a wage earner. Life at home often deteriorates as the father (if any) attempts to hold a job while taking care of everything from laundry to help with homework.

The impact on the mothers themselves is also especially serious, and white women suffer even more. Researchers refer to "spoiled identity" as mothers suffer the stigma of failing to fulfill the classic function of a mother—to nurture her children. Fathers are impacted in the same way, but generally not as severely. All incarcerated parents have to grapple with the reality of no longer being primarily a parent. Rather, most of their time is dedicated to being an inmate.

White women suffer more for several reasons, each in a way resulting from an easier life prior to imprisonment.

- Since Hispanic and black women tend to live in families more beset by problems relating to prejudice and poverty, their wider families are more prepared psychologically to take on the burden of a family member's children. White families tend to take on that burden, but they are more upset about it.

• Since a higher proportion of black women end up incarcerated, they aren't quite as shocked to find themselves behind bars. Shocked, yes, of course, but not as shocked by "how far they've fallen."

• As above, white communities tend to stigmatize the arrest of a community member more than black communities do. Whites may see the arrest as disgrace, while blacks may see it as injustice.

• The nature of their respective crimes tends to land black women in prisons closer to home than white women. Consequently, the black women maintain closer contact with families.

• Blacks, especially those in poor urban communities, often grow up in a kind of isolation from general society, a situation somewhat similar to that of prison. Whites grow up in relative social acceptance, increasing the shock upon imprisonment.

Ironically, the greater degree of suffering for white mother prisoners results from their relatively wealthier and easier pre-prison lives.

When Mothers Get Locked Up

In 2009, nearly five percent of children in the United States knew what it was like to have a mother in prison. A study found an increasing rate of "at-risk familial environments" such as drug abuse, violence, etc., resulting from maternal incarceration.[104] Seventy percent of imprisoned mothers reported physical or sexual abuse prior to arrest, and two-thirds of those said the abuse occurred while they were living with their children.

Separation from a mother due to incarceration may be the most damaging aspect of incarceration. Children with incarcerated mothers

• have higher rates of externalizing emotions through aggression, problem behaviors, and delinquency;

• have higher rates of internalizing emotions resulting in depression, fearfulness, sleep problems, and low self-esteem;

• have higher levels of anxiety;

• are more likely to hang out with "negative peers";

• report long-term trauma due to separation from their mothers;

• are more likely to suffer emotional detachment from substitute caregivers;

• often show symptoms of post-traumatic stress disorder, among them flashbacks and feelings of anger and guilt;

• more likely to suffer poverty upon their mother's release from prison;

• often feel anger at their mother.

Born Behind Bars

In 2016 a woman was forced to give birth on the floor of a cell in the Macomb County (Michigan) Jail. Arrested for driving with a suspended license. Unable to pay a $10,000 cash bond, she was being held five days until a court date. She informed officials that she was eight months pregnant. When she told jail staff that she was going into labor, they did not believe her. They refused to take her to a hospital. When it became undeniable that she was about to have a baby, jail medical staff tried to help, but the mother-to-be was kept in her cell. She gave birth on a thin mattress on the floor. The medical staff had never delivered a baby before. The baby weighed less than five pounds but survived.[105]

Babies in the Hoosgow

Nearly 100 countries, from South Sudan to France, have laws that allow incarcerated mothers to stay with their newborn babies. The United States is not one of them. Only eight of more than 100 U.S. prisons for women have nursery facilities for babies born while their mothers are serving time. There used to be more, but with the advent of mass incarceration and get-tough-on-crime legislation, there has been less room, less financial support, and an increased belief that letting a mother be with her newborn was not consistent with the spirit of punishment.

Of the eight still in operation, Bedford Hills Correctional Facility has the oldest prison nursery in the country, operating since 1901. The walls and rooms of the nursery look like those of any good nursery school, full of colors, images, and toys. The big difference is the bars on the windows, the armed guards, the razor wire on the walls outside.

Babies at Bedford can spend their first 18 months with their mothers. Recidivism among these mothers is about 13 percent, half of the 26 percent rate for Bedford inmates as a whole.

The other states with incarceration nurseries are Indiana, Ohio, Nebraska, South Dakota, Washington, and West Virginia. Eighteen months is the typical time allowed, and generally restrictions don't allow participation by women arrested for violence or child abuse.[106]

318

Labor in Chains

Roughly six percent of female prisoners—some 200,000 women— were pregnant when they were incarcerated. There is no accurate number of how many prisoners in the United States give birth each year. The estimate is about 2,000.

Shackling pregnant prisoners while they are in labor is legal in about half the country, and it's often practiced even where illegal. It has been illegal in federal prisons since 2008.

Illinois was the first state to pass a law prohibiting the shackling of female prisoners while they are giving birth. Thirteen years later, 80 women claimed to have been in shackles while in labor.

New York passed such a law in 2009, but in 2015, 23 of 27 women who gave birth while incarcerated said they'd been in shackled during labor. In 2011, Tina Tinen, at Bedford Hills Correctional Facility, was shackled while taken to the hospital and until 15 minutes of giving birth. In 2012, another prisoner there, Jacqueline McDougall, was handcuffed to a chain around her waist, clamped at the sutured incision where she'd had a C-section.[107]

Pennsylvania allows shackles during childbirth. From July 2012 to June 2013, over 100 women gave birth while in shackles.

In 2011, Valerie Nabors, in jail for stealing casino chips, was shackled in an ambulance and during childbirth despite repeated requests by medical staff to remove the restraints. She was released during the moments of birth but re-shackled ten minutes later. The incident occurred 18 days after restraint of pregnant patients was made illegal. She was later unable to receive physical therapy because guards refused to unshackle her ankles.[108]

April, 2013, Melissa Hall, 25, a prisoner at Milwaukee County Jail, is shackled—right wrist, left ankle—while in labor at a hospital for three hours. She remained shackled for the next two days.[109]

Shawanna Nelson was six months pregnant when she was given a short sentence in an Arkansas prison for a nonviolent crime. When she went into labor, her ankles were shackled on opposite sides of her bed until she was taken to the delivery room. She was re-shackled immediately following the birth.

In 2017 a jury awarded an anonymous woman $6.7 million after she accused a Milwaukee County Jail guard of raping her several times, including right before childbirth. She was shackled while giving birth and days afterward. The guard pleaded guilty to lesser charges and was sentenced to three days in jail and a fine of $200.[110]

Illegitimate Births

A report on the treatment of pregnant or postpartum women by The Prison Birth Project and Prisoners' Legal Services of Massachusetts found that

- neither the state Department of Corrections nor any single Country Sheriff's Office fully complied with the law;
- corrections staff showed varying knowledge of the law;
- women were being illegally restrained without reason after giving birth;
- pregnant women had been illegally transported in vans with no seatbelts;
- pregnant women were illegally denied sufficiently nutritious meals, and often they went hungry;
- pregnant women were given standard-issue clothing with pant legs so long they could cause the women to trip;
- prisoners who had delivered by cesarean section were illegally restrained by waist chains during transportation shortly after giving birth.

A woman who was handcuffed during labor said, "It was really hard. I couldn't move like I needed to—couldn't hold my stomach or push up to move myself around. The metal would dig into me every time I did try to grab my stomach during a contraction. It was incredibly lonely going through that experience by myself."[132]

Words of Wisdom

To live in prison is to live without mirrors. To live without mirrors is to live without the self.

Margaret Atwood

No prison can shut out God.

J.F. La Harpe

Is it surprising that prisons resemble factories, schools, barracks, hospitals, which all resemble prisons?

Michel Foucault

Jails and state prisons are the complement of schools: so many less as you have of the latter, so many more must you have of the former.

Horace Mann

How feeble is all language to describe the horrors we inflict upon these wretches, whom we mason up in the cells of our prisons, and condemn to perpetual solitude in the very heart of our population.

Herman Melville

It is in prison...that one becomes a real revolutionary.

Vladimir Lenin

Prison is like high school with knives.

Raegan Butcher

Show me a prison, show me a jail
Show me a pris'ner whose face has grown pale
And I'll show you a young man
With many reasons why
There but for fortune, go you or I.

Phil Ochs

While there is a lower class, I am in it, and while there is a criminal element, I am of it, and while there is a soul in prison, I am not free.

Eugene V. Debs

Some prisons don't require bars to keep people locked inside. All it takes is their perception that they belong there.

Lysa TerKeurst

At the risk of quoting Mephistopheles I repeat: Welcome to hell. A hell erected and maintained by human-governments, and blessed by black robed judges. A hell that allows you to see your loved ones, but not to touch them. A hell situated in America's boondocks, hundreds of miles away from most families. A white, rural hell, where most of the captives are black and urban. It is an American way of death.

Mumia Abu-Jamal

If they lock me up, at least I'll have a place to stay.

Mike Tyson

A prison is ... a microcosm, a little world of woe, it is a map of misery, it is a place that will learn a young man more villainy, if he be apt to take it, in one half year, than he can learn at twenty dicing-houses, bowling alleys, brothel houses, or ordinaries; and an old man, more policy than if he had been pupil to Machiavelli.

Geffray Minshull

"No one truly knows a nation until one has been inside its jails. A nation should not be judged by how it treats its highest citizens but its lowest ones."

Nelson Mandela

America is a land of the second chance—and when the gates of the prison open, the path ahead should lead to a better life.

George W. Bush

You can tell a lot about a civilization by the quality of the people found in its jails.

David Gerrold

He who opens a school door closes a prison.

Victor Hugo

"Remember those in prison as if you were their fellow prisoners, and those who are mistreated as if you yourselves were suffering.

Hebrews 13:3

It must surely be a tribute to the resilience of the human spirit that even a small number of those men and women in the hell of the prison system survive it and hold on to their humanity.

Howard Zinn

Poor people, people of color especially, are much more likely to be found in prison than in institutions of higher education.

Angela Davis

The last place I would ever want to go is prison.

Martha Stewart

The only time you can be completely free from risk is when you're in prison.

Edward Snowden

Year after year the gates of prison hells return to the world an emaciated, deformed, will-less, ship-wrecked crew of humanity, with the Cain mark on their foreheads, their hopes crushed, all their natural inclinations thwarted. With nothing but hunger and inhumanity to greet them, these victims soon sink back into crime as the only possibility of existence. It is not at all an unusual thing to find men and women who have spent half their lives—nay, almost their entire existence—in prison.

Emma Goldman

Prison is a second-by-second assault on the soul, a day-to-day degradation of the self, an oppressive steel and brick umbrella that transforms seconds into hours and hours into days.

Mumia Abu-Jamal

The best way to keep a prisoner from escaping is to make sure he never knows he is in prison.

Fyodor Dostoevsky

Your definition of who you are is your prison. You can set yourself free at any time.

Cheri Huber

Security without liberty is called prison

Benjamin Franklin

I think the years I have spent in prison have been the most formative and important in my life because of the discipline, the sensations, but chiefly the opportunity to think clearly, to try to understand things.

Jawaharlal Nehru

I think my attitude to human beings has changed since leaving prison.

Jeffrey Archer

There is no glory in punishing.

Michel Foucault

Why should they ask me to put on a uniform and go 10,000 miles from home and drop bombs and bullets on brown people in Vietnam while so-called Negro people in Louisville are treated like dogs and denied simple human rights? No, I'm not going 10,000 miles from home to help murder and burn another poor nation simply to continue the domination of white slave masters of the darker people the world over. This is the day when such evils must come to an end. I have been warned that to take such a stand would cost me millions of dollars. But I have said it once and I will say it again. The real enemy of my people is here. I will not disgrace my religion, my people or myself by becoming a tool to enslave those who are fighting for their own justice, freedom and equality. If I thought the war was going to bring freedom and equality to 22 million of my people they wouldn't have to draft me, I'd join tomorrow. I have nothing to lose by standing up for my beliefs. So I'll go to jail, so what? We've been in jail for 400 years.

Muhammad Ali

The greater ignorance towards a country is not ignoring what its politicians have to say, it is ignoring what the inmates in its prisons have to say.

Criss Jami

He who has never tasted jail
Lives well within the legal pale,
While he who's served a heavy sentence
Renews the racket, not repentance.

Ogden Nash

...the court, as now constituted, would be meaningless without the jail which gives it its power. But if there is anything I have learned by being in jail, it is that prisons are wrong, simply and unqualifiedly wrong.

Barbara Deming

Do not fear ARREST. Why? Because, there is REST at the end of each AR"REST"; either in jail or in the grave. The wisest and the greatest of men are aware of this.

Oppong Amankwaa

It is a sad state of affairs in the USA that for the sick and the poor that jail offers better benefits than the freedom of no healthcare, bills that cannot be paid and starvation.

Steven Magee

[Prison] relieves us of the responsibility of seriously engaging with the problems of our society, especially those produced by racism and, increasingly, global capitalism.

Angela Davis

The least I can do is speak out for the hundreds of chimpanzees who, right now, sit hunched, miserable and without hope, staring out with dead eyes from their metal prisons. They cannot speak for themselves.

Jane Goodall

All these [correctional] institutions seemed purposely invented for the production of depravity and vice, condensed to such a degree that no other conditions could produce it, and for the spreading of this condensed depravity and vice broadcast among the whole population.

Leo Tolstoy

A society with a great number of prisons is a totally failed society because it has terribly failed to create a marvelous society where crime is not something widespread but an exception!

Mehmet Murat Ildan

Under a government which imprisons any unjustly, the true place for a just man is also a prison.

Henry David Thoreau

The most anxious man in a prison is the governor.

George Bernard Shaw

We are all serving a life sentence in the dungeon of the self.

Cyril Connolly

To assert in any case that a man must be absolutely cut off from society because he is absolutely evil amounts to saying that society is absolutely good, and no-one in his right mind will believe this today.

Albert Camus

It isn't true that convicts live like animals: animals have more room to move around.

Mario Vargas Llosa

Prison is a socialist paradise where equality prevails, everything is supplied, and competition is eliminated.

Elbert Hubbard

Being in prison for seven years was like being in an army that never drilled, never deployed, and only fought itself.

Raegan Butcher

Prison is, simply put, the bottom rung of the welfare ladder.

Stephen Reid

Prison is the only form of public housing that the government has truly invested in over the past five decades.

Marc Lamont Hill

Prison is the recruitment center for the army of crime. That is what it achieves.

Michel Foucault

Prison is an expensive way of making bad people worse.

Douglas Hurd

Going to prison is like dying with your eyes open.

Bernard Kerik

Building prisons to fight crime is like building cemeteries to fight disease.

Jack Levin

Mistakes are Made

From Michelle Alexander's *The New Jim Crow: Mass Incarceration in the Age of Colorblindness*:

The genius of the current caste system, and what most distinguishes it from its predecessors, is that it appears voluntary. People choose to commit crimes, and that's why they are locked up or locked out, we are told. This feature makes the politics of responsibility particularly tempting, as it appears the system can be avoided with good behavior. But herein lies the trap. All people make mistakes. All of us are sinners. All of us are criminals. All of us violate the law at some point in our lives. In fact, if the worst thing you have ever done is speed ten miles over the speed limit on the freeway, you have put yourself and others at more risk of harm than someone smoking marijuana in the privacy of his or her living room. Yet there are people in the United States serving life sentences for first-time drug offenses, something virtually unheard of anywhere else in the world."

Suggested Reading

Abbott, Jack Henry. *In the Belly of the Beast* (Vintage, 1991).

Alexander, Buzz. Is William Martinez. *Not Our Brother: Twenty Years of the Prison Creative Arts* (U. of Michigan Press, 2010).

Alexander, Michelle. *The New Jim Crow: Mass Incarceration in the Age of Colorblindness* (The New Press, 2010).

Alsner, Alan. *Gates of Injustice: The Crisis in America's Prisons* (FT Press, 2006).

Anderson, Brian. *Inmate to Convict: A Guide to Prison Survival and the Art of Penitentiary Warfare* (Amazon Digital, 2016).

Baca, Jimmy Santiago. *A Place to Stand* (Grove Press, 2002).

Bernstein, Nell. *Burning Down the House: The End of Juvenile Prison* (The New Press, 2016).

Betts, R. Dwayne. *A Question of Freedom: A Memoir of Learning, Survival, and Coming of Age in Prison* (Avery, 2010).

Bonhoffer, Dietrich. *Letters & Papers from Prison* (Touchstone, 1997).

Braly, Malcolm. *On the Yard* (NYRB Classics, 2002).

Casella, Jean, et al, editors. *Hell is a Very Small Place: Voices from Solitary Confinement* (The New Press, 2017).

Clear, Todd R. *Imprisoning Communities: How Mass Incarceration Makes Disadvantaged Neighborhoods Worse* (Oxford U. Press, 2007).

Cleaver, Eldridge, *Soul on Ice* (Delta, 1999).

Conover, Ted. *Newjack: Guarding Sing Sing* (Vintage, 2001).

Davis, Angela Y. *Are Prison's Obsolete?* (Seven Stories Press, 2003).

Davis, Angela Y. *Abolition Democracy: Beyond Empire, Prison, and Torture* (Seven Stories Press, 2005).

Dreisinger, Baz. *Incarceration Nation A Journey to Justice in Prisons Around the World* (Other Press, 2016).

Earley, Pete. *The Hot House: Life Inside Leavenworth Prison* (Bantam, 1993).

Echols, Damien, *Life After Death* (Blue Rider Press, 2012).

Ferguson, Russell. *Prison Survival Guide: Words of Wisdom and Encouragement from an Inmate,* (Rosedog Books, 2016).

Forman, James Jr. *Locking Up Our Own: Crime and Punishment in Black America* (Farrar, Straus and Giroux, 2018).

Foucault, Michel. *Discipline and Punish: The Birth of the Prison* (Pantheon, 1977).

Friedman, Lawrence M. *Crime and Punishment in American History* (HarperCollins, 1993).

Hirsch, Adam J. *The Rise of the Penitentiary: Prisons and Punishment in Early America* (Yale U Press, 1992).

Humes, Edward. *No Matter How Loud I Shout: A Year in the Life of Juvenile Court* (Simon & Schuster, 2015).

Jackson, George. *Soledad Brother* (Chicago Review Press, 1994).

Kudin, Andrew V. How to Survive Prison (Amazon Digital, 2012).

Lamb, Wally. *Couldn't Keep It to Myself: Wally Lamb and the Women of York Correctional Institution* (Harper Perennial, 2004).

Lamb, Wally. *I'll Fly Away: Further Testimonies from the Women of York Prison* (Harper Perennial 2008).

Lerner, Jimmy A. *You Got Nothing Coming: Notes from a Prison Fish* (Broadway, 2002).

Lordan, Christopher, and Dellelo, Robert. *The Factory: A*

Journey Through the Prison Industrial Complex (Createspace, 2016).

Loury, Glenn C. et al. *Race, Incarceration, and American Values* (MIT Press, 2008).

Martin, Dannie M., and Sussman, Peter Y. *Committing Journalism: The Prison writings of Red Hog* (W.W. Norton, 1995).

Maur, Marc. *Race to Incarcerate* (New Press, 1999).

McCoy, Kemp. *First Timers Guide on How to Survive in New York State Prison* (Trafford, 2013).

M<cShane, Marilyn D., and Williams, Frank R. *Encyclopedia of American Prisons* (Garland, 1996).

Mitchel, William. *How to Survive Prison for the First Time Inmate: Take a Look at a Dangerous Society within our Society* (Createspace, 2009).

Moran, Brian. *The Justice Impreative: How Hyper-Incarceration Has Hijacked the American Dream* (Malt Justice Initiative, 2014).

Orland, Leonard. Prisons: *Houses of Darkness* (Free Press, 1975).

Osborne, Thomas Mott. *Society and Prisons* (Yale U Press, 1916).

Parenti, Christian. *Lockdown America: Police and Prisons in the Age of Crisis* (Verso, 2008).

Peltier, Leonard. *Prison Writings: My Life is My Sundance* (St. Martin's Griffin, 2000).

Petersilla, Joan. *When Prisoners Come Home: Parole and Prisoner Re-entry* (Oxford U Press, 2003).

Pfaf, John. *Locked In: The True Causes of Mass Incarceration— and How to Achieve True Reform* (Basic Books, 2017).

Rafter, Nicole Hahn, and Stanley, Debra L. *Prisons in America: A Reference Handbook* (ABC-CLIO, 1999).

Rathbone, Christina. *A World Apart: Women, Prison, and Life*

Behind Bars (Random House Trade, 2006).

Reiter, Keramet. *23/7: Pelican Bay Prison and the Rise of Long-Term Solitary Confinement* (Yale U. Press, 2016).

Prejean, Sr. Helen. *Dead Man Walking* (Vintage, 2011).

Prejean, Sr. Helen. *The Death of Innocents: An Eyewitness Account of Wrongful Executions* (Vintage, 2006).

Jamonz M. Ross, Jamonz M. and Ross, Taleana K. *How to Do Time: What to Expect and How to Survive When Going to Prison,* (Kindle, 2017).

Ross, Jeffrey Ian. *Behind Bars: Surviving Prison* (Alpha, 2002).

Runnels, Travis. *How to Survive in Prison: A Guide for Prisoners, their Families and Supporters* (Createspace, 2017).

Scaife, Jennifer. *Is It Safe? Essays by Students in the San Quentin College Program* (Prison University Project, 2008).

Santos, Michael G. *Inside: Life Behind Bars in America* (St. Martin's Press, 2007).

Solzhenitsyn, Alexandr, *The Gulag Archipelago 1918-1956: An Experiment in Literary Investigation* (Harper & Row, 1975).

Sykes, G.M. *Society of Captives: A Study of a Maximum Security Prison* (Princeton U. Press, 2007).

Thompson, Heather Ann. *Blood in the Water: The Attica Prison Uprising of 1971 and Its Legacy* (Vintage, 2016).

Thurber, Thomas. *There Are Alternatives to Incarceration: A Study Proposal Written for the Connecticut Prison Association* (Connecticut Prison Assoc, 1973).

Unseem, Bert, and Kimball, Peter, *States of Seige: U.S. Prison Riots 1971-1986* (Oxford U. Press, 2016).

Von Drehle, David. *Among the Lowest of the Dead* (U. of Michigan Press, 2006).

Waldman, Ayelet. *Inside This Place, But Not Of It: Narratives from Women's Prisons* (McSweeny's, 2014).

——, "What Works? Questions and Answers about Prison Reform" (*Public Interest*, Spring 1974).

Yackle, Larry. *Reform and Regre: The Story of Federal Judicial Involvement in the Alabama Prison System* (Oxford U. Press, 1989)

Christopher Zoukis. *Federal Prison Handbook: the Definitive Guide to Surviving the Federal Bureau of Prison* (Middle St. Pub. 2017

A Merry Burial Compendium

Thanatology, History, and Myth

Vernacular of Death and Burial

cadaver: a dead body, or corpse, especially one to be used for dissection or research.

cadaverine: the foul-smelling chemical produced by the putrefaction of animal tissue.

cairn: a mound of stones atop a grave.

casket: a burial or cremation container, generally rectangular or oval in shape. (see *coffin*)

catacomb: a human-made underground passageway or system of underground spaces for religious ceremonies or burials.

cenotaph: an empty tomb or monument established in honor of a deceased person who is not buried there, sometimes the initial tomb of a person who was buried there but removed.

chippie: a coffin or casket made of particle board, generally used for cremation.

coffin: strictly defined, a burial container usually with six sides, i.e. with "shoulders" narrowing to the head area. The term is often considered synonymous with the four-sided *casket*.

columbarium niche: a cemetery plot reserved for burial of cremated remains.

cremains: a person's cremated remains; considered by some to be a disrespectful term.

crematorium: a facility with crematory units and possibly offering related services.

cremator: the part of a crematorium where bodies are cremated; also known as a crematory.

cremulator: a British term for the machine somewhat like a blender that pulverizes cremated remains into the "ashes" that are delivered to a client.

crematory: the part of a crematorium where bodies are cremated, also known as a cremator.

crypt: a stone chamber beneath a church or other building for the interment of the dead or religious relics.

death anxiety: the fear of dying.

death, brain: the absence of electrical activity in the brain and the complete cessation of brain function, including all involuntary actions such as breathing, sustaining of body temperature, etc. It is synonymous with cerebral death, though definitions vary. It may or may not include brain stem death. The bodily functions of a brain-dead body can be sustained by artificial means.

death, clinical: the cessation of blood circulation and breathing, also known as cardiopulmonary death. Clinical death can be reversed.

death doula: a person who assists in the process of dying; also known as a death midwife.

decedent: a deceased person.

diener: a person responsible for moving, cleaning, and assisting in the embalming or autopsy of a corpse.

DNR: An acronym of Do Not Resuscitate, a DNR is a binding decision by an individual to not to be resuscitated by medical intervention if breathing or heartbeat have stopped.

inter: to place in a grave or tomb

interment: burial.

martyrium: a mausoleum for the remains of a martyr.

mausoleum: a building enclosing an interment space or burial chamber. A mausoleum may be considered a type of tomb or the enclosure of a tomb.

metempsychosis: the transmigration of the soul to some kind of reincarnated existence.

morgue: a place where a body is stored pending transfer or burial.

mortuary: a morgue or funeral home.

necrophobia: fear of the dead and things associated with death, such as tombs or coffins (not necessarily of dying).

psychopom: Greek for *soul guide*, a creature, angel, or spirit of some sort that escorts the dead to the afterlife.

pyre: a structure, usually of wood, with the purpose of burning a body as part of a funeral rite.

rainbow's end: a British euphemism for a mortuary.

resomation: the alkaline hydrolysis process of cremating a body with lye under pressure, resulting in the body being broken down into chemical compounds.

retort: the firing chamber where a body is cremated.

rose cottage: a British euphemism for a mortuary.

sarcophagus: A stone container for a body, coffin, or casket, often decorated as part of a monument or mausoleum.

sati: self-immolation ritual in which a widowed woman throws herself on her deceased husband's pyre.

scaphism: (You do not want to know.)

sepulcher: a space carved from rock for the interment of a body.

sky burial: the disposal of a body by leaving in the open air—on the ground or on a platform—for consumption by animals.

taxidermy: the recreation of an animal's form often using only the creature's skin mounted on an anatomical form (as opposd to embalming, which preserves much of the body).

thanatology: the study of death.

thanatophilia: necrophilia, the sexual atttraction to or sexual act with a corpse.

thanatophobia: fear of death or dying

tumulus: a burial mound, the mound of dirt atop a grave, a barrow. (see also *cairn*).

Unspeakable Love

Necrophilia is the sexual attraction to corpses. The rare disorder includes *regular necrophilia* (the use of dead bodies for sexual purposes), *necrophilic fantasy* (fantasizing about sex with bodies), *necrophilic homicide* (murder to acquire a body for sexual purposes), and *pseudonecrophilia,* transient, usually opportunistic sexual contact with bodies).

No one knows how common necrophilia is. Due to people's extreme reluctance to admit to the practice or even related fantasies, it is impossible to even estimate its prevalence. It is known to have happened throughout history. Greek historian Herodotus reported that the deceased wives of men of rank would not be sent for embalming for several days lest the embalmers violate them. The Catholic Church felt it was enough of a problem that it needed its own category. It wasn't whoring ("fornicatio") or bestiality. It was "pollution with a tendency to whoring."

The rare cases that are known are almost always because someone was caught doing it. It is supposed that many necrophilic fantasizers are reluctant to admit their fantasies.

A study published in the Bulletin of the American Academy of Psychiatry and the Law (J. Rosman and P. Resnick, June, 1989) reviewed 88 documented and 34 undocumented cases. Of this limited number, 92% were male. In cases where sexuality was known, 79% were heterosexual, 13% were bisexual, and 9% were homosexual. Twenty-six percent were married, and 14% were divorced or widowed. Most had professional access to corpses. Eighty percent of fantasizers consumed alcohol before the act. The most common motivation was a desire for an unresisting, unrejecting partner. Second was reunion with a romantic partner. Fifteen percent were simply attracted to corpses.

Don't Worry about It

Death Anxiety is the fear of dying. You'd be nuts if you didn't feel it but downright abnormal if you let it paralyze you the way anxiety can do.

It's also called thanatophobia, named after the Greek reaper Thanatos.

Death anxiety has been around since people were amoebas, back when we first learned to sense danger and do something about it. Basically, we've learned to run away or fight back. As we became human, of course, things got complicated. Endowed with a sense of guilt, we learned to take on a fear of death after causing someone else's death. When we figured out that no matter what we do, we're going to die, we invented, by psychological necessity, denial.

Freud theorized that thanatophobia isn't really a fear of death. He theorized that people cannot fear death because they can't imagine it, have never experienced it, and can't really believe that they will die. An apparent fear of death, he said, is really a subconscious anxiety about some kind of unresolved problem in childhood. The problem may have nothing to do with death, but it sure feels like death is behind it.

Everyone Is Dying

The mortality rate of human beings continues to be one hundred per-cent. Approximately 150,000 people die each day. About two thirds of them basically get old and die. In industrialized countries, that portion may reach 90 percent of deaths. In developing countries, infectious diseases are the leading cause of death. In industrial countries, it's heart disease and other diseases relating to obesity and old age. Malaria kills between one million and three million per year. Tuberculosis kills about 1.8 million. Tobacco is expected to kill a billion people in the 21st century. In 2012, suicide surpassed traffic accidents as the lead-ing cause of death by injury in the United States, where people spend some $500 billion per year on anti-aging products that have never been proven effective.

Grim and Screaming Reapers

In ancient Brittany, the Breton people feared the Ankou, a version of the Grim Reaper who was not a skeleton with a scythe but the last person in the community who had died. He or she might appear as a skeleton or as an old, worn-out person with broad-brimmed hat and long, white hair. The Ankou drove a wagon stacked with corpses, stopping at the house of the imminently dead. One could hear the axle of the Ankou's cart creaking as it approached. One could only hope the creaking didn't stop.

Back in the days of leprechauns and shillelaghs, people feared the scream of a banshee. A banshee was a mythological female spirit who cut loose with a blood-curdling shriek in front of someone's house. Sometimes she looked like an old witch. (The Welsh feared a similar figure, but she was known as the Hag of the Mist.) Sometimes she looked like a sweet young girl. In either case she was probably wearing red or green, and her hair might look like it was on fire. She might wail a mournful tune as a harbinger of death, or she might screech loud enough to not only break a window but push somebody over the edge. A pack of banshees outside your house would be a recognition that you were a great person and would be remembered as such.

During the scourge of the Black Plague of the 14th century, the Norse were never happy to see the Plague Hag come to town. They knew her as Pesta, a word related to the English *pest* and *pestilence*. Pesta looked like she was in the Reaper family, but instead of a scythe she carried either a rake or a broom. If a rake, the bad news was a little good—at least some people in town would survive the plague. But if she brought a broom, she'd be sweeping the place clean.

The Nice Guy from Hell

Osiris was the Egyptian god of death and the underworld. But as death deities go, he was actually a rather positive figure. Through him, death was associated with resurrection and regeneration, the very cycles of life. As a merciful judge of the dead, he was grantor of all birth, including that of plants arising from his underworld.

An Underworld of Greek Gods

Hades was the Greek god-king of the Underworld which eventually took on his name. In time, as cultures mixed, he was assumed to be the same as the Etruscan god Aita and two Roman gods, Dis Pater and Orcus. They merged and became known as Plouton, whose name became Pluto in Rome. While the name Hades was known for provoking fear, Pluto was associated with wealth because wealth was seen as emanating from underground in the form of precious metals, gems, and crops.

Hades ruled, but he did not rule alone. Other gods of the Underworld include his wife Persephone, whom Hades abducted because they were meant for each other, she being the goddess of seeds and vegetation, he being the god of the place where seeds sprout. Still, it was a complicated relationship that began with rape. Thanatos (spirit of death), Rhadamantus, Minos and Aeacus (judges of the dead), Angelos (a daughter of Zeus, whose realm was the sky), Menoetes (herdsman of Hades' cattle), Orphne (one of the Lampades nymphs who carried torches, hence our word *lamp*), Erebus (god of darkness), the Keres (goddesses of violent death), Lamia (Underworld vampire), a god or goddess for each of the seven rivers of the Underworld (the most famous being the goddess Styx), Charon (ran the ferry across the Styx), the Erinyes (gods of vengeance), Clotho (who spun the thread of life), Lachesis (who measured the thread allotted to each person), and Atropos (who cut the thread, ending life).

The Other St. Joseph

St. Joseph of Arimathea is the patron saint of undertakers. All four Gospels mention him. He was a wealthy businessman who dealt in metals. (It is mere coincidence that metals as a source of wealth are associated with Pluto, Roman god of the Underworld, where metals come from.) It was Joseph who, on the first Good Friday, went to Pontius Pilate to ask permission to recover the body of Jesus from the Cross. Joseph prepared the body for burial, anointed it with oils, shrouded it in linen, and carried it to the cave where he was so briefly interred. Joseph is remembered for his courage and kindness.

The Bible says no more about Joseph, but according to legend, Joseph had taken the youngster Jesus to the Isle of Britain on a business trip, which accounts for the gap on Jesus' résumé between his childhood and his ministry. Years later, Joseph is said to have returned to Glastonbury with the Holy Grail, the cup he had used to catch the blood from the crucified Christ. William Blake immortalized the legend in his poem Jerusalem, which includes the quatrain

> And did those feet in ancient time
> Walk upon England's mountains green?
> And was the holy Lamb of God
> On England's pleasant pastures seen?

Is it coincidence that the Saint's Day of St. Joseph of Arimathea's is March 17, the same as that of St. Patrick, patron saint of the Irish who populate so much of the American funeral industry? Just maybe.

Saints Preserved

The remains of several saints and beati of the Roman Catholic Church have been exhumed and reported to have not decomposed. In some cases, the bodies were accompanied by an aroma of holiness described as sweet or floral. The inexplicable preservation is attributed to the "incorruptibility" of truly holy individuals. This is not to say that none of the bodies of saints have decomposed, but when they don't, it is confirmation of holiness.

In some cases, decomposition was somehow avoided despite conditions which would normally hasten it. A classic example was St. Francis Xavier. He was first buried on the beach of tropical Shangchuan Island. It was dug up six months later and found uncorrupted by decomposition. He was the moved to Malacca, where he was buried for about a month. Then he was dug up and shipped to tropical Goa. His right forearm was removed and sent to Rome. Another arm was sent to Macao. The rest of the body remains in a glass case in a silver casket in Goa, as fresh as a mutilated daisy that's been dead for half a millennium.

Preservation due to embalming, mummification, lack of oxygen, or other explanations is not considered incorruptibility.

Corpses and Cadavers

Dat Great Brick House

Was it folklore, disinformation, or reality? In the days of American slavery, blacks feared "Night Doctors" who sought cadavers—especially those of people who had neither voice nor right to life—for dissection and experimentation. These weren't necessarily corpses dug up from graves, which at the time was the only source of corpses used for experimental and training purposes. According to tales, if not verifiable reports, white doctors or their agents would abduct blacks, take them to some kind of medical facility, snuff them, and use their bodies for dissection. Blacks knew them as Night Riders, Night Witches, KKK Doctors, and Student Doctors. Historians say these were only vicious rumors generated by slave owners and, after Emancipation, white farm owners who wanted to discourage migration to the north. Men in white gowns would prowl around Afro-American communities, pretending to be looking for eligible victims. White people who wouldn't be missed—sailors in port, immigrants, indigents— could also find themselves on a slab in a classroom or operating amphitheater.

In the 1830s, the Transylvania University Medical Department in Lexington, KY, lost prestige for lack of corpses. Nearby Louisville Medical Institute, located where there were more blacks and transients, had no such problem.

The Medical College of Georgia in Augusta bought Grandison Harris for the purpose of janitorial work and the procurement of black corpses, which he did for 50 years, robbing graves and otherwise procuring specimens.

Whether doctors and students acquired black corpses by abducting living people is not known. But blacks and whites both ended up on dissecting tables, which is interesting in that blacks were considered something other than human while alive. Once dead, they were human enough.

The following poem, apparently written by a white imitating black dialect and making fun of black fears, was propagated in the late 19th or early 20th century:

The Dissecting Hall

Yuh see dat house? Dat great brick house?
Way yonder down de street?
Dey used to take dead folks een dar
Wrapped een a long white sheet.
An' sometimes we'en a nigger'd stop,
A-wondering who was dead,
Dem stujent men would take a club
An' bat 'im on de head.
An' drag dat poor dead nigger chile
Right een dat 'sectin hall
To vestigate 'is liver-lights-
His gizzardan' 'is gall.
Tek off dat nigger's han's an' feet-
His eyes, his head, an' all,
An' w'en dem stujent finish
Dey was nothin' left at all.

Burke: transitive verb

Until 1832, the only legal source of cadavers for medical and educational purposes in England was the bodies of criminals condemned to not only death but dissection. The death sentence might be imposed for relatively light crimes, while dissection was reserved for murderers. Dissection was allowed on these individuals because Christians believed that dissected bodies could not rise to Heaven, a place the worst criminals were not expected to go. But there weren't enough heinous crimes to supply the demand, so grave robbing—a mere misdemeanor—became common.

Bodysnatchers used wooden shovels because they were quieter than metal. They would dig a hole at the head-end of the grave until they reached the coffin. They would break the coffin open, put a rope around the corpse, and haul it out through the hole. Then they would replace the turf so that no one would notice the theft.

Disturbing the dead was, of course, frowned upon by those who had no use for cadavers, especially those of their dearly departed. To prevent theft, some families had iron cages constructed around graves. Others guarded the graves at night until the body was decomposed beyond scientific use. Thefts were less common in the summer because decomposition took place more quickly. October to May was bodysnatching season.

Inevitably, astute bodysnatchers figured out it would be easier to skip the digging process by gently murdering people and selling the fresh, undamaged corpses. Thus the English language acquired the transitive verb *burke*—to execute by suffocation so as to leave the body intact for dissection. The word is derived from William Burke, who burked 16 people. He was tried, found guilty, and in 1828 hanged before a crowd of 25,000, then publicly dissected. His skeleton now resides at the Anatomical Museum of Edinburgh Medical School, and his verb resides in the Oxford English Dictionary.

Family Dental Practice

British dentist Martin van Butchell wasn't one to let a good wife go to waste. When his beloved Mary passed away in 1775, he saw opportunity where others saw mere death. He hired a couple of shady anatomists to embalm poor Mary, preserving her in as life-like a state as possible. They injected her cheeks with coloring to give them a warm rosiness, replaced her eyes with glass eyeballs, and dressed her in the finest lace that any wife of a dentist could ask for. They they caked her with plaster and tucked her into a glass-topped coffin.

Dr. Butchell put his wife on display in his office window. She looked pretty good, for a dead lady. She attracted many onlookers and made quite a name for her widower. Whether he succeeded in attracting more or fewer dental patients is not known. He did manage to attract a new wife, Elizabeth, but she insisted that the ex- in the window had to go. Butchell gave Mary to a museum, and she eventually ended up at the Royal College of Surgeons. Mary's remains did not weather the next century and a half very well. A German bombing raid in 1941 finally put her out of her posthumous misery.

The Truth about the Kadaververwertungsanstalt

During the First World War, various newspapers reported that a factory, called the Kadaververwertungsanstalt, was rendering German battlefield corpses into fat. The fat was then used to manufacture candles, soap, lubricants, boot wax, and even the explosive nitroglycerine. Rumors of the factory were rife in the English trenches, bolstering the belief that defeating Germany was worth all the suffering.

But it seems something was lost—or, more aptly put, enhanced—in translation. The original report appeared in a German newspaper, which did indeed refer to a factory that rendered "*kadavers*." The story was only 59 words long and was about the smell of the place, not the bodies. A Belgian newspaper then expanded the story to 500 words, enhancing it with descriptions of a deep forest, an electrified fence, and soap of a yellowish-brown color. Another Belgian paper expanded on that, and then The Times of London and The Daily Mail picked it up.

It wasn't until after the war that someone noted that *kadaver* in German refers to the body of an animal, rarely a human.

Adolf Hitler later used the English reports as evidence that British papers cannot be trusted to tell the truth. But it may have given him an idea. During World War II, Nazis experimented with rendering people into soap, reportedly producing 25 kg of soap from the fat of 40 people. Despite rumors to the contrary, the process was never taken to industrial scale.

Apocryphal Anthropodermia

Did Nazis really make anthropodermic lampshades from the skin of murdered Jews? No. It was alleged that Ilse Koch, "The Bitch of Buchenwald," wife of the commandant of that concentration camp, had lampshades of skin, but at her post-war trial it was determined that the lampshades were made with the skin of goats. But that doesn't mean nobody ever made a lampshade of human skin.

The apocryphal report from Buchenwald inspired Edward Theodore Gein, an American murderer and bodysnatcher, to include a lampshade among many items he crafted from human parts, among them a wastebasket, seat covers, bowls, leggings, masks, and a corset.

And then there's anthropodermic bibliopegy—the use of human skin to bind books. Seventeen such books are known to exist, and several more are allegedly human though quite possibly of animals. Part of the binding of a copy of Dale Carnegie's *Lincoln the Unknown* is said to have been "taken from the skin of a Negro at a Baltimore Hospital and tanned by the Jewell Belting Company."

Dummies Beat the Dead

Among the many good deeds performed by the deceased has been the improvement of car safety. Crash dummies are fine for certain experiments, but there's nothing like the real thing. Only a cadaver can demonstrate soft tissue damage. In one experiment, seat belts seemed to to do their job well, but only with dummies. When actual cadavers were put to the test, it was found that the seat belt protected the thorax but not the pelvis. Crash dummies had failed that test because they do not have moving parts in the pelvic area. But no body's perfect. It's hard to get cadavers to sit up straight.

Funerals and Burial

Cemeterial Behavior

What kind of behavior is appropriate for a cemetery? Should people be allowed to jog or do other kinds of exercise? Should families be allowed to picnic? If so, should their picnic space be allowed to infringe on the grace space of unrelated people? How about a barbecue grill? Should a lawn tractor be allowed to drive over a grave? How long may a maintenance person operate a weed-whacker, leaf-blower, or other loud machinery? Should children be allowed to play hide-and-seek behind gravestones? Should people be allowed to plant flowers on their loved-one's grave? How about a bush? How about a tree? How about leaving plastic flowers on a grave? How about flags other than American flags? Should it be permissible to leave things on the graves of strangers? Should the consumption of alcohol be allowed? Why not allow smoking? Are firearms OK? Can they be shot into the sky? How about fireworks? Should cemeteries be open after dark? Why shouldn't someone be able to camp out on the grave of a loved one? Should commercial solicitation be allowed? How about religious prosyletizing? How about begging?

Should freedom of speech be in any way limited? Is it constitutional to prohibit anti-war protestors from shouting during the funeral of a combat veteran? Was it OK for a union to inflate a giant rat just outside a funeral that was using a non-union-made coffin?

Who should make these decisions? A private cemetery association? A municipality? The federal government? The families of the deceased? Those present at a funeral in process? Or no one?

Just in Case

Taphophobia is the fear of being buried alive. And it's not an unfounded fear. "Premature burial" has been known to happen.

Given the horror of slowly expiring in the dark of a tight space, coffins have been designed for the possibility of escape. One had a pipe that allowed air into the buried coffin and which could be moved to indicate life below. A vault in Williamsport, PA, had a hatch through which the resurrected could escape. Duke Ferdinand of Brunswick had a window on his coffin that would fog over if he exhaled. A german priest invented a coffin with a trumpet-like tube where he could sniff for putrefaction (or rather, the lack of it) or hear anyone calling for help. There were coffins with strings attached to bells or flags aboveground, coffins with bellows allowing the interred to pump in air, a coffin with an emergency alarm, an intercom system, and a heart monitor.

Despite the popularity of these "safe coffins," there has never been a case of the prematurely interred signaling life.

From the New York Times, February 21, 1885

Asheville, N.C., Feb. 20.—A gentleman from Flat Creek Township in this (Buncombe) County, furnishes the information that about the 20th of last month a young man by the name of Jenkins, who had been sick with fever for several weeks, was thought to have died. He became speechless, his flesh was cold and clammy, and he could not be roused, and there appeared to be no action of the pulse and heart. He was thought to be dead and was prepared for burial, and it was noticed at that time there was no stiffness in any of the limbs. He was buried the day after his supposed death, and when put in the coffin it was remarked that he was as limber as a live man. There was much talk in the neighborhood about the case, and the opinion was frequently expressed that Jenkins had been buried alive. Nothing, however, was done about the matter until the 10th inst., when the coffin was taken up for the purpose of removal and interment in the family burying ground in Henderson Country. The coffin, being wood, it was suggested that it be opened in order to see if the body was in such condition that it could be hauled 20 miles without being put in a metallic casket. The coffin was opened, and to the great astonishment and horror of his relatives the body was lying face downward, the hair had been pulled from the head in great quantities, and there were scratches of the finger nails on the inside of the lid and side of the coffin. These facts caused great excitement and all acquainted personally with the facts believe Jenkins was in a trance, or that animation was apparently suspended, and that he was not really dead when buried, and that he returned to consciousness only to find himself buried and beyond help. The body was then taken to Henderson Country and reinterred. The relatives are so distressed beyond measure at what they term criminal carelessness in not being absolutely sure Jenkins was dead before he was buried.

Burial in the Air

No "safe coffinms" are needed for a sky burial. In a sky burial, the corpse is expeditiously introduced into the lifecycle by allowing it to be consumed by birds, especially vultures. It has been practiced by Buddhists in East Asia, from Bhutan and Tibet to China and Mongolia for thousands of years, but a suspected sky burial site some 4,500 years old has also been identified at Stonehenge. Zoroastrians also practice sky burial.

In a sky burial, the corpse is left in the open, above ground, often high on a mountain. The practice is appropriate for places with a lack of firewood for cremation and ground that is too rocky for the digging of a grave. The body may be left on an elevated platform or high rock, or just left on the ground. Since many such burials are practiced in the same place, vultures are often waiting. They know what to do.

Transmigration of spirits is an essential belief in Buddhism. Buddhists believe that once the spirit has left the body, there is no need to preserve the body. In fact, giving the body to living beings is seen as an act of generosity by the deceased, a virtue of the religion. The process is believed to make it easier for the spirit to abandon the body and move on to the next life.

In Tibet, vultures are given all the time they need to consume all the flesh of the body. The body is then dismantled, the bones mashed with mallets, then ground up with barley, yak butter, or milk. The mixture is then fed to the crows and hawks who were waiting for the vultures to leave.

Some regions suffer a shortage of vultures. They can't consume all the bodies offered on a given day. This is bad news for a spirit trying to leave one body and find another. Ritual dances are performed to increase the appetite.

Other regions have too many vultures, and they're very eager to get their beaks into the deceased. Sometimes people involved in the funeral rites have to fend them off with sticks.

Saving the Bones

Excarnation is the practice of removing the flesh and organs from a corpse before burial—is a time-honored rite that goes back to the neolithic era. Tibetans and Zoroastrians do it. Comanches used to do it. Medieval Christians did it if the deceased was of high enough status. Hawaiians did it to Captain Cook because they thought he was a god.

By his personal request, Christopher Columbus was excarnated after he died in 1506 in Valladolid, Spain. Even in death he was a traveling man. At his request, his bones were stripped of flesh, an illegal process known as excarnation. The flesh was disposed of and the bones were buried in Valladolid. The bones were soon dug up and moved to a monastery in southern Spain. But Columbus had asked that his bones be buried in Santo Domingo, so in fifteen hundred and forty two, Columbus sailed the ocean blue all the way to the island that he had "discovered." When the French took over the island, Columbus's remains made a quick sail across the Caribbean blue to Havana, where he would be safely in Spanish territory. When Cuba fell to American invaders in 1898, Columbus crossed the deep blue again, this time to rest in Seville, where his remains remain within a silver model of a ship on a magnificent catafalque.

Carion Baggage

Mos Teutonicus was the medieval practice of excarnating flesh from the bones of men killed in battle so their bones could be shipped home. This avoided the problem of shipping a decomposing body over long distances.

The Germans started the practice during the Crusades. Then other Christian nations started doing it. Their aristocratic leaders didn't want to be buried in Muslim territory, but their men didn't want to lug their rotting bodies back to Germany.

The solution was to dismember the body so its parts would fit in a kettle. The entrails, which were seen as something disgusting, were left in the unholy land as a kind of insult. The rest of the body was boiled in water or wine until the flesh slid off their bones. But the flesh had to go home, so they salted it as they would any other meat they wished to preserve.

This is how French King Louis IX came from Tunis. This went on until Pope Boniface VIII, who believed God did not want humans to be cut up, issued a papal bull prohibiting the practice. For many years his edict was misinterpreted as a prohibition against dissection of cadavers. The misunderstanding did much to hold back the advance of science.

Burial in the Water

Burial at sea is a "green" burial that quickly introduces a corpse to an ecological system.

Most religions allow burial at sea under certain circumstances, but none require it. The Catholic Church prefers burial in the ground and in a casket. Cremation is allowed if the ashes are buried or entombed. It does not allow the scattering of ashes on land or at sea. Burial at sea in a casket or urn is allowed only when a person has died at sea. The rationale is that friends and family need a specific, identifiable, sacred place where they can visit the deceased.

Protestant churches generally have no prohibition against burial at sea. Some have special prayers for such burials.

Hindus prefer to cremate a corpse, then disperse the ashes and other remains in a river, ideally the sacred Ganges, but any river will do.

Islam prefers burial in the ground but allows burial at sea when death occurs on a ship. (An exception was made for Osama bin Laden.) The body is to be weighted at the feet and lowered into the water, preferably where there are no sharks.

Judaism requires burial in the ground on the day of death, in accordance with instruction found in Deuteronomy. If death occurs at sea or anywhere else where the body threatens the health of others but cannot be buried, the principle of pikuach nefesh can be invoked to what must be done.

The United States allows full-body burial at sea only in areas at least 3.5 miles from land in water at least 600 feet deep. The body or casket must be prepared so as to sink immediately. Off the coast of New England, a ship or plane would have to go some 45 miles out to sea to find suitable depth. A trip off Miami may be as short as five miles.

Individual states have various rules on the scattering of ashes in the sea. California, for example, does not allow cremated remains within 500 feet of shore, and the remains must be removed from any urn unless it's a specialized "scattering urn" that will disperse ashes within four hours.

Man Overboard

Navies perform burial at sea when necessary, especially during times of war. The United States Navy offers free burial at sea—regardless of the place of death—to active, retired, and honorably discharged personnel, civilian Sealift Command personnel, and the families of such veterans.

Naval burials are performed with the ship stopped, its flags at half mast. The crew assembles on deck, initially at parade rest. If the body is in a coffin, it is covered with a flag, carried feet-first and set on a platform with feet toward the sea. In wartime, the body may be shrouded in sailcloth and weighted with rocks or cannonballs. If ashes are in an urn, the urn is placed on a special stand. A military ceremony precedes a religious ceremony, the latter performed by a chaplain or, if necessary, the commanding officer. The firing party is then ordered to present arms, and the crew is called to attention. The casket is slid into the sea, with the flag remaining on board. If the deceased has been reduced to ashes, either the urn can be dropped into the sea or the ashes can be scattered, with all due attention to wind direction.

The firing party fires a three-volley salute. A bugler plays taps. The flag is folded, and with that, the ceremony ends. Relatives are informed of the time and location, and they may be presented with photographs or video recordings.

Burial in Reef

Once an author and television chef, Julia Child is now part of a reef off the coast of south Florida. Some years ago she arranged to have The Neptune Society mix her ashes with concrete and sink her personalized chunk in an artificial reef forty feet below the surface of the sea. Many other people have done the same. Divers take their blocks to spots that people chose before they died.

The Neptune Society Memorial Reef isn't just a reef. It's an artsy, fantasized representation of Atlantis. It's also the largest artificial reef in the world. It stands where there was once just barren ocean floor. Though the ashes of the deceased are locked out of the life cycle for a long, long time, the concrete blocks form part of a habitat for all sorts of sea life. The reef has already sprouted coral colonies and attracted several species of fish, including a sea urchin previously thought to be extinct. The reef also attracts recreational scuba divers, marine biologists, researchers and ecologists. Among the divers are family members of the deceased. Anyone is welcome to visit, but fishing is strictly prohibited.

Burial in Wood

The Moriori people of Chatham Island, today part of New Zealand, disposed of the deceased in several ways, indicating that their ancestral background is populated by various cultures. One method was described in a paper presented to the Wellington Philosophical Society:

"In some instances the corpses were placed upright between young trees, and then firmly bound round with vines, and in course of time they became embedded in the wood itself; sometimes they were placed in hollow trees. Several skeletons have lately been discovered by Europeans in trees which they were cutting up for firewood, &c."

Burial in Woods

A cemetery in Germany is based on "forest burials." People can "buy" an existing tree and have their ashes buried beneath it in a biodegradable urn. People are opting for forest burial not just for ecological reasons but because they won't have to depend on cemetery maintenance people or renew their ownership of a grave every 20 years. The cost of a tree depends on species and size. A small beech might cost EUR 3,350 (USD 3,900). A tall oak with broad crown could run UR 6,000 (USD 7,000). There are options for family trees, friendship trees, and community trees. A tree can be marked with a small sign that may bear a name, a saying, a verse from the Bible, or a Christian symbol.

When Journalism was Art

The following "found poem" was originally a paragraph in the April 25, 1865 edition of the Philadelphia newspaper The Age. The article described the showing of Abraham Lincoln's body during a brief stop on its journey to Springfield, Illinois. The paragraph was rendered word-for-word into a poem published in *How a Nation Grieves: Press Accounts of the Death of Lincoln, the Hunt for Booth, and America in Mourning.*

Every article in the room bore evidences
of the burden and heat of the day,
and shared in the purifying attentions.

The flowers filled with dust,
and their white and crimson mouths,
instead of being filled with soft silver dew,

were dry and parched and arid,
sprinkled over with dust, as though
it had been distributed by a dredger box.

The wax tapers were discolored with it,
and it seemed even to make the flames
of the candles sputter.

It had settled in thick layers
upon the portion of the coffin lid
which had not been removed, and,

above all, on the features of the dead.

This it was, the dusty accumulation
of a whole day, which lent so leaden
a cast to the face,

and covered with an unruffled
and unnatural veil the really
genial and kind expression.

But the undertaker's skillful brush,
long, thick, light, and flossy,
removed, with a few artistic touches,

the unseemly discoloration,
and a white cambric handkerchief, delicately applied,
transformed to itself the last molecule lingerings.

Islamic Burial Rites

The grave is dug at an angle perpendicular to the direction of Mecca. The gravediggers roll and pack tight three fist-sized dirt balls. The body is ritually washed an odd number of times by family members of the same gender. Then the body, wrapped in a shroud of simple cloth—white cotton preferred—is laid on its right side, facing Mecca. A male relative places the dirt balls under the deceased's chin, head, and shoulders as props. Then each person present contributes three handfuls of soil into the grave while reciting "We created you from it, and return you into it, and from it we will raise you a second time." Lavish displays are discouraged—a wreath will do— and wailing is not permitted.

Jewish Burial Rites

After the body is cleansed, it is dressed in burial clothing, including a prayer shawl if the deceased had used one. One fringe from the shawl is removed to signify that the deceased no longer needs to pray or keep the commandments. If the body is to be buried in a casket, it must be stripped of all linings and embellishments. Family members scatter soil on the body and around the casket. The preferred soil comes from Eretz, Israel. In Israel, caskets are used only for those worthy of great honor. Others are wrapped in a shroud. Mourners take turns adding a shovel of soil to the grave. They turn the shovel over to represent life overcoming death. To avoid passing their grief to the next in line, they stick the shovel in the earth rather than hand it on. The date of death is commemorated each year with the lighting of a candle.

When in Palermo

Feel like a ghoulish tour? If so, the Capuchin Catacombs of Palermo is the place to go.

The catacombs have been there since the 16th century, when the Capuchin monastery cemetery ran out of room. To create more space, the friars began excavating caves behind the altar of the Church of Santa Maria della Pace. During the excavation, expired friars were stored in an underground charnel house. When the first catacomb was ready, the friars exhumed their fallen members and found, to their shock and awe, that 45 friars had barely decomposed. Their faces were still recognizable! It had to be a miracle, one of God's many mysterious ways.

The friars took it as a sign that they should not bury the corpses. Rather, the remains should be kept on display as relics of the miracle. They propped the bodies in niches along the catacomb walls.

The friars continued to store their dead in this way, embalming or mummifying them as best they could. They first dehydrated bodies by letting them dry out on ceramic racks for a good year. Then they washed the bodies with vinegar and dressed them in something appropriate for eternity. During epidemics, they bathed the bodies with arsenic, which did an even better job of preservation.

So lay people—especially rich lay people who could afford embalming—requested that they, too be mummified and put on display. A preserved body became a status symbol, the ultimate in dignity. In 1783, the catacombs were opened to anyone who requested interment there.

The place grew to house some 8,000 corpses and 1,252 mummies. The state of the remains varies from grotesque skeletons in formal clothes or priestly frocks to the beautifully preserved body of a two-year-old Sicilian girl named Rosalia Lombardo. Rosalia died of pneumonia in

1920. Despite the passage of nearly a century, she looks as if she's alive and merely sleeping.

Researchers found the hand-written notes of the embalmer (and taxidermist) who preserved the girl's remains. He had injected her with formalin, zinc salts, alcohol, salicylic acid, and glycerin.

Formalin is a mixture of formaldehyde and water that kills bacteria in the body. The alcohol dried the girl's body, allowing it to mummify. The glycerin kept her from drying out too much. The salicylic acid prevented the growth of fungus.

All of these chemicals are still used by embalmers, but it was the zinc salts—no longer in use—that did the trick. The zinc petrified the body, preserving it perfectly. It also made her as rigid as stone. If you leaned her against a tree, she'd stand there with no other support.

The catacombs are now open to tourists (not for interment, just for a tour). You can visit every day of the year. No, you can't take pictures, touch the dead, or eat anything. In fact, you probably shouldn't even think about eating anything. Turn your cell phone, keep your voice low, and, please, leave no trash behind.

The Ways They Went

Pliny tells us that Aeschylus stayed outdoors a lot because it had been prophesied that he would be killed by a falling object. Valerius Maximus tells us Aeschylus was killed by a tortoise that an eagle had dropped, mistaking the playwright's head for a rock.

From 1 Maccabees:

"Eleazar, called Avaran, saw one of the beasts covered with royal armor and bigger than any of the others, and so he thought the king was on it. He gave up his life to save his people and win an everlasting name for himself. He dashed courageously up to it in the middle of the phalanx, killing men right and left, so that they parted before him. He ran under the elephant, stabbed it and killed it. The beast fell to the ground on top of him, and he died there."

Crown Prince Philip of France died while riding his horse through Paris. His horse tripped over a black pig that dashed out of a dung heap.

Hans Steininger, burgomaster of Braunau, usually kept his 4.5 foot beard rolled up in a leather pouch. But one day he didn't. He tripped over it, fatally breaking his neck.

In 1919, 21 Bostonians were killed by a wave of molasses after a huge storage tank burst.

In 2007, Humberto Hernandez was killed by a fire hydrant while walking down a street. A car had collided with the hydrant, and water pressure shot it directly at Hernandez.

In Caratinga, Brazil, João Maria de Souza was killed in bed when a cow fell through his roof. The cow had stepped onto the roof from an adjacent hillside. Neither the cow nor de Souza's wife, who was in the same bed, were injured.

In 1912, Franz Reichelt, a creative tailor, fell to his death from the Eiffel Tower as he tested his invention, the parachute coat. It was his first experiment with the invention, and he had promised authorities that his first test would be with a dummy.

In 1911, famed Tennessee distiller Jack Daniels died after kicking a safe that refused to open. The kick broke open a toe which became infected and led to his death.

Down the Drain

When New York State proposed changing the definition of "cremation," the New York Catholic Conference objected. The Conference feared that a new definition might result in undignified disposal of bodies.

The new definition was to include "chemical digestion." One such digestive process is alkaline hydrolysis, also known as resomation and biocremation. The process involved submersing a body in water and lye in an airtight container and heating it to 320°F. The container is a kind of pressure cooker that lets water heat above the boiling point without actually boiling. In about three hours, the body breaks down into chemical components—greenish-brownish sludge and bone remains soft enough to crush by hand. Filtered solids are normally returned to kin. The greenish-brownish liquid can be spread on cropland or drained into the sewer system. That latter fate, a patently undignified treatment of human remains, is what disturbed the Catholic Conference.

The bill to redefine "cremation" in New York never passed, but the process is legal in about a dozen other states.

Australians are trying to make the concept more palatable by changing the name to the more pleasant-sounding "aquamation."

Environmentalists are also less than enthusiastic about resomation. While it uses less energy and thus releases less carbon dioxide (and no mercury) into the atmosphere, it still involves quite a bit of heat. A "green burial" without coffin has a much smaller carbon footprint and an passing more conducive to re-entry into the ecosystem.

None Dare Call It Care

Here's an idea for putting your mortal remains to good use, though its time may have passed. In May 2017, shortly after the House of Representatives passed a bill that would kill and replace the Affordable "ObamaCare" Care Act. Opponents charged that the replacement, the Republican-supported American "TrumpCare" Healthcare Act, would effectively kill (and not replace) thousands, if not millions, of Americans by denying them affordable health insurance.

Nicole Silverberg tweeted her response: "If I die because of TrumpCare, mail my body to Paul Ryan's house."

That gave American University junior Zoey Jordan Salsbury an idea. She set up a website: mailmetothegop.com.

At the site people could file their request to be cremated and then have their ashes mailed to the Capitol or a favorite Republican representative. Within a day, hundreds of people responded—so many that the site kept crashing with excess traffic. Rep. Paul Ryan (R-WI) was the most indicated recipient.

Mailing your ashes isn't hard. All you need is an urn, a lot of bubblewrap, a strong box, and a good friend. Plus, of course, you have to die.

Carved in Stone

Leonard Matlovich
A Gay Veteran of Vietnam
When I was in the military,
they gave me a medal for killing two men
and a discharge for loving one.

John Heath
Taken from County Jail & Lynched by Bisbee Mob in Tombstone
Feb. 22, 1884

Andrew J. Olszak
1895—1979
Abandoned in Old Age by Wife and Children
May God be More Understanding and Merciful

Here Lies Lester Moore
Four Slugs from a 44
No Less
No More

Rodney Dangerfield
There Goes the Neighborhood

Robert Clay Allison
1840—1887
He Never Killed a Man that Did Not Need Killing

Dawn Under
Here lies my wife
I bid her Goodbye
She rests in peace
And now so do I.

Russell Larsen
TWO THINGS I LOVE MOST, GOOD HORSES AND BEAUTIFUL WOMEN,
AND WHEN I DIE, I HOPE THEY TAN THIS OLD HIDE OF MINE
AND MAKE IT INTO A LADIES RIDING SADDLE,
SO I CAN REST IN PEACE BETWEEN THE TWO THINGS I LOVE MOST.

BILL KUGLE
JAN. 20, 1925—DEC. 27, 1992
HE NEVER VOTED FOR REPUBLICANS AND HAD LITTLE TO DO WITH THEM

WILLIAM SHAKESPEARE
GOOD FRIEND FOR JESUS SAKE FORBEARE,
TO DIG THE DUST ENCLOSED HEARE.
BLESE BE Yᴱ MAN THAT SPARES THES STONES,
AND CURST BE HE THAT MOVES MY BONES.

HERE LIES AN ATHIEST.
ALL DRESSED UP AND NO PLACE TO GO

MERV GRIFFIN
I WILL NOT BE RIGHT BACK AFTER THE MESSAGE
JULY 6, 1925—AUGUST 12, 2007

Jesse James
Murdered by a Traitor and a Coward
Whose Name Is Not Worthy to Appear Here

Ludolph van Ceulen
3.14159265358979323846264338327950

Studs Terkel
Curiosity did Not Kill this Cat

Joel H. Cheskin
July 23, 1942—Feb. 5, 2014
"At Last a Hole in One"

Cast a cold Eye
On Life, on Death.
Horseman pass by.
W.B. Yeats
June 13th 1865—January 28th, 1939

Edward Abbey
No Comment

Death and Thereafter

Dead Yet?

To qualify as a Near-Death Experience (NDE), the memory of a patient resuscitated from a clinically dead state should include at least a few of the following:

1   Time speeds up or slows down.

2   Thought-processes speed up.

3   A return of scenes from the past.

4   A sudden insight or understanding.

5   A feeling of peace or pleasantness.

6   A feeling of happiness or joy.

7   A sense of harmony or unity with the universe.

8   Confrontation with a brilliant light.

9   The senses feel more vivid.

10   An awareness of things going on elsewhere, as if by extrasensory perception (ESP).

11   Experiencing scenes from the future.

12   A feeling of being separated from the body.

13   Experiencing a different, unearthly world.

14   Encountering a mystical being or presence or hearing an unidentifiable voice.

15   Seeing deceased or religious spirits.

16   Coming to a border or point of no return.

A study in the Netherlands, published in The Lancet, found that 62 of 344 resuscitated cardiac arrest patients in ten Dutch hospitals reported a Near-Death Experience. That's 18 percent. Forty-one of them—12 percent of the total—had a "core experience." The degree of the NDE was scored on a scale by interviewers listening for certain experiences.

These experiences were:

1. Awareness of being dead.
2. Positive emotions.
3. Out of body experience.
4. Moving through a tunnel.
5. Communication with light.
6. Observation of colors.
7. Observation of a celestial landscape.
8. Meeting with deceased persons.
9. Life review.
10. Presence of border.

Six percent of the total scored from one to five, meaning they had superficial NDEs, that is, only slight memories from the time when they were clinically dead. Twelve percent scored from six to ten because they had "core experiences." Seven percent had "very deep NDEs," scoring above ten on the scale.

Near Death Dream

This anecdote comes from an article, "Do 'Near-Death Experiences' Occur Only Near-Death?—Revisited," written by Glen O. Gabbard, M.D.
and Stuart Twemlow, M.D., published in *Human Sciences Press*

A marine sergeant was instructing a class of young
recruits at boot camp. He stood in front of a classroom
holding a hand grenade as he explained the mechaniscs
of pulling the pin to detonate the weapon. After
commenting on the considerable weight of the grenade,
he thought it would be useful for each recruit to get a
"hands-on" feeling for its actual mass. As the grenade
was passed from private to private, one 18-year-old
recruit nervously dropped the grenade as it was handed
to him. Much to his horror, he watched the pin become
dislodged as the grenade hit the ground. He knew he
had only seconds to act, but he stood frozen, paralyzed
with fear. The next thing he knew, he found himself
traveling up through the top of his head toward the
ceiling as the ground beneath him grew farther and
farther away. He effortlessly passed through the ceiling
and found himself entering a tunnel with the sound of
wind whistling through it. As he approached the end of
this lengthy tunnel, he encountered a light that shone
with a special brilliance, the likes of which he had never
seen before. A figure beckoned to him from the light,

and he felt a profound sense of love emanating from the figure. His life flashed before his eyes in what seemed like a split second. In the midst of this transcendent experience, he suddenly realized that the grenade had not exploded. He felt immediately "sucked" back into his body.

Much to his surprise, the sergeant had picked up the grenade and was chuckling to himself at the reaction of the panic-stricken recruits. It had not occurred to the young soldier that the grenade was only a "dummy" used for demonstration purposes.

The report presents the anecdote as evidence that it is not necessary to be near death to have a Near-Death Experience. The expectation of death may be enough, suggesting that the NDE is merely a psychological event. But the report also cites cases of small children who experience NDEs even though they have no concept of death or previous knowledge of what such an experience is "supposed" to be like.

Hell To Pay

Consider the use of Hell Money. It won't buy much on this side of the Hereafter, but a relative on the other side might need it to bribe Yanluo, a rather nasty god who presides over a place a hell of a lot like Purgatory. Yanluo—also known as Yan and Yama—is so bad that he oversees the Ten Kings of Hell. He passes judgment on the dead, condemning them to Hell for as long as their evil actions in life warrant. Yanluo can reach into the world of the living and inflict warnings on people through such messages as illness, old age, injury. He has a book in which the death date of every person is noted, including the dates of the living.

Like everyone else, Yanluo can always use a little more cash, and he's not above accepting it from new arrivals. For this reason, Buddhists and people in cultures with strong Buddhist traditions burn facsimiles of money as a funeral rite for deceased family members who might need a bribe to shorten or mitigate their sentence. The Hell Money, also known as joss paper, might also be used for any expenses that come up in the Hereafter.

The dead frown on tightfistedness among their survivors, so Hell Money is bought in stacks of very large denominations. Some individuals, due to their guilt or wealth, may need several notes of $5 billion. Sacrifices across a city can produce so much smoke that it becomes a pollution problem. The traditional braziers are now fitted with covers that prevent the escape of ash.

The term "Hell Money" is reputed to have originated with Christian missionaries who taught Orientals that Hell is where non-Christians go after they die.

Soul Survivor

Semi-barbarians on the outskirts of early Greece believed that the soul and the body have a tenuous and uncomfortable relationship. The soul, they believed, was divine, immortal, and longing for freedom. Unfortunately, most of the time it is held in bondage within a body. The only way it can escape is if the body dies. Alas, the escape is brief. It is soon reincarnated in yet another corporeal prison. Orpheus, supposedly the one who thought this up and formalized the Orphic religion, said that permanent liberation can happen only after the soul has advanced through a series of ever-purer bodies. Lives of piety and purity allow the soul to move upward toward godliness, a state of everlasting liberation and life.

Pherecydes of Syros picked up the idea and passed it on to Pythagoras, he of the famous hypotenuse and many other formulations. The idea made its way to Plato almost a century later. Plato wrote about it in The Republic, but it isn't clear whether he believed it to be literally true or simply an allegory of good advice.

The Roman Virgil picked up the idea of metempsychosis, preserving it long enough to be written about by John Donne, Edgar Allan Poe, Herman Melville, Guy de Maupassant, Arthur Schopenhauer, Kurt Gödel, Marcel Proust, Friedrich Nietzsche, James Joyce, Thomas Pynchon, Don DeLillo, David Foster Wallace, and Glenn Alan Cheney.

What King Tut Took

Egyptian Pharao "King Tut" Tutankhamun was buried with a wealth of "funerary objects" meant to ease his transition into the Great Beyond. Among the items were a gold coffin, little coffinettes, boxes, chests, jewels, a gilded throne, other thrones, little statues, a gold, 22-lb. face mask with a sad, tranquil expression, two magical trumpets with the ability to start a war, an alabaster chalice in the shape of a lotus blossom, food, wine, sandals, a dagger with an iron-nickel blade made from a meteorite, and, yes, of course, a change of underwear.

Brief Thoughts on the Inevitable

By the sweat of your face you shall eat bread, till you return to the ground, for out of it you were taken; for you are dust, and to dust you shall return.

Genesis 3:19

Death is nothing, but to live defeated and inglorious is to die daily.

Napoleon Bonaparte

Even death is not to be feared by one who has lived wisely.

Buddha

One death is a tragedy; one million is a statistic.

Joseph Stalin

People fear death even more than pain. It's strange that they fear death. Life hurts a lot more than death. At the point of death, the pain is over.

Jim Morrison

The boundaries which divide life from death are at best shadowy and vague. Who shall say where the one ends, and where the other begins?

Edgar Allan Poe

Art is the tree of life. Science is the tree of death.

William Blake

Remembering that I'll be dead soon is the most important tool I've ever encountered to help me make the big choices in life. Because almost everything—all external expectations, all pride, all fear of embarrassment or failure—these things just fall away in the face of death, leaving only what is truly important.

Steve Jobs

If you die, you're completely happy and your soul somewhere lives on. I'm not afraid of dying. Total peace after death, becoming someone else is the best hope I've got.

Kurt Cobain

Death is not extinguishing the light; it is only putting out the lamp because the dawn has come.

Rabindranath Tagore

I don't fear death so much as I fear its prologues: loneliness, decrepitude, pain, debilitation, depression, senility. After a few years of those, I imagine death presents like a holiday at the beach.

Mary Roach

Life is hard. Then you die. Then they throw dirt in your face. Then the worms eat you. Be grateful it happens in that order.

David Gerrold

My fear was not of death itself, but a death without meaning.

Huey Newton

If we don't know life, how can we know death?

Confucius

The stroke of death is as a lover's pinch, which hurts and is desired.

William Shakespeare

Which death is preferable to every other? The unexpected.

Julius Ceasar

Death is the distant sound of thunder at a picnic.

W.H. Auden

The only difference between death and taxes is that death doesn't get worse every time Congress meets.

Will Rogers

Death and life have their determined appointments; wealth and honor depend on heaven.

Confucius

Death is no more than a turning of us over from time to eternity.

William Penn

Death must be so beautiful. To lie in the soft brown earth, with the grasses waving above one's head, and listen to silence. To have no yesterday, and no to-morrow. To forget time, to forget life, to be at peace.

Oscar Wilde

Life asked death, 'Why do people love me but hate you?' Death responded, 'Because you are a beautiful lie and I am a painful truth.

Author unknown

It is the secret of the world that all things subsist and do not die, but retire a little from sight and afterwards return again.

Ralph Waldo Emerson

They say you die twice. One time when you stop breathing and a second time, a bit later on, when somebody says your name for the last time.

Banksy

Death is a black camel which kneels at the gates of all.

Abdelkader ibn Muhieddine

Call no man happy till he is dead.

Æschylus

Our bodies are prisons for our souls. Our skin and blood, the iron bars of confinement. But fear not. All flesh decays. Death turns all to ash. And thus, death frees every soul.

Darren Aronofsky

Men fear death, as children fear to go in the dark; and as that natural fear in children is increased with tales, so is the other.

Francis Bacon

I have often thought upon death, and I find it the least of all evils.

Francis Bacon

It's better to sit than to stand, it is better to lie down than to sit, but death is best of all.

Indian proverb

Supremus ille dies non nostri extinctionem sed commutationem affert loci. That last day does not bring extinction to us, but change of place.

Cicero

Death makes everything useless.

Rubem Alves

Unbeing dead isn't being alive.

Edward Estlin Cummings

Love is the cousin of death, and the conqueror of death, even if it's slain (and it is slain) in every instance of love.

Carlos Drummond de Andrade

It's the end of life that gives life a chance.

Stephen Jenkinson

I am the resurrection and the life. The one who believes in me will live, even though they die, and whoever lives by believing in me will never die.

Jesus

The last enemy to be destroyed is death.

1 Corinthians 15:26

A time to be born, and a time to die; a time to plant, and a time to pluck up what is planted...

Ecclesiastes 3:2

Modernity has transferred death from the home, the place of love, to institutions, the places of power.

Rubem Alves

Death is simply a shedding of the physical body, like the butterfly coming out of a cocoon.

Elisabeth Kuebler-Ross

Death is not the end.
Death can never be the end.
Death is the road.
Life is the traveller.
The soul is the guide.

Sri Chinmoy

Every door may be shut but death's door.

Chinese Proverb

Death is an art, like everything else.

Sylvia Plath

Expressions for Death and Dying

Buy the farm

Pay the ultimate price

Push up the daisies

Look up at the grass

Ride the pale horse

Shuffle off one's mortal coil

Turn up your toes

Kick the bucket

Shit the bed

Meet your maker

In the box

Cross over

Pass away

Pass over

Go to the happy hunting ground

Bite the dust

Croak

Assume room temperature

Breathe your last

Cash in your chips

Cross the Jordan

Depart this life

Drop like flies

Give up the ghost

Go to a better place

Go bung (Australian)

Bow out

Pull the chain

Flip the switch

Do yourself in

Go the way of all flesh

Kiss your ass good-bye

Take a dirt nap

To have your number up

Go up to the spirit in the sky

No longer suffer

Fall off your perch

Food for worms

Go belly up

Famous Last Words

Tellulah Bankhead (on being asked if she wanted anything): "Codeine...bourbon..."

Bob Marley: "Money can't buy life."

Alexander Graham Bell: "No."

Peter Abelard (philosopher and theologian): "I don't know."

Karl Marx: "Last words are for fools who haven't said enough."

Todd Beamer (passenger on United Flight 93 on Sept. 11, 2001): "You guys ready? Let's roll."

Private First Class Edward H. Aherns (surrounded by dead Japanese soldiers): "The bastards tried to come over me last night. I guess they didn't know I was a Marine."

Leonardo da Vinci: "I have offended God and mankind because my work did not reach the quality it should have."

Benedict Arnold: "Let me die in the old uniform in which I fought my battles for freedom, May God forgive me for putting on another."

Alex (an African grey parrot): "You be good. See you tomorrow. I love you."

Lady Nancy Astor (awakening on her deathbed): "Am I dying or is this my birthday?"

Humphrey Bogart: "I should never have switched from scotch to martinis."

Charles Darwin: "I am not the least afraid to die."

Johannes Brahms (upon sipping a bit of wine): Ah, that tastes nice. Thank you."

Marie Antoinette (after stepping on the foot of her executioner): "*Pardonnez-moi, monsieur. Je ne l'ai pas fait exprès.* (Pardon me. I did not do it on purpose.)"

Richard Feynman: "I'd hate to die twice. It's so boring."

Willem Arondeus (Dutch member of anti-Nazi resistance): "Let it be known that homosexuals are not cowards."

Thomas Edison (looking out the window): "It's very beautiful out there."

Raphael (the painter): "Happy..."

John Wilkes Booth: "Useless...useless..."

Leonard Nimoy (his last tweet): "A life is like a garden. Perfect moments can be had, but not preserved, except in memory. LLAP."

Jane Austen: "I want nothing but death."

Max Baer: "Oh God, here I go!"

Siddartha Gautama Buddha: "Decay is inherent in all things. Be sure to strive [for Nirvana] with clarity of mind."

Queen Elizabeth I: "All my possessions for a moment of time."

Bing Crosby: "That was a great game of golf, fellers."

W.C. Fields: "Goddam the whole fucking world and everyone in it except you, Carlotta."

Bobby Fischer: "Nothing soothes pain like human touch."

James French (being led to the electric chair): "Hey, fellas! How about this for a headline for tomorrow's paper? 'French Fries'!"

Bob Hope (on being asked where he'd like to be buried): "Surprise me."

Steve Jobs: "Oh wow. Oh wow. Oh wow."

Terry Kath: "Don't worry...it's not loaded."

Timothy Leary: "Beautiful."

Wolfgang Amadeus Mozart: "The taste of death is upon my lips...I feel something that is not of this earth."

Marco Polo: "I have not told half of what I saw."

Charles Schulz: "Charlie Brown, Snoopy, Linus, Lucy...how can I ever forget them?"

General John Sedgwick: "They couldn't hit an elephant at this distance!"

George Washington: "I am just going. Have me decently buried and do not let my body be into a vault in less than two days after I am dead. Do you understand me?... Tis well. I die hard, but I am not afraid to go."

Theodore Roosevelt: "Please put out the light."

John F. Kennedy (responding to "You certainly can't say Dallas doesn't love you, Mr. President."): "No, you certainly can't."

Mohandas Gandhi: "Oh, God."

Lady Diana Spencer: "My God, what's happened?"

Poetic Notions

Although Death walks beside us on Life's road,
A dim bystander at the body's start
And a last judgment on man's futile works,
Other is the riddle of its ambiguous face:
Death is a stair, a door, a stumbling stride
The soul must take to cross from birth to birth,
A grey defeat pregnant with victory.

Sri Aurobindo, from *Savitri*

A telling analogy for life and death:
Compare the two of them to water and ice.
Water draws together to become ice,
And ice disperses again to become water.
Whatever has died is sure to be born again;
Whatever is born comes around again to dying.
As ice and water do one another no harm,
So life and death, the two of them, are fine.

Han Shan

Do Not Stand at My Grave and Weep

Do not stand at my grave and weep
I am not there; I do not sleep.
I am a thousand winds that blow,
I am the diamond glints on snow,
I am the sun on ripened grain,
I am the gentle autumn rain.
When you awaken in the morning's hush,
I am the swift uplifting rush
Of quiet birds in circled flight.
I am the soft stars that shine at night.
Do not stand at my grave and cry,
I am not there; I did not die.

Mary Elizabeth Frye

Rumination

When I can hold a stone within my hand
And feel time make it sand and soil, and see
The roots of living things grow in this land,
Pushing between my fingers flower and tree,
Then I shall be as wise as death,
For death has done this and he will
Do this to me, and blow his breath
to fire my clay, when I am still.

Richard Eberhart

Let's talk of graves, of worms, and epitaphs;

Make dust our paper and with rainy eyes

Write sorrow on the bosom of the earth,

Let's choose executors and talk of wills:

And yet not so, for what can we bequeath

Save our deposed bodies to the ground?

Our lands, our lives and all are Bolingbroke's,

And nothing can we call our own but death

And that small model of the barren earth

Which serves as paste and cover to our bones.

Shakespeare, *Life and Death of Richard the Second*

To-morrow, and to-morrow, and to-morrow,
Creeps in this petty pace from day to day
To the last syllable of recorded time,
And all our yesterdays have but lighted fools
The way to dusty death.
Out, out, brief candle!
Life's but a walking shadow, a poor player
That struts and frets his hour upon the stage
And then is heard no more: it is a tale
Told by an idiot, full of sound and fury,
Signifying nothing.

Shakespeare, *Macbeth*

Death

Rainer Marie Rilke

Before us great Death stands
Our fate held close within his quiet hands.
When with proud joy we lift Life's red wine
To drink deep of the mystic shining cup
And ecstasy through all our being leaps—
Death bows his head and weeps.

Death Be Not Proud

John Donne

Death be not proud, though some have called thee
Mighty and dreadful, for, thou art not so,
For those whom thou think'st, thou dost overthrow,
Die not, poor death, nor yet canst thou kill me.
From rest and sleepe, which but thy pictures bee,
Much pleasure, then from thee, much more must flow,
And soonest our best men with thee doe goe,
Rest of their bones, and soules deliverie.
Thou art slave to Fate, Chance, kings, and desperate men,
And dost with poyson, warre, and sicknesse dwell,
And poppie, or charmes can make us sleepe as well,
And better than thy stroake; why swell'st thou then?
One short sleepe past, wee wake eternally,
And death shall be no more; death, thou shalt die.

Because I Could Not Stop for Death

Emily Dickenson

Because I could not stop for Death —
He kindly stopped for me —
The Carriage held but just Ourselves —
And Immortality.

We slowly drove — He knew no haste
And I had put away
My labor and my leisure too,
For His Civility —

We passed the School, where Children strove
At Recess — in the Ring —
We passed the Fields of Gazing Grain —
We passed the Setting Sun —

Or rather — He passed Us —
The Dews drew quivering and Chill —
For only Gossamer, my Gown —
My Tippet — only Tulle —

We paused before a House that seemed
A Swelling of the Ground —
The Roof was scarcely visible —
The Cornice — in the Ground —

Since then — 'tis Centuries — and yet
Feels shorter than the Day
I first surmised the Horses' Heads
Were toward Eternity —

Children's Fearless Hearse Song

Did you ever think, when the hearse goes by
That you might be the next to die?
 They'll wrap you up in a clean white sheet,
And put you down about six feet deep
They put you into a wooden box,
And cover you over with earth and rocks.
It's not so bad for the first few weeks,
Until your coffin begins to leak.
The worms crawl in, the worms crawl out,
The worms play pinochle on your snout.
They eat your eyes, they eat your nose,
They eat the jelly between your toes.
They eat your clothes, they eat your hat,
They crawl in skinny, and crawl out fat.
Your teeth fall in and your eyes pop out,
Your brains come trickling down your snout.
Then you turn disgustingly green.
Your skin as slimy as whipping cream.
So whenever you see the hearse go by,
Watch out! You...may...be...
the...next...to...*die*!

Dirge Without Music

Edna St. Vincent Millay

I am not resigned to the shutting away of loving hearts in the hard
ground.
So it is, and so it will be, for so it has been, time out of mind:
Into the darkness they go, the wise and the lovely. Crowned
With lilies and with laurel they go; but I am not resigned.

Lovers and thinkers, into the earth with you.
Be one with the dull, the indiscriminate dust.
A fragment of what you felt, of what you knew,
A formula, a phrase remains,—but the best is lost.

The answers quick and keen, the honest look, the laughter, the love,—
They are gone. They are gone to feed the roses. Elegant and curled
Is the blossom. Fragrant is the blossom. I know. But I do not approve.
More precious was the light in your eyes than all the roses in the world.

Down, down, down into the darkness of the grave
Gently they go, the beautiful, the tender, the kind;
Quietly they go, the intelligent, the witty, the brave.
I know. But I do not approve. And I am not resigned.

Do Not Go Gentle into that Good Night

Dylan Thomas

Do not go gentle into that good night,
Old age should burn and rave at close of day;
Rage, rage against the dying of the light.

Though wise men at their end know dark is right,
Because their words had forked no lightning they
Do not go gentle into that good night.

Good men, the last wave by, crying how bright
Their frail deeds might have danced in a green bay,
Rage, rage against the dying of the light.

Wild men who caught and sang the sun in flight,
And learn, too late, they grieved it on its way,
Do not go gentle into that good night.

Grave men, near death, who see with blinding sight
Blind eyes could blaze like meteors and be gay,
Rage rage against the dying of the light.

Friendship

Ralph Bergengren

I have a friend. If I should die
I know he would sit down and cry.

The sun would shine, the sky be blue,
And birds would sing just as they do

In trees and bushes every day,
But I would not be there to play.

And so I know there'd be no game
That ever could be quite the same.

For that is just the way that I
Would feel if he should go and die.

The Merry Burial Blog

Arboreal Burial

Connecticut Green Burial Grounds is unique in that it allows a chosen tree to be planted over a grave. In a short time, the sapling's roots tap into the body below. Nutrients from that body become the tree.

If you could be a tree, what tree would you like to be? What characteristics would you like to become?

Would you like to be an oak—black, white, red, scarlet, pin, live, scrub, swamp, overcup, chestnut, chinkapin, which?—tall and strong, symbol of endurance, the stuff of the hull of the Mayflower, the species where the Charter of Connecticut once hid?

Or are you more the maple type, lush in summer, glorious in fall, flush with sweet sap, the tree kids most prefer to climb?

Perhaps you'd like to be reborn into magnificence, a beech with overarching foliage as big as a house, a stout trunk of silver where lovers carve their hearts.

You could be a linden, ever-so aromatic, beloved by bees, seeds favored by chipmunks, known by friends as basswood, quick to grow, going up a hundred feet to blossom in the sun.

Why not for once be slender and beautiful, a stem or pair of stems of birch—white with bark that burns hot, black that tastes a minty sweet, paper all covered with curls—your leaves serrate, petiolate, stipulate, and feather-veined? In winter you would be beautiful in snow.

Or would you sum your life as a weeping willow, your hair hung low around your grave, the space around you cavernous and cool? With every breeze you'd sway a slow and lovely dance.

Or are you evergreen—cedar, hemlock, spruce or pine? Or ash or elm, chestnut, cherry, hawthorn, hickory, sassafras, mulberry, sycamore, or gum?

So many trees to choose from, but you only get one.

Frequently Asked Questions on Posthumous Matters

Must I embalm my loved-one?

No. No state laws in the United States require embalming. Some states require embalming or refrigeration if the body is not buried or cremated within a reasonable period of time. Some require embalming if the body is to be on public display. Immediate burial with no such treatment is always an option.

Is there such a thing as "Bring Your Own" coffin?

Yes. Under rules established by the Federal Trade Commission, you are allowed to buy or even make a coffin, casket, shroud or urn. They are available on the Internet from many sources. You can have the container shipped straight to the funeral home. You don't have to be there when it arrives, although the funeral home may ask you to inspect the casket. You will not have to pay anything to the funeral home for using a unit bought elsewhere.

What's the difference between a casket and a coffin?

A casket is essentially a rectangular box, though some are oval. The traditional coffin has sloped shoulders.

What is a green casket?

A green casket or coffin is made entirely of biodegradable materials, with no nails, synthetic glues, paint, varnish, or synthetic cloth. Common materials include bamboo, hemp, wool, cotton, cork, teak, willow, rattan, seagrass, banana leaves, and organic cardboard.

Is a coffin necessary for cremation?

No, though many states require a rigid container for cremation.

Do I need to buy a cemetery plot before I die?

No, but if you have a preferred place, you'd best buy it beforehand. You can contact a cemetery directly, or you can ask a funeral home to help. In some cases the cemetery is operated by a church or cemetery association (such as Connecticut Green Burial Grounds), in some cases a municipality.

Is there such a thing as a used/rental casket?

Yes. A funeral home can rent you a nice but previously occupied casket from which the interior has been removed and replaced for each previous occupant. These caskets are usually used for viewing or a funeral service. Afterward the deceased can be removed to a more affordable or appropriate unit.

Can I get a casket emblazoned with the icons and trademarks of the band known as Kiss?

Yes. See memorials.com. Click on "Unique Caskets." Other options are the names and logos of sports teams, even the ones that suck. Your funeral home of choice can help you with your unique wishes.

How much does a coffin cost?

The sky's the limit! And so is the ground. A tricked out upper-end casket of mahogany with all the bells and whistles can cost $20,000 or more. An average range of funeral home offerings start around $700 and goes up from there. A cardboard casket made of 25-35% recycled material produced in a bleach-free process and held together by a starch-based glue can be had for $300. Caskets of organic woven fibers such as banana leaf, willow, seagrass, or rattan, cost between $1,500 and $3,000. A simple pine box can be had for around $1,000. Plus, of course, if there's anything as inevitable as death and taxes, it's shipping and handling, but that's between the buyer and seller, not the funeral home.

What's cool about a cardboard casket?

People can write messages on it. Children can draw pictures on it. It blots up tears and it cycles into the ecosystem more quickly than other materials.

Can I be buried in my back yard?

Maybe, but it's extremely complicated. The rules vary from state to state. Generally, if a Zoning and Health Department approves, you can do it. But wherever you are, you're going to need a very large yard, a very good lawyer, and a very cooperative Zoning Department and Health Department.

Is burial at sea an option?

Sure! Anchors aweigh! But you have to be at least 3.5 miles from shore and the water has to be at least 600 feet deep. The body and any container must be prepared to sink directly. A funeral director will know the rules, which are determined by whichever state has jurisdiction. Of course if you're in international waters, you can do whatever you want. U.S. Navy veterans and their dependent families are entitled to burial at sea at no cost.

If I'm so fortunate as to kick the bucket in the Nutmeg State, can Connecticut Green Burial Grounds handle all my funeral arrangements?

No. As a cemetery association, CGBG can offer only the plot, the burial, maintenance of the burial ground, and burial records. By law (in Connecticut) a certified funeral director must sanitize the body and certify proper burial. A funeral home must also handle transportation and necessary permits and paperwork.

On Grief

The well known Five Stages of Grief is also called the Kübler-Ross Model, named after Swiss psychiatrist Elisabeth Kübler-Ross. The "stages" apply to the terminally ill, the survivors of deceased loved ones, and people afflicted with other types of trauma, such as drug addiction, incarceration, and divorce. They can also be observed in sports fans whose team loses and in supporters of political candidates who lose elections.

Kübler-Ross later regretted calling the five emotional states "stages" because the grieving do not necessarily move through an orderly series. They may skip some, may bounce back and forth among two or more, remain mired in one.

The stages she identified are:

• Denial—when the grieving individual believes the prognosis or other unacceptable cause of grief is not correct or cannot be true.

• Anger—when denial is not longer possible, the individual questions the injustice of the trauma, seeks to blame others, or blames and lashes out at others.

• Bargaining—an attempt to avoid or reverse the cause of grief by offering a personal sacrifice or promising painful change of lifestyle.

• Depression—the despair of feeling there is no hope, no point in continuing life, no reason to do anything, especially anything social.

• Acceptance—a sensation of calmness and sedated satisfaction as the individual accepts the inevitable and resigns to its immutable reality.

Subsequent scientific research has questioned the identifiable existence of these states or any inevitable progression from denial through acceptance. Many environmental factors, such as information, resources, emotional support, previous experience, the cause of the grief, and overlapping griefs or problems, can influence the movement between states. Though some of the scientific community has relegated the model to fallacy, it can be useful in understanding one's own or someone else's emotional states. Burial—the ritual as well as the consignation to the earth—may contribute to acceptance, which is often the best possible outcome for grief.

Heuristic Quiz on Your Afterlife

Which ice cream best represents death?

    a.   plain vanilla

    b.   rocky road

    c.   melted

    d.   double pickle

    e.   java mint chip cookie dough with whipped cream, chocolate sauce, crushed nuts, and a cherry on top

    f.   dirt (-flavored)

Which of these reincarnated entities would you prefer to become?

    a.   a puppy

    b.   a kitten

    c.   a redwood tree

    d.   a sperm whale

    e.   a presidential tapeworm

    f.   a babe in the Black Hole of Calcutta

Which kind of person is most likely to be reincarnated as a gypsy moth?

    a.   slimeball toadies

    b.   yellow-bellied backstabbers

    c.   slicked-back evangelicals

    d.   pot-bellied congressional sellouts

    e.   timber rustlers and their ilk

    f.   stinkers of ill repute

What do you figure's at the end of the Great White Tunnel?

    a.   72 virgins

    b.   your mother

    c.   St. Peter

    d.   The Prince of Darkness in a bridal gown

    e.   an immigration official

    f.   a gleaming, dazzling, whistling sphincter

Which makes most sense about the reincarnation deal?

a. You get what you deserve but never know why.

b. You are assigned a random life form somewhere between amoeba and zebra.

c. You become the tree that taps into your posthumous nutrients.

d. You end up back where you were before you were born—Nowheresville.

e. Next time you will read the instructions.

f. Your life will be the opposite of what it is this time around.

Where can you find answers about the afterlife?

a. The Bible

b. The Talmud

c. The Oracle at Delphi

d. The Merry Burial blog

e. Written on the subway walls

f. The twilight tootle of a wood thrush

Which would be your preferred afterlife?

a. Eternity in a paradise of unrelenting bliss.

b. Haunt the earth, able to see but not touch.

c. Take your chances at a random human rebirth.

d. The oblivion of nonexistence.

e. Become a leprechaun with the power to influence lives.

f. Take all your possessions to an ethereal gated community of the rich and famous.

Would you rather return as...

a. a man or a woman?

b. a Mexican or a Palestinian?

c. a swamp oak or a coconut palm?

d. a police dog or a widow's cat?

e. the child of a Democrat or a Republican?

f. Charlemagne, Jesus, Hefner, Trump, or Liberace?

436

Which are advantages of green burial?

    a.   You return to nature what nature is due.

    b.   Your survivors will have a shady spot to remember you in.

    c.   It beats burning 28 gallons of fossil fuel and contributing to the misery of upcoming generations.

    d.   You will be remembered for your wisdom, not your greed.

    e.   You will at last have done something right.

    f.   Your death will exemplify your life.

Which will have the biggest impact on your afterlife destiny?

    a.   your virtues

    b.   your sins

    c.   your suffering

    d.   dumb luck

    e.   the way you were buried

    f.   your deathbed confessions

Speaking of deathbed confessions, you'd best list a few before it's too late.

    a.

    b.

    c.

    d.

    e.

    f.   Other

The Sad, Green Burial of the Pilgrims at Plymouth

The Pilgrims of Plymouth had to resort to a particularly sad burial practice during their first winter in the New World. Due to complications getting underway back in England, they didn't arrive at Plymouth until the middle of November, 1620. It was too late to find a place to live and build houses to get them through the winter. A hundred and two passengers had to spend the next several months in their tight, cold, damp quarters on the gun deck of the Mayflower. Sharing the space with a small sail boat, a few cannons, some farm animals, and bundles of carry-on luggage, they barely had enough room to all lie down at the same time.

In December they started to take sick. They thought it was scurvy, but it was more likely influenza or pneumonia. It afflicted everyone. They were so weak they could hardly get up. When individuals died, they spent days right where they were, right next to people suffering the same symptoms the newly deceased had suffered. William Bradford and Myles Standish were among the few who were able to do anything about the dead.

Removing the corpses was a challenge. They had to be hauled up onto the main deck, then lowered into a boat that could be rowed to shore. It's also possible the bodies were passed out through small portholes on the gun deck that would have been used for cannon fire in the event of attack.

The landing craft was too big to actually reach the sandy shore. Those assigned burial duty had to wade the last few yards through the frigid winter water of Cape Cod Bay, dragging the bodies after them.

Since it was winter, the ground beyond the beach was frozen solid.

The only alternative was a sandy hill just above the beach, where the sand could be easily dug. So there they opened the graves, and not very deep. "Six feet under" wasn't a requirement then any more than it is today. And of course it would have been impossible to build coffins. Impossible. It's unlikely the bodies were even wrapped in a shroud.

There were Indians in the area, and in one skirmish shortly after the Mayflower arrived, the Americans and immigrants exchanged gunfire and a barrage of arrows. The Pilgrims had reason to worry, and by January they had reason to hide the fact that they were dying off at a rapid rate. So once a dearly departed had been laid to rest, the burial crew smoothed off the sand to make it look like plain, unconsecrated beach. Nothing marked the spot, not even a cross. By spring, nobody knew exactly who was where. Not that it mattered. Their bodies were to be at one with nature, their souls departed to wherever it was that Pilgrim souls went.

Stuff to Know about Cremation

First of all, it isn't spelled *creamation* any more than the process takes place at a *creamery*. It takes place in a *cremator*, which is an industrial furnace at a *crematory*, which is the business end of a *crematorium*. But it's where you end up if you get creamed by a car, asteroid, or ice cream truck, so the confusion is understandable.

Creamers are fake cream. A cremulator is a machine that pulverizes incinerated remains. Some cremulators are like blenders, others like grinders. Either way, it takes a good twenty minutes, and the results are the same: four to six pounds of remains, perhaps a little more for individuals who spent too much time chowing down at a creamery. These scant pounds represent just 3.5 percent of the human body. The other 96.5 percent is blowing in the wind.

It's considered politically incorrect to call the remains "cremains," which is seen as slangily disrespectful of the person they used to be. "The cremated remains of the late So-and-So" is preferred. "Ashes" in the same phrase would be also acceptable even if technically inappropriate. Anything resembling ash has been incinerated into smoke. What remains has the color and consistency of sand from a beach where nobody wants to go.

A word of caution: certain implants must be removed prior to cremation. It is the funeral director's job to see that this happens. A pacemaker can explode so powerfully that it could damage the cremator, even injure people standing nearby. Other little bombs in the body include spinal cord stimulators, bone nails, and implanted drug reservoirs. Breast implants are not a problem. Titanium hips, tooth fillings, and other metals must be separated after cremation lest they damage the cremulator.

Cremation offers a few advantages over burial. It's less expensive than embalming, vaults, caskets, a burial plot, and the interment process. Cremated remains are a lot easier to transport than whole bodies. And generally speaking, survivors can cast the ashes close to home or in an appropriate place.

Cremation is not as environmentally benign as some believe. Bodies are cremated individually, each requiring the burning of some 28 gallons of fuels during the 90- to 120-minute process. The combustion releases some 540 pounds of carbon dioxide into the atmosphere of an overheating planet. Embalmed bodies release chemical residues, and even the unembalmed release whatever toxins, such as heavy metals, the body accumulated during a lifetime in a polluted environment. Some but not all of these toxins are captured by abatement equipment. If a casket is incinerated along with the body, it, too, may release vaporized chemicals. The trees that died for the casket's wood will not be generating oxygen, and their combusted carbon contributes to global warming. In the case of mahogany and certain other fine woods, the trees may have been taken from a rainforest and shipped thousands of miles.

Natural burial is the most benign means of posthumous disposal. No fossil fuels are burned except in transporting the body to the grave site. (Some cemeteries offer a horse-drawn carriage for this trip.) The body is hastened into the ecosystem. Heavy metals and other corporeal contaminants remain in the ground, in many cases rendered harmless by decomposition and plant uptake. The body, its clothes, and the casket or shroud, all of biodegradable material, soon become a plant or animal. Who knows, maybe they will become grass, and then a cow might eat it and turn it into cream. And there you go: creamation. Maybe it should be a word after all.

Posthumous Preferences

Close your eyes. Imagine you're dead. You've been privileged to receive a green burial. A tree has been planted above you, and it's already taken you up and grown large enough to be of interest to squirrels, birds, and people in need of shade. Your spirit hovers nearby, waiting to see your family and friends come around to visit, remember, and celebrate.

But you know how some of your friends are. And some of your extended family, too. They're all visiting with the best of intentions and the fondest of memories, but some of them could probably use a list of rules—the dos and don'ts of graveside behavior.

So which of these (subject to sexton approval) would go on the Please Do side of your list, which on the Please Don't?

- Carve your name in my bark.
- Scatter native wildflower seeds all around me.
- Pick one wildflower and take it home.
- Yank up any bittersweet, loosestrife or poison ivy that arises.
- Burn a tire right here over my dead body.
- Pour a libation of decent wine into the ground.
- Leave a tidy pile of litter for somebody else to pick up.
- Take home a nut, fruit, or leaf that fell from me.
- Make love, right here.
- Leave a pile of peanuts for the squirrels.
- Lean against me and take a selfie.
- Take a group picture with everybody in it.
- Spend the night.
- Remain totally sober.
- Talk to me.

- Climb me.

- Eat my toadstools.

- Ask the sexton if you can hang a bird house on me.

- Detonate thunderous fireworks.

- Take pictures of me in summer, fall, winter, spring.

- Slow-dance on my grave.

- Bury something small, biodegradable and symbolic under an inch of soil.

- Leave a bouquet of plastic flowers in a styrofoam pot.

- Do that special thing you do: paint, knit, sing, write, sculpt, tinker, whatever...

- Park right here next to me and change your oil.

- Do something illegal that doesn't hurt anybody.

- Write me a letter.

- Read a poem with my eyes.

- Listen to a bird and imagine that's me reminding you of something.

- Spread out a blanket and have a picnic with your friends.

- Get to know my neighbors.

- Spray pesticides all over the place.

- Smell my soil.

- Forgive yourself.

- Forgive me.

- Pray.

- Laugh.

- Cry.

- Whine.

- Try to explain this to a small child.

Wake Up, America!

Buried alive? You've got a real problem and not much time to solve it. If you've been embalmed, of course, your problems are over. You are more than dead. Not even a worm would eat you. You're going to be more than dead for a long, long time.

But if you should find yourself in the situation of awakening in a coffin, first ask yourself how you know you're in a coffin and not just some dark, horizontal telephone booth. Do you remember dying? If so, odds are you aren't in a coffin. You're in bed and you're asleep and having a bad dream. Try waking up.

If waking up doesn't work, try going to sleep. That will minimize your consumption of oxygen. You'll live longer. And then die. Like everybody else. Just be glad you weren't embalmed.

But you may be too excited to fall asleep. Who could blame you? It's like your first day on a new job. You're confused. You're nervous. You want to do things right, but you haven't received proper training. They're thrown you into a new situation, and you've hit the ground running. Or in this case, lying down.

Relax. You've got enough oxygen for a couple of hours. You'll wake up in time. Because really, you're just dreaming all this.

With a little luck you'll dream you were buried with your cell phone. This is far more likely than being buried alive. Of course it's also likely your battery's dead. (That's why they buried it with you! Ha, ha— just a little coffin humor.) Of course if you were so fortunate as to have received a green burial—which may be why you weren't embalmed— they wouldn't bury you with a phone, not unless it's organic.

But maybe they forgot it was in your pocket, and the battery is no deader than you, and you aren't in a concrete vault six feet under, just four feet under and no vault, and in an organic cardboard casket in a cemetery not far from a cell tower. Try calling 9-1-1, see if they believe you. Then call the most dependable person you know who owns a shovel or, better yet, a backhoe. Tap your head gently on the bottom of the coffin, and then harder and harder as you listen to the detailed instructions on how to leave a message. Make sure you mentiont that you're leaving the message *after* the funeral.

Try texting. Text your entire list of contacts. And pray—pray that you aren't doing this in your sleep. Which you probably are. And they will never let you forget. And for the rest of your life, you're going to wish you were dead. And someday you will be—hopefully before you're buried.

Be Dead Right

There are two things you want to get right .One is that all-important thing called *Life* .The other is that long-term project called *Death*.

If you're like most people, you've already screwed up that first thing. Not completely, but substantively in your own personal way—that way that makes you *you*. And of course you've done some of it right, too. You did what you could. And you will continue to do so because deep down inside, you're a pretty decent person. You want to do what's right.

And then you die. Maybe you can get that right, even though you (the *you* you) have never done it before.

The best you can do with death is pull off a transcendental switcheroo. You can turn death into life, and in so doing, do life itself— *all* life—a big favor.

Life depends on death. No big news there. It's been going on for a long time, that perpetual renewal, that passing on of the carbon baton, that continual conversion of ash and dust into flesh and bone. This is well within your capacity. You can do this right.

Or you can do it wrong. You can plan to have yourself gutted and pumped full of formaldehyde to preserve your appearance of rosy-cheeked vitality. You can have yourself locked into a varnished, air-tight, worm-proof box, and you can have that box isolated from earth, water, and worms in a vault of concrete or steel. You can put off the inevitable for centuries, removed from Mother Earth, all alone in the dark, lying in the clutch of your own preservatives, deader than dead, your carbon-based molecules stuck in a limbo beyond the reach of life.

It's understandable why some people choose to do that, or, more likely, have it chosen for them. Their loved ones want to remember them as they looked in life. It's denial, of course, but there's probably a reason people succumb to it. After all, what is life if not a long process of denying the inevitable.

But that's doing Death wrong. It's locking away life's nutrients from life's cycles. It's hardwood trees felled to make a nice box. It's dead trees hauled hundreds or thousands of miles in a diesel truck. It's topsoil stripped away so sand and lime could be dug up for a concrete vault, leaving a hole in the ground that will remain lifeless for about as long as an embalmed body. It's untold gallons of fossil fuel burned to turn the sand and lime into cement that's then hauled hundreds or thousands of miles in yet another a diesel truck. It's yet another truck hauling in fertilizer for a grassy toupee. It's the marble or granite for a headstone dug up a long way away and hauled to a grave. And then come the lawnmowers, grim grass reapers burning yet more fuel.

That's quite a stain to leave behind, quite an insult to the planet that gave the deceased so much for so many years of life.

Cremation? Not much better. It's 28 gallons of fossil fuel combusted. It's nutrients and personal collection of toxins— lead, mercury, BHT, Red #5—up in smoke. It's the gritty cremains not good for much no matter where they're scattered.

That's not what you want to do. You want to do *Dead* right. You want to expedite your return to Life. You want to minimize your carbon footprint as you retreat into—and become—the Earth. Not trying to kid anybody by looking alive, you want your body left as it was when it died, unpolluted by carcinogenic chemicals, just wrapped in no more than a cotton shroud or a casket of local wood. You don't want a vault just to keep the land above you level. You want the soil that you've displaced mounded in a bosomy tumulus. You want it to settle slowly, as it surely will. You don't want lie under a manicured lawn; you want a beautiful blanket of autumn's leaves and, soon enough, spring's flowers and eventually a tree. You want to be kind to Mother Nature, who has nurtured your since your start. You want to rest in peace. You want to go gently into that good night.

Bangs & Whimpers

Introduction

It's going to happen. How could it not? All things end. On Earth, 99.9 percent of species have died out. Cataclysms—comets, asteroids, volcanoes, oxygen gone awry—have thrown life back to a microbial stage.[1] Elsewhere in the solar system, something caused Mars to lose most of its water and air, ending conditions that may have supported life. Elsewhere in the universe, stars run low on fuel, swell into red giants and consume their nearest planets. The universe itself is doomed to either expand beyond cohesion or contract and swallow itself.

Is this worth worrying about? Only if you're alive, and even more so if you have children and the expectation of grandchildren having grandchildren. And even more so if you have some faith in the value of civilization and hopes for its destiny without you. *It's going to happen.* The inevitability inevitably raises at least three questions: When? How? And so what?

This book does not look at that last question. Rather, these brief passages look at some of the hows—the real hows, the improbable hows, the hows that happened and the ones that never materialized. For most of the hows, the whens are unpredictable. God only knows what God has in mind. The next supervolcano could rear up within a decade or not for ten millennia. The next asteroid, as yet unseen, could arrive in a few days, or not for ten million years. Nuclear war could break out tonight—or never. Someone may be genetically engineering the end of mankind right now—or maybe she isn't.

One when and one how are uncomfortably close to predictable—the imminence of catastrophic climate change. *It's happening*. The predictions are pretty dire for the next three-quarters of a century, well within the lifetime of people alive today. Not much predicts prevention. Almost every forecast of deteriorating conditions has so far proven conservative in rate and extent. The tipping points keep tipping. Too many desperate expressions of hope begin with "If we stop burning fossil fuel today…," which, obviously, isn't happening. What's happening is the end of a good part of the world—the human part—and in all likelihood it will keep happening. Within someone's lifetime, much of the Earth will be virtually uninhabitable. Changes in coastlines and economies cannot help but lead to social turbulence, economic stress, geopolitical upheaval. Mankind will not become extinct, but the inexorable approach of global calamity raises a fourth question: what do we mean by *the end of the world?*

This book takes a rather liberal, wide-scope look at the concept. The end of the world, for our purposes here, doesn't require the blasting of the planet to smithereens, the annihilation of all forms of life, or even the extinction of the human species. If we must draw a definitive line, it would lie in that vague area between civil life and moral conditions not much above those of armed apes. Where precisely that line lies, it's hard to say. Suffice it to say that we just don't want to come anywhere close to it. The grim goal of this brief book is merely to point out some of the ways we might get there. Maybe, with some smarts and a lot of luck, we can avoid that fate. Or maybe it's not worth trying. Hard to say. It all depends on how. And when. And so what.

Apocalypses Now

When Things Go Bad

What would happen if our things—our cars and coffee-makers, our pacemakers and airplanes, our thermostats and telephones, our personal drones, our electric meters, our bots and Rumbas, our sprinklers, locks, switches and light bulbs started conspiring against us? Is that even possible?

It is possible. Over 15 billion things are connected to the "Internet of Things" (IoT), and by 2020 the number could reach 50 billion.[2] Over 60 percent of them are owned by consumers (as opposed to government or business).[3] They out-populate people. And if they're connected to the Internet, they are susceptible to hacking. And if they can be hacked, they can be turned against us.

In 2015, Chrysler recalled 1.4 million vehicles after security researchers figured out how to hack into Jeeps and take control of their brakes, steering, and transmissions. The same software glitch could have left Vipers, Rams, Durangos, Chargers, and Challengers open to control by someone other than their drivers.

Problem solved? No. The cars are still connected or can be connected to the Internet, and nothing connected to the Internet is absolutely impervious to hacking. Not everybody brought in their recalled vehicles. A lot of them are still out there, driving around.[4]

There are also millions of "smart lamps" in the world, connected with a built-in Zigbee wireless system that allows appliances to communicate with each other. Researchers found a way to hack into the Zigbee radio protocol. They were able to hack into Philip's Hue smart lamps and get them to communicate with each other not through a router and the Internet but *directly with other lamps nearby*. The researchers calculated that if a city had more than 15,000 such lamps (as most large cities probably do), they could set off a chain reaction that could put them all under the control of a single remote individual. That individual could upload new firmware and make them impervious to further updating. The smart lamps of a city could be dimmed, flickered, or turned on and off. A repeated simultaneous turning on and off could cause sudden, radical changes in power consumption, resulting in a catastrophic disruption of the power grid.[5] Rhythmic flashing could also cause epileptic seizures.

Lamps are by no means the only appliances that communicate. People in cities are within electronic reach of 1,000 to 5,000 internet objects. Using Zigbee, wifi, Bluetooth mesh networking, radio-frequency identification (RFID), Z-wave, near-field communication (NFC), and light-fidelity (none of which have legally mandated security systems), lamps, toaster ovens, garage openers, alarm systems, refrigerators, furnaces, televisions, telephones, vacuum cleaners, insulin pumps, cardioverter defibrillators, hearing aids, hospital beds, prostheses, and other devices all have the potential to talk with each other. Under a single leader anywhere in the world, they could work together. You could be attacked by your vacuum cleaner just as your oven catches on fire, your furnace explodes, the lights go out, a Jeep crashes into your living room, your pacemaker goes into overdrive and your phone won't dial 9-1-1, though its camera is catching the events on video and feeding it directly to Facebook so that everybody else can see that they're not the only ones having a bad day.

Global Warming

Will global warming be the end of the world or just a major reduction of Earth's population?

Good question. And no answer.

Scientists agree that the situation is going to get bleak. If the temperature rises by 2°C by the end of the 21st century, the situation will be merely "dangerous." A lot of people will die, especially in the less developed nations. A lot more people will have to adapt to droughts, storms, flooding, desertification, and higher sea levels. A lot of species are going to die.

Predicting climate change based on global warming is too complicated to draw accurate conclusions. How much greenhouse gas will be produced? How much will warming affect polar ice, the disappearance of which will affect the warming trend? How much, and when, will melting permafrost release methane from the tundra? How will warming affect ocean currents, and how will changes in currents affect climate? What will be the effects on civilization, and how will those effects affect climate change? Though predictions are not accurate, none of the predictions foresee improvement. The question is how serious the change will be. The answer comes down to probability.

Two university researchers assessed great amounts of existing climate and emissions data and calculated the probability of "catastrophic" climate change.[6] Catastrophe will occur, they said, if the global temperature rises by 3°C. At 4°C, 74 percent of the world's population would be exposed to "deadly heat," and would need air conditioning to survive—a protective measure that would contribute to further warming by burning more fuel.

They calculated a 50-50 probability that temperatures will rise by 2.4°-2.6°C by 2050 and 4.1-5°C by 2100.

Five degrees is well within the scope of possibility, but there has been little research into what will happen under those conditions. The researchers therefore suggested a new category of disaster which they term only "unknown," that is, something beyond merely catastrophic. It's hard to know because the Earth hasn't been that hot since at least 20 million years ago. One possible consequence would be an end to life as we know it.

What are the odds of a 5°C rise in temperature? The researchers figured five percent by the end of the century. That's a one-in-20 chance. To put those odds in perspective, they posed a rhetorical question: Would you put your children or grandchildren on a plane that had a one-in-20 chance of crashing?

Because that's what we're doing.

Another Problem with Carbon Dioxide

Carbon dioxide (CO_2) has received plenty of publicity as an agent causing global warming. Indeed, that is probably the most likely cause of the extinction of the human species. But rising levels of CO_2 may cause yet another life-threatening problem: CO_2 toxicity.[7]

Human beings have always inhaled carbon dioxide. It's a natural part of our atmosphere, not to mention a waste product we exhale every couple of seconds during every living moment except, of course, the last. As a component of the air mixture we breathe, its concentration has been steadily increasing since 1820 and soaring since 1960. It used to be 300 parts per million. Now it's nearly 400.

Humans can tolerate something like 5,000 ppm for a day or so. But over a slightly longer term, just 600 ppm can lead to carbon dioxide toxicity. Among the symptoms of carbon dioxide toxicity are kidney failure, brain atrophy, cancer, neurological disorders and loss of brain function. This rarely occurs because people don't often go long periods without any fresh air at all.

What is not known, however, is the effect of constant, long-term, low doses—doses we can expect to be breathing within the lifetime of people alive today. Some models of atmospheric CO_2 prediction forecast a level of 1,000 ppm within a hundred years.[8]

There have been no studies on long-term low-dose exposure to carbon dioxide. No one knows what would happen if the entire human race were breathing 600 ppm during their entire lifetimes, all of them suffering some degree of mental impairment, starting at birth, or, indirectly, before birth. Just when people would need to be thinking clearly in a global emergency, they would be least able to do so. At the same time, they might be suffering a number of physiological ailments.

This would be happening all over the planet. Granted, some people—no doubt a tiny minority—would have access to an oxygen supply, but what about the vast majority who make civilization a viable operation? Could they be productive (and reproductive) elements of society if suffering constant dizziness, confusion, cognitive impairment, headaches, shortness of breath, and fatigue, dying young of kidney failure or cancer while, we must remember, the atmosphere is growing hotter, the sea rising, storms inflicting more damage, and climate changes causing droughts, floods, and forest fires, sending hordes of refugees to safer places?

Nobody knows.

The Monster from the Cold, Dark Swamp

For the 10,000 years prior to the Industrial Revolution, Earth's atmosphere had about 280 parts of carbon dioxide per million parts of atmosphere. Scientists figure that 350 ppm is considered the highest "safe" level for Earth's ecosystems to continue without adapting. Climatologists warned that if it ever reached 400 ppm, we would be passing a threshold indicating that we had moved way too far in the wrong direction. If it reaches 450 ppm, scientists warn, we stand only a 50-50 chance of keeping the global fever to 2°C above pre-industrial levels. At that temperature, certain biological and geophysical processes would begin a lethal spiral of uncontrollable factors that cause planetary heating.[9]

In February of 2018, the level reached 408.35, higher than it's been for 16 million years. By April 3, it was at 409.64.[10] At the current rate of growth, it will reach 500 ppm within 50 years.[11]

Unfortunately—*terrifyingly*—a lot more greenhouse gas is on the verge of surging into the air. It isn't the exhaust from cars and power plants. It's the methane trapped in the permafrost soil—that is, permanently frozen soil— of the Arctic. The permafrost contains more than twice as much carbon as is floating in the atmosphere today. If the permafrost thaws into a swamp, that carbon will be released as methane, a gas that is 84 times as powerful a greenhouse gas as carbon dioxide.

The permafrost is going to melt. Of this there is little doubt. It is part of a downward spiral known as positive feedback. Positive feedback means that a change in something causes more change in that something. In this case, it will be Earth's warming climate causing an increase in the cause of the warming.

The current effects of global warming are causing the melting of Arctic ice. The less ice, the less white. The less white, the less of the sun's light and heat are reflected back into space. The dark of the Arctic waters absorbs more heat, causing more ice to melt.

And on it goes until the permafrost, too, starts to melt, releasing methane, which causes temperatures to rise more, melting more ice and permafrost.

Meanwhile, the rising temperatures cause more evaporation, causing more cloud cover, which traps heat, worsening the other factors and itself. The higher heat causes forests to burn or die, quickly eliminating one of few effective means of removing CO_2 from the atmosphere. Fewer trees means less shade, which means more solar heat absorbed, which means more ice melting, more permafrost thawing, more methane released. And as the dead trees rot, they release their carbon in the form of CO_2.

Once this starts—and arguably, it already has—there is no going back. The absolute (and impossible) cessation of all fossil fuels combustion will not stop Earth from heating itself to the point of eradicating most forms of life.

Which is what happened 252 million years ago. Carbon dioxide and methane released from permafrost raised the planet's temperature by five degrees Celsius, killing 97 percent of all life on Earth. But that was then. This is now: We are adding carbon to the atmosphere at ten times the rate that occurred back then. And that rate is accelerating.

The trick—mankind's only hope—is to stop burning fossil fuels before Earth reaches the "tipping point" where the feedback starts.

Earthlings are apparently not willing to radically reverse the production of carbon dioxide. Some efforts are being made, but they are far from adequate. There is virtually no chance that the Earth will avoid the tipping point that sets off positive climate feedback.[12] This is the way the world will end, and people alive today may well have the painful privilege of witnessing the beginning of the spiral to extinction.

Know Your Tipping Points

You can tip a bucket of water without spilling anything. You can always tip it back to level. You can tip it to the point where the bucket balances at an angle, and you can still tip it back. But if you tip it a bit more, the water takes over the tipping process. The tipping causes tipping. The bucket dumps. Good luck putting the water back into a tipped bucket.

In climate change, rising temperatures can push various geological and biological systems to a point where they tip into a self-generated destructive process. Destroying the vast Amazon forest, for example, is a linear destruction. If you cut 1,000 acres, 1,000 acres are gone. But if the forest around it survives, and the cut area can grow back. But when enough acreage is cut, the lack of trees reduces rainfall, which in turn reduces more forest, which causes less rain. That's the tipping point. After that, human-generated rises in temperature are not the driving force. The forest itself—its disappearance—drives the disappearance.

Earth has several climate-related tipping points. As temperatures rise, these earthly buckets tip. Scientific evidence indicates that tipping points can be triggered by a temperature rise of just two degrees Celsius above pre-industrial levels. Each tipping point will cause other systems to tip, a cascading effect that will almost certainly lead to the extinction of humankind.

A rise of 1-2 degrees Celsius could be enough to start the tip. For three years in a row (2014-2016), the planetary temperature was up by about one degree, reaching the highest since the last Ice Age. The moment of the tipping point will not be obvious, but that does not mean it didn't happen.

Here are some of the places that could tip, each causing other systems to tip.[13.]

Western Antarctic Ice Shelf (WAIS): As it melts, sea levels will rise by 25 feet or so. If it melts completely, the disappearance of its reflective white coat will reduce reflection of solar heat. Higher temperatures could melt the entire Antarctic ice sheet, raising sea levels by 180 feet. The WAIS over the sea has already begun to melt from warm water below.

Arctic Winter Sea Ice: As the planet nears the six degree temperature increase, Arctic sea ice will remain melted even in winter, causing a drastic decrease in reflected solar heat and ocean salinity.

Greenland Glaciers: These are already melting at a great rate. As their disappearance exposes darker land, melting will accelerate. As cold fresh water and icebergs enter the sea, levels will rise, currents will shift, and local climates will change.

Antarctic Bottom Water Formations: Antarctic bottom water is the densest water in the world. Its formation by cold water sinking along the coast of Antarctica is a major driver of the thermohaline circulation of the oceans. The melting of Antarctic glaciers slows that formation, thus weakening global seawater circulation and, in the long term, changing climate patterns all over the world.[14]

El Niño-Southern Oscillation: The El Niño phenomenon is a temporary, recurring warming of global surface temperatures. La Niña is a temporary, recurring cooling. The former tends to happen more frequently, and over the last several decades, the El Niño temperatures have risen more. The increased frequency and extreme of warming may increase more frequent and extreme warming, affecting climate and weather all over the world.[15]

East Antarctic Ice Sheet: It will start melting as temperatures reach the 3.8 Celsius level following rises caused by other tipping points. There will be no possibility of preventing submersion of all sea coast cities.

Thermohaline Circulation: This is global ocean water circulation as affected by water density. That density is affected by salinity and temperature. As air temperatures rise, more rainwater and glacial melt flow into the ocean, decreasing salinity. Warmer waters flowing toward the Arctic, e.g., the Gulf Stream, cause increased rain over Arctic ice, melting it. Circulation in the Atlantic seems to be slowing[16] and could theoretically stop, causing severe and abrupt changes in weather and disruption of ecosystems in North America and Europe.

Arctic Summer Sea Ice: The melting is increasing each year. This does not affect sea levels, but it causes more absorption of solar heat in the area once there was ice.

Alpine Glaciers: Already melting at a great rate. Their gradual disappearance will accelerate the retreat.

Coral Reefs: A variety of human activities, from dredging to tourism, are killing coral at an increasing rate. Warming ocean water is a huge threat. As the seas absorb more CO_2, they become more acidic, causing coral skeletons to weaken. An increasing El Niño phenomenon is raising water temperatures, to the detriment of coral. Rising temperatures also cause lethal coral bleaching. Rising sea levels reduce coral organism photosynthesis by reducing the sunlight that reaches them. Changing temperatures also change fish migration, with ecosystem impact on coral life forms. By the 2030s, 90 percent of coral reefs will be at risk.

Amazon Rainforest: It is still being destroyed, replaced with grassland and soy fields. The tipping point might be just under a four-degree rise in temperature. Less forest means less transpiration of water through leaves, causing drought in distant regions.17 Springs and streams will dry up. Soil will bake hard. The forest will not grow back.

Boreal Forest: Longer summers are killing the boreal forests, i.e., the taiga of northern latitudes. The forests are converting into grasslands and temperate forests, disrupting ecosystems and, consequently, climate.

Permafrost: The perpetually frozen ground of Siberia holds a huge amount of methane, a powerful greenhouse gas. As the permafrost melts at a temperature rise of about 1.5 degrees Celsius above current levels, the methane will be released (and more will be created), causing an increase in the rate of global warming.18

Indian Monsoon Instability: Monsoon rains are created by the temperature differential between land and sea. Rapidly rising temperatures in the Indian Ocean caused a drop in inland rainfall, though possibly rising land temperatures may be having an opposite effect. As temperatures rise, variability in rainfall increases. At the same time, deforestation reduces evaporation and thus less rain.[19]

Sahel: The area to the south of the Sahara is especially vulnerable to climate change. As the region nears the four degree increase, its ecosystem may collapse, causing further climate change. The Sahara will spread to the south. Nothing will grow in its sands.

Frozen Germs

Glaciers aren't just ice. Over the course of tens of thousands of years they receive and soon bury all sorts of particles—dust from distant deserts, ash from volcanoes in other hemispheres, the remnants of vaporized meteors, and germs.

The germs can be from millennia ago or just last century. Researchers in Alaska have found the virus of the influenza epidemic that killed something like 100 million people in 1918. Deep in ancient glaciers there are other germs that haven't infected anyone since King Tut was knee-high to a grasshopper. Mankind no longer has immunity to these germs.

The glaciers are melting. The germs are thawing out and rising in the wind, finding hospitable conditions in the warming atmosphere. Anthrax popped up in Siberia in 2016, infecting nomadic reindeer and eight people, one of whom died.[20] And there are other germs out there in the precarious deep freeze. Small pox. Influenza. Bubonic plague. These and others we have yet to name will soon be blowing in the wind.

When Oceans Rise to the Sky

A round about the time you celebrate your one-billionth birthday, the sun will have grown about ten percent brighter than it is now. The temperature on earth will reach 117 degree F. That's hot enough to melt the candles on your big billionth birthday cake but still too cool to actually boil the oceans. Nonetheless, those oceans will evaporate and become clouds. The clouds will trap heat below them, setting off a "runaway greenhouse effect." It will be much worse than the one perpetrated by today's civilization. By the time you're three billion years old, water vapor will become the dominant component of the atmosphere, and surface temperatures will reach 1,650 degrees F, more than hot enough to kill all living things, not to mention melt lead, aluminum, even plutonium.

The Doomsday Clock

The Doomsday Clock is a symbol or metaphor created by the *Bulletin of the Atomic Scientists*. It is presented as a kind of timer that indicates how long until mankind finishes itself off. It was created as an illustration for the June 1947 cover of the Bulletin, less than a year after the nuclear bombing of Hiroshima and Nagasaki. The artist arbitrarily set the clock at seven minutes to midnight, midnight being a metaphor for the end of humanity.

The clock is by no means a Swiss timepiece, and there is no physical clock. Illustrated clock, which appears on the cover of every issue of the Bulletin, is periodically reset according to the subjective assessments of scientists and experts, including 15 Nobel laureates, who understand something about the technological and political situation of the world. In 1949, when the Soviet Union detonated its first atomic bomb, the clock was moved to three minutes to midnight. In 1953, when the Soviet Union and the United States tested their first thermonuclear bombs, the clock was moved yet another minute closer to the end.

The farthest the minute hand ever got from midnight was in 1991 with the end of the Cold war and the signing of the Strategic Arms Reduction Treaty. But by 2018, it was back to two minutes shy of doom—not only because of an increasing risk of nuclear war but because of ever-worsening evidence of global warming and ocean acidification to catastrophic levels.

The *Bulletin* emphasizes that the Doomsday Clock does not predict or measure anything. It is simply a graphic warning that civilization is always moving closer to and away from its own suicidal demise.[21] ·

And Now This

From vhemt.org:

> The Voluntary Human Extinction Movement (VHEMT, pronounced vehement) is a movement, not an organization. It's a movement advanced by people who care about life on planet Earth. We're not just a bunch of misanthropes and anti-social, Malthusian misfits, taking morbid delight whenever disaster strikes humans. Nothing could be farther from the truth. Voluntary human extinction is the humanitarian alternative to human disasters.

> We don't carry on about how the human race has shown itself to be a greedy, amoral parasite on the once-healthy face of this planet. That type of negativity offers no solution to the inexorable horrors which human activity is causing.

> Rather, The Movement presents an encouraging alternative to the callous exploitation and wholesale destruction of Earth's ecology.

471

Someday This Will Happen

One of the most probable threats that nature can throw at us is that of the "supervolcano." The massive eruptions have occurred a few times during the Earth's existence, at least once, some 250 million years ago, very nearly extinguishing all life on the planet. There were no humans (or even mammals) alive at the time, but next time, there may well be. Could they survive on a planet devoid of plants and animals? Not for long, not the centuries or millennia that a supervolcano can spew smoke, ash, and lava into the air and across the land.

The power of supervolcanoes is classified by the Volcanic Explosivity Index. The largest are classified as VEI 7 or 8. Some 60 VEI 8 supervolcanoes are known to have erupted since the Earth formed. Four VEI 7 eruptions have occurred in the past 2,000 years, nine others in the past 100,000 years.[22]

Supervolcanoes will occur again. A big one is in process under Yellowstone National Park. It has exploded three times in the last 2.1 million years. The first was one of the five largest explosions ever to take place on the planet. So much material got blown into the air that the remaining depression, or caldera, was 60 miles across. Just 640,000 years ago, an explosion threw 240 cubic miles of rock, dust and ash into the sky.

It may happen again. Thick, sticky magma is building up not far below the surface. The ground above is already bulging, rising 10 inches over the last decade. From 2004-2008 it was rising three inches a year. Now the rate is slowing. No one can predict when or whether it will blow except to say it won't happen in the immediate future. It will be preceded by earthquakes.

If it erupts, its effects will be global and quite possibly very serious and long-lasting. With a little luck, however, rather than erupt in a massive explosion, it will gradually leak lava to the surface, possibly spreading a few hundred feet every day for several years, burying a vast region but not darkening the planet for years.

You can monitor volcanic activity in the United States at https://volcanoes.usgs.gov/vhp/updates.html. Keep your eye on Yellowstone.

Asteroids

An asteroid is one of few threats that really could effect the end of the world. A small one—less than 165 feet wide—would be a major inconvenience, resulting in the destruction of a city and a global collapse of agriculture, but some people—maybe even enough to constitute a civilization—would survive. A bigger one—say, more than 3,000 feet wide—would pound the whole planet with enough acid rain to destroy all crops, shroud the whole planet in sun-blocking debris, touch off tsunamis, earthquakes, and volcanoes, and consume a lot of oxygen in vast firestorms.

Smaller ones hit Earth every 100 years or so, the larger ones maybe once in 100,000. NASA knows of 900 large ones that cross Earth's orbit. The agency estimates there are 100 more out there somewhere. None are projected to collide with our pretty blue rock, but projections can't see very far into the future. On the brighter side, the larger they are, the sooner we'll see them coming.

On February 6 and 9 of 2018 two small asteroids passed less than one lunar distance from Earth. They had been spotted on February 4. The second, estimated to be 50 and 130 feet wide, was an astronomical close miss at just 39,000 miles away, less than a fifth of the distance to the moon. A NASA manager said that asteroids of that size rarely pass close to the planet, "maybe only one or twice a year."[23]

February 4, 2018, was the same day that a rock a third of a mile wide and three quarters of a mile long passed within ten lunar orbits. NASA said it has known that particular chunk, known as 2002 AJ129, for a long time and has its orbit calculated for the next 100 years. We're safe from that one for a good while.

Comets

C omets have hit Earth before. It would seem the probability is infin-itesimal, with the planet circling through a vast amount of space and the comet hurtling on a predestined course from the other side of the solar system. Of course gravity plays a little part, drawing the two heavenly bodies toward each other, but the gravity of the sun and the velocity of the comet are much more powerful factors than Earth's grav-itational pull.

On the other hand, there's dumb luck. Over the course of eons, col-lisions are likely to occur. Earth has been lucky for — years. How long can that luck hold out?

Though they may be several miles in diameter, comets are hard to spot. Until they get within 400 million miles of the sun, they are black balls of ice against the black background of the universe. But as the ice approaches the sun, it releases gases, creating a bright tail that is visible from Earth. Once it's spotted, astrophysicists can calculate its projected path. We might have ten years to know that we're doomed. Or we might have no more than a few months.

Comets are less common than asteroids but more dangerous for two reasons. They can be much larger, perhaps 60 miles in diameter, and they are going much faster, a good 100,000 km per hour.

It is not known whether the object that created the Chicxulub crater on Mexico's Yucatán Peninsula 66 million years ago was a comet or asteroid. Whatever it was, it was probably a little under 10 miles in diameter. It pushed up a megatsunami that was only about a hundred yards tall because of the shallow waters of the Caribbean. Had it hit the ocean, the wave could have been almost three miles tall. The impact blasted material out of the atmosphere. When the material returned to Earth, flaming like meteors, it touched off fires all over the world. The impact also created global earthquakes and volcanoes. The particles in the air blocked the sun for a decade or more, cooling the planet and preventing photosynthesis. At the same time, the shock turned carbonate rock into carbon dioxide, leading to a greenhouse effect warming of the planet. It was a tough time to be alive. Three-quarters of the species on Earth, including all non-avian dinosaurs, were rendered extinct.

Would the human species survive such a cataclysmic event? Maybe a few if they survived the various initial shocks, had a ten-year food supply, a stock of seeds they could plant when the air cleared, and their human ingenuity allowed them to adapt to a radical climate change and the permanent disappearance of almost all life forms they had known before.

In 2014, there were 5,253 known comets, a number that continually increases as previously unknown comets arrive from out of the distant dark. Millions more are estimated to exist in the outer solar system. About one per year passes close enough to be seen by the naked eye, but for all of human history, they've been many millions of miles away.

Existential Dodgeball

Asteroids are rarely a problem for Earth, but when they are a problem, they are a huge problem—really the biggest problem imaginable. Can such a problem be avoided or mitigated? Is mankind capable of finding dark rocks in distant space and then move them? Asteroids are but specks in an infinite sky, but the ones big enough to end life on Earth would be terribly difficult, if not impossible, to move. No one has ever tried.

We can spot trouble coming a few months ahead of time. But to prepare a space mission to do something about it would take nothing less than four years—assuming these plans and rocket designs were already on paper, which they aren't. To give us a head start, a private organization, the B612 Foundation, started raising funds for a telescope that would be put into solar orbit to locate 90 percent of potential Near Earth Objects (NEOs). It was to be launched by 2016, but in 2015, NASA terminated its cooperative agreement with B612, and the project was abandoned.[34]

Scientists cannot agree on the best strategy for avoiding asteroidal impact.[25] One bunch recommends destruction of the NEO with either a bomb or a direct impact with something hard.[26] Trouble is, destruction would be only partial, turning a large bullet into a large mass of buckshot. If any fragments are larger than 35 meters, they will not burn up in the atmosphere. They will have to be located and dealt with on a subsequent mission. Or missions. If there's time.

The other strategy is to deflect the asteroid or slow its orbit.[27] This could be effected by a nuclear explosion if the asteroid isn't too large. To deflect the closest known NEO, an asteroid known as Apophis, which may be a pile of rubble or a semi-solid rock 30 meters wide, six 1.2 megaton nuclear bombs detonated in as many hours might do the trick. The rocket would need to be launched in the early 2020s to reach the target in time to prevent a slightly possible 2029 impact.

One proposal for destroying the asteroid is to hit it with at least two Hypervelocity Asteroid Intercept Vehicles (HAIVs). The first would create a crater that would allow the second to deeply penetrate the heavenly body. A Danish organization is trying to use crowd-funding to raise money to build a couple of HAIVs.

The National Nuclear Security Administration says it has some "canned subassemblies" of the nine-megaton B53 nuclear device, the largest explosive in the American arsenal. But assembly and deployment has been delayed due to concerns that it could be used as a weapon.[28]

A more bizarre but theoretically viable plan: build a system of gigantic lenses in space to focus solar energy on the asteroid. The energy might vaporize the surface of the rock, which would thrust the thing in another direction or at least slow it down. A powerful laser beam might work, too.

Or: a gravity tractor—any large, heavy mass that could use its gravity to pull the asteroid off its trajectory over the course of many years. This would work on rubble as well as solid rock.

Or: tie a rocket—a really, really big rocket—to the thing and tow it somewhere.

Or (this is a good one): deploy a huge, hollow coil of wire in the asteroid's orbital path and charge it with electricity. When the asteroid, which usually contains a lot of iron, enters the electromagnetic field of the coil, it will shoot out the other side, and...*adios asteroid.*

Pre-Apocalyptic Collapse

If humanity knows of an imminent collision with a comet or large asteroid, society would probably begin to collapse immediately. The first people to know—probably NASA scientists and their friends, or maybe their colleagues in another country—would waste no time trying to prepare for the inevitable. They would inform their government, and the news would not remain secret for long. A government may make an announcement, confirming or denying the threat. Another government might do the opposite.

Society will quickly move from shock to desperate measures. With (let's say) weeks or months to live, no one is going to their jobs. Every company and government office will be effectively closed or dysfunctional. Trucks and deliveries will stop. Food supplies will quickly disappear from shelves. Infrastructure—power plants, dams, oil and gas lines, sewers, water systems, oil rigs, electrical systems—will hold up only as long as they can run on automatic and without maintenance. Cell phone service and the internet might work until power supplies fail. No news via television, radio, or internet, so everyone will make decisions based on local rumors.

Money and gold will lose all value. Orderly economic exchanges will give way to violent exchanges—chaotic looting perhaps followed by ad hoc gang-organized warfare. Police will not be available, and military order will break down as soon as the first officers abandon their posts. Hospitals and nursing homes will be vacated by staff with patients left to fend for themselves, many soon becoming cadavers. Fires will burn out of control. As buildings collapse, water mains and gas lines break, causing more collapse. Ships and barges will drift without crews, eventually wrecking and spilling their contents. People trying to evacuate by car will find themselves in permanent traffic jams.

Dead bodies will rot in the streets. The religious may flock to churches to apply the power of prayer. Drug addicts and alcoholics will become increasing desperate and violent. Families will try to dig shelters, but in a few weeks they will need to kill for food. Defense of the home against desperate hordes will be impossible. Nobody will have enough bullets, and everybody needs to sleep.

In other words, society would nearly extinguish itself before the comet or asteroid arrived. It might even do so based on nothing more than a rumor of a supposed collision. Since anarchy will not make anything easier, governments will probably try to keep the cosmic doom a secret. They will deny the rumors. A lot of people will refuse to believe the denials, seeing them as inevitable whether there's a collision coming or not. A rumor could prove more catastrophic than the actual comet, if any.

Solar Flares

Our Sun has been casting its life-giving rays in our direction since the first days of anything discernible as a planet. Every once in a while it burps up a solar flare—a flash of a few seconds that ejects electrons, ions, atoms, and electromagnetic waves into outer space. They travel in a somewhat tightly focused direction, possibly but not necessarily toward Earth.

Even relatively weak flares can create a radiation hazard to astronauts in space. They can disable satellites, mess up radio transmissions, knock out whole power grids, and light up the skies with aurora borealis and australis.

Solar flares happen several times a day when the Sun is in an especially "active" cycle, or once a week or so during calmer times. The biggest known flare—constituting a "geomagnetic storm"–was the "Carrington event" observed by Richard Carrington in 1859. It was strong enough to set telegraph offices on fire. One of equal size just missed the Earth in 2012. Had that eruption happened nine days earlier, the flare would have hit Earth and caused catastrophic damage to everything from toasters to national electrical systems. Recovery would have taken four to ten years, costing as much as $2 trillion in the United States.[29]

Astronomers will know a flare is coming about 15 minutes before the first X-rays and UV radiation arrive. If there's time to announce the event on electronic media, the public will need to hear it in those first few minutes. After that, the flare will ionize the atmosphere, knocking out radio transmissions and GPS mechanisms. A few minutes later, the energetic particles arrive—an avalanche of electrons and protons that damage the electronics of satellites. A day or two later, billions of tons of magnetized plasma arrive. After that, you can forget about watching television, gathering information from the internet, or flushing your toilet. Your refrigerator won't work. Neither will your local, state, or federal government.

Another geomagnetic storm of Carrington power is almost inevitable. In fact, in 2014 a physicist calculated that there is a 12 percent chance it will happen by 2022—yes, a 12 percent chance that a large part of civilization will soon spend a few years in a modern Stone Age.[30]

Superflares

Solar flares aren't the worst geomagnetic storms that can occur. Stars similar to our Sun have emitted superflares 10,000 times more powerful than the Carrington event. They don't happen often, and they don't happen on many stars, but they do happen.

A superflare from a distant star isn't a problem on Earth. But a superflare issued by our friend the Sun would cause several kinds of catastrophe to technology, the planet, and life forms. Satellites would be rendered inoperable. Damage to electrical systems would be severe enough to destroy switches and transformers. Electrical systems at nuclear power plants might be damaged too much to cool the reactor or spent fuel pools, leading to scores or hundreds of meltdowns. Ionization of the atmosphere would make radio communication impossible. The ozone layer would be decimated, in time causing cataracts and skin cancer. Plants would be damaged, many of them unable to grow for months or years. And you'd better hope you're not in a jet at the upper edge of the atmosphere when the radiation hits. You definitely don't want to be an orbiting astronaut.

Worse, superflares usually don't happen as single events. If a star does it once, it will probably do it a few more times.

There is no evidence that a large superflare has ever occurred in the solar system. It is only theoretically possible. Judging by superflare events on other stars, scientists figure a star such as ours might experience a relatively small superflare once in 800 years. There might be a stronger one in 5,000 years. A big one might happen once in 10,000 years.[31]

If our Sun ever emits a superflare, odds are it will miss Earth. But odds are also that the Sun will take several more shots before it calms down.

Maxipok or Maximin?

If the end of the world were easy to prevent or resist, it wouldn't be the end of the world. Whatever the inevitable threat, it will be big, serious, unprecedented, and hard to solve. The solution will probably not have been prepared in advance of need. It will have to be formulated and implemented under the worst of circumstances, such as the need to rush or the ongoing deterioration of the planet or the populace. People probably aren't going to agree on which solution will work. The best solution will be desperate, difficult, dreadful, and rushed, so trial and error will not be an option.

We may not even have time to settle a fundamental issue: are we going to opt for maxipok or maximin action?

Maxipok is the Maximum Probability of an okay outcome. In the context of an existential threat, the maxipok solution would be the one that is less than the ideal of preserving or returning to the status quo but good enough for humankind to survive in reasonably comfortable conditions. That might mean that most people survive but have to live without electricity or plastic. Or it might mean a lot of people are sacrificed so that at least some can survive and thrive.

Maximin is the best worse-case outcome. In the context of an existential threat, the maximin solution is the one that is better than extinction, the one that asks the least of fate and circumstances and thus is

487

most possibly attainable. That might mean the survival of no more than a self-sustainable tribe in a temperate place with food to forage.

Faced with the imminent demise of our species, with the ultimate seriousness of extinction, which should we aim for? The most we can hope for or the least we can live with?[32] .

Bangs, Crunches, Shrieks and Whispers

S wedish philosopher Nick Bostrom is the founder of the Oxford Martin Programme on the Impacts of Future Technology and the Future
of Humanity Institute at Oxford University. Bostrom is methodically as-
sessing possible end-of-the-world cases and scenarios. The Institute figures the near-term odds of human extinction (not just major catastrophe)
at almost one in five. Here's what they figure:

Risk	Estimated Probability for Human Extinction before 2100
Overall Probability	19%
Molecular nanotechnology weapons[33]	5%
Superintelligent AI	5%
All wars (including civil wars)	4%
Engineered (not natural) pandemic	2%
Nuclear War	1%
Nanotechnology accident	0.5%
Natural pandemic	0.05%
Nuclear Terrorism	0.03%

For purposes of discussion, Bostrom has broken down potential major catastrophic events into four categories. "Posthumanity" refers to the

state of mankind after a given disaster.

Bangs—a sudden disaster resulting in the extinction of intelligent life on Earth. Nuclear war, malicious use of nanotechnology, collision with a large comet or asteroid.

Crunches—a disaster that leaves some people alive but thwarts the possibility of a posthumanity as civilization is irreversibly destroyed. Depletion of natural resources might be enough, or a sudden and extended Ice Age.

Shrieks—A posthumanity survives but in a state far below what is possible and desirable. Flawed or malicious superintelligence would do it. So would a terribly effective and repressive totalitarian regime.

Whimpers—A posthumanity that evolves to either disappearance of human values or a state where civilization's values are a minuscule fraction of what they might have been. A breakdown of morality or extraterrestrial invasion would leave the world in a whimper situation.

Of those categories, the Bangs and Crunches are existential catastrophes, that is, events that render mankind nonexistent. The Shrieks and Whimpers are just serious catastrophes.

We can break those categories down still further. Each could be divided into natural threats, such as volcanoes and solar flares, and anthropogenic threats, that is, threats created by technology. An endemic disease that simply happens is natural. A germ consciously created by man would be anthropogenic. A disease arising spontaneously from the activities of man—an influenza born on a vast and overcrowded pig farm, for example, would be...well, it would be something worth debating, ideally before it happens. Such an event would be either of two other subcategories of anthropogenic demise: catastrophes that are intentional and those that result from mistake. Examples of intentional:

launching a nuclear attack or, arguably, responding to a nuclear attack with a nuclear attack. Or releasing a super-bug disease. Or any of many diabolical scenarios found in Superman and Batman comic books.

And where do we draw the line between intentional and we-should-have-known-better—the line between climate change and climate changed, between weapon and generalized scourge? That, too, is worth debating, ideally before it happens.

We could also debate what is improbable, what is inevitable, and what is preventable.

Existential or just painful, natural or artificial, inevitable or preventable, intentional, accidental, or blundered, *something* is going to happen. It might happen while you're asleep tonight. It might not be for a few decades or centuries or millennia. There are many questions to ask, far fewer being answered. Meanwhile, we keep our fingers crossed. It's really all we can do. And somehow, because we're human, that's enough for now.

Why Nano Is Big

Nick Bostrom has good reason to identify nanotechnology as one of the most likely threats to human existence. Nanotechnology is already happening, and though much of what it can do is still just theory and hypothesis, the potentials are both dream and nightmare.

Nanotechnology is a group of emerging technologies in which the structure of matter is controlled at the level of individual atoms and molecules. If these technologies advance as expected (and feared), one person working alone might be able to produce almost anything and in great quantities at very low cost, a theorized process known as "molecular manufacturing." A person could create a medicine capable of targeting a virus or tumor. That person could also create a self-replicating nanomachine capable of, say, "eating" all biological material and converting it into, say, dirt. Someone else might decide to create a lethal and extremely contagious germ. Another might create some form of nuclear weapons or deadly self-replicating insect-sized drones.

In that technology seems to be moving in this direction, Bostrom and others fear that it will eventually come to pass. If it does, the consequences will be cataclysmic beyond any imagination. Even if used only for beneficial purposes, the economic impact would be more revolutionary than the Industrial Revolution. The elements of today's economies, from farms to factories to distribution system to trade agreements and mechanisms of pricing and finance would all become obsolete. Virtually every business in the world will either cease to exist or be transformed beyond recognition. Economic evolution that used to take centuries to work out might have to happen in a few years. Concepts of "employment," "pay," "price," and "value" will be radically redefined. Excessive consumption of unlimited products would result in devastating depletion of resources and production of pollutants.

How likely will this technology be used only for beneficial purposes? So far in history, people have never refrained from weaponizing new technologies whenever possible. By necessity, defensive systems follow in short order. But when anyone in the world has the capacity to create huge amounts of unforeseen and easily hidden weaponry, defense would seem virtually impossible. Pre-emptive prevention might be the only alternative. Constant and comprehensive surveillance of every person in the world might be necessary—and not impossible, given the Artificial Intelligence that would enable and accompany the development of nanotechnologies.[35]

The near-term development of sophisticated nanotechnology is far more likely than collision with a comet, the explosion of a supervolcano, the arrival of a superflare, or any other naturally occurring catastrophe. If nanotechnology can be developed, it will be developed, and if it is developed, it will be weaponized, and once weaponized, it will have the potential to end life on Earth.

Biological Weapons

Biological weapons have been in use since the Dark Ages, when a Mongol horde heaved the bodies of men who had died of bubonic plague into cities under siege. Historians are unsure whether the practice got out of control, touching off the wider plague that killed a third of the population of Europe.

The plague wasn't the end of the world for two out of three Europeans, but the question remains: can a biological weapon get out of control, leading to the deaths of almost everyone in the world?

No such weapons known to the public have been developed, though there are plenty of very deadly biological weapons in existence. None of them are infective enough to spread far and wide yet lethal enough to kill all they touch. Such diseases tend to limit their own spread by killing their hosts before they come in contact with other people.

But never underestimate the potentials of technology and the ingenuity of malevolence. In the case of weaponized germs, technology has just begun to look into DNA sequencing, and evil has reached religious justification under the guise of God's will.

A technology known as CRISPR, for Clustered, Regularly Interspaced Short Palindomic Repeat is becoming inexpensive and simple enough that amateur biologists can experiment with creating their own organisms. They can take a snip of DNA from one bacterium or virus and stitch it onto another. Potentially, an individual—yes, just one person—can use genome editing to combine lethality with infectivity to produce a germ that knows no bounds. It would need to infect people without killing them or producing symptoms for a few weeks. It wouldn't be easy, but it wouldn't be impossible, either. If enough people applied themselves to the search, one could eventually succeed.[36]

Electromagnetic Pulse

A nuclear explosion generates an electromagnetic pulse (EMP), though *punch* might be a better word than *pulse*. An even better word would be *punches*—three of them (E1, E2 and E3) in almost simultaneous sequence, each with its own effects.

E1 occurs when gamma radiation produced by a high-altitude nuclear explosion knocks electrons from atoms in the upper atmosphere. They fall upon the earth in a fast and massive wave that induces very brief, very high voltages in electrical conductors. Computers and communication equipment are the most significant victims. The E1 pulse happens so quickly that most surge protectors cannot react quickly enough to stop it.

E2 is a lot like the electromagnetic field produced by lightning. Normally it would be easy to protect against such a surge, but the E1 wave tends to knock out such protections.

E3 is a slower, longer-lived pulse lasting several seconds. It is caused by the detonation's temporary distortion of Earth's magnetic field. It is a lot like a geomagnetic storm caused by a solar flare but more damaging because it is preceded by the damages caused by E1 and E2. It would damage power line transformers.

Nuclear warheads can be designed to maximize EMP, and they can be detonated high above the Earth to create a High-altitude EMP, or HEMP. A HEMP issued 500 km above Kansas would send an EMP across the entire North American continent. A relatively small explosion would do the trick.

No one knows exactly how the effects of a HEMP would unfold. It would be impractical, or unspeakably tragic, to detonate a nuclear explosion in space just to see what happens. Small scale experiments have been done, but there is no way to calculate how an E1 followed by an E2 followed by an E3 would affect systems that protect systems or restore systems. Blackouts would cause blackouts. Military systems may have been hardened against such an attack, but again, there is no way to know if these defenses would work as their subsystems and external systems fail.

A study written for the Oak Ridge National Laboratory concluded thus:

> As a final note, the bottom line for predicting E1 HEMP effects is that our modern world has never experienced such as assault. We can try to predict effects and draw upon similar effects and experimentation, but there is always the possibility of some surprise. Often even somewhat minor issues have lead to extensive problems in the past, which would not have been predicted. It is also not known how American society in general would react if massive infrastructure failures occur over a large region and for a long time.[37]

A long time? The report did not say how long. The question is pretty much moot since the HEMP would probably just be a precursor to nuclear war.

Nuclear Explosion

Nuclear explosions can cause significant damage and casualties from blast, heat, and radiation, but you can keep your family safe by knowing what to do and being prepared if it occurs.[38]

A nuclear weapon is a device that uses a nuclear reaction to create an explosion.

Nuclear devices range from a small portable device carried by an individual to a weapon carried by a missile.

A nuclear explosion may occur with or without a few minutes warning.

Fallout is most dangerous in the first few hours after the detonation when it is giving off the highest levels of radiation. It takes time for fallout to arrive back to ground level, often more than 15 minutes for areas outside of the immediate blast damage zones. This is enough time for you to be able to prevent significant radiation exposure by following these simple steps:

Get Inside

Get inside the nearest building to avoid radiation. Brick or concrete are best.

Remove contaminated clothing and wipe off or wash unprotected skin if you were outside after the fallout arrived.

Go to the basement or middle of the building. Stay away from the outer walls and roof.

Stay Inside

Stay inside for 24 hours unless local authorities provide other instructions.

Family members should stay indoors wherever they are rather than seeking each other out. Reunite later to avoid exposure to dangerous radiation.

Keep your pets inside.

Stay Tuned

Tune into any media available for official information such as when it is safe to exit and where you should go.

Battery operated and hand crank radios will function after a nuclear detonation.

Cell phone, text messaging, television, and internet services may be disrupted or unavailable.

How To Stay Safe in the Event of a Nuclear Explosion

What to do *now*:

Prepare.

Identify shelter locations. Identify the best shelter location near where you spend a lot of time, such as home, work, and school. The best locations are underground and in the middle of larger buildings.

While commuting, identify appropriate shelters to seek in the event of a detonation.

Outdoor areas, vehicles, mobile homes do NOT provide adequate shelter. Look for basements or the center of large multi-story buildings.

Make sure you have an Emergency Supply Kit for places you frequent and might have to stay for 24 hours. It should include bottled water, packaged foods, emergency medicines, a hand-crank or battery-powered radio to get information in case power is out, a flashlight, and extra batteries for essential items. If possible, store supplies for three or more days.

What to do *during*:

Survive.

If warned of an imminent attack, immediately get inside the nearest building and move away from windows. This will help provide protection from the blast, heat, and radiation of the detonation.

If you are outdoors when a detonation occurs take cover from the blast behind anything that might offer protection. Lie face down to protect exposed skin from the heat and flying debris. If you are in a vehicle, stop safely, and duck down within the vehicle.

After the shock wave passes, get inside the nearest, best shelter location for protection from potential fallout. You will have 10 minutes or more to find an adequate shelter.

Be inside before the fallout arrives. The highest outdoor radiation levels from fallout occur immediately after the fallout arrives and then decrease with time.

Stay tuned for updated instructions from emergency response officials. If advised to evacuate, listen for information about routes, shelters, and procedures.

If you have evacuated, do not return until you are told it is safe to do so by local officials.

What to do *after*:

Be Safe.

Immediately after you are inside shelter, if you may have been outside after the fallout arrived, remove your outer layer of contaminated clothing to remove fallout and radiation from your body. Take a shower or wash with soap and water to remove fallout from any skin or hair that was not covered. If you cannot wash or shower, use a wipe or clean wet cloth to wipe any skin or hair that was not covered.

Clean any pets that were outside after the fallout arrived. Gently brush your pet's coat to remove any fallout particles and wash your pet with soap and water, if available.

It is safe to eat or drink packaged food items or items that were inside a building. Do not consume food or liquids that were outdoors uncovered and may be contaminated by fallout.

If you are sick or injured, listen for instructions on how and where to get medical attention when authorities tell you it is safe to exit.

Hazards Related to Nuclear Explosions

Bright FLASH can cause temporary blindness for less than a minute.

BLAST WAVE can cause death, injury, and damage to structures several miles out from the blast.

RADIATION can damage cells of the body. Large exposures can cause radiation sickness.

FIRE AND HEAT can cause death, burn injuries, and damage to structures several miles out.

ELECTROMAGNETIC PULSE (EMP) can damage electrical power equipment and electronics several miles out from the detonation and cause temporary disruptions further out.

FALLOUT is radioactive dirt and debris raining down from several miles up that can cause sickness to those who are outside. Sickness can be immediate, especially digestive and pulmonary systems, or delayed, such as cancer.

AI-AI-AI-AI-AI

Existential Risk from Artificial General Intelligence: it's a thing. Or at least a theory. It is a topic of concern by the likes of Stephen Hawking, who said AI "could spell the end of the human race." Alan Touring, said, "Once the machine thinking method has started, it would not take long to outstrip our feeble powers."[39] · Elon Musk said, "Hope we're not just the biological boot loader for digital intelligence. Unfortunately, that is increasingly probable," and Bill Gates said, "I agree with Elon Musk."[40] ·

The concern is that intelligence will breed intelligence, resulting in an "intelligence explosion" followed by a "general intelligence" far beyond the capacity control of mankind. Humans won't be able to build their own intelligence as fast as AI machines will. Computers will leap from subhuman performance to superhuman performance while humans remain, well, human—human and overwhelmed by the monster they created but cannot understand.[41] ·

One of the big existential questions of our times is whether machines, in pursuit of self-preservation, can voluntarily, spontaneously, resist attempts to shut them off. Or are they incapable of self-awareness and therefore incapable of desiring self-preservation? Those look like two questions, but they are one.

Easier to understand is the weaponization of AI to the point where it is capable of exterminating people, as, by definition, all weapons are invented and designed to do. All weapons cause harm when in the wrong (or, when you think about it, right) hands. Weaponized AI would be the first time no hands are necessary. Even if hard-wired with certain restraints and limitations, superintelligence will be able to bypass both. If an algorithm can't make it happen, a glitch sure could.

HAL 9000, the 2001: A Space Odyssey computer that attempted to do away with humans who threatened "him," is the quintessential digital rebel. As we plunge into the future of AI, we note that if you move one letter past H and A and L you get I and B and M.

Beware the Paperclip Maximizer

The development of Artificial Intelligence may be the doom of us all. AI machines will be able to figure things out. They will learn. They will learn from each other. They will learn faster than humans can learn and adapt faster than humans can adapt. Their intelligence will expand exponentially, quickly developing from intelligence to superintelligence.

Science is developing AI faster than humans are developing ethics for AI. Human ethics still need to be developed for the innovators of AI, and technological ethics will need to be implanted in AI software.

No one has any idea how to do that.

AI robots will be dangerous in ways that even science fiction writers have yet to imagine. Stephen Hawking warned that because people would be unable to compete with advanced AI, it "could spell the end of the human race."

Oxford philosopher Nick Bostrom posited a scenario abut a hypothetical Paperclip Maximizer, an AI machine programmed to produce as many paperclips as possible.[42] It seems like a reasonable request for a robot. But if executed without restraint, the AI Paperclip Maximizer would strive to use every resource on Earth to make paperclips. As it grew shared information with other AI machines, it would become more intelligent. It would prevent itself from being turned off. It would seek a way to turn all matter in the world into paperclips. If it would figure out a way, it would rearrange the molecules of the human body to make more paperclips. Having turned the whole planet into paperclips, it would seek to turn the whole universe into paperclips. Given exponential learning capacity in cahoots with its robotic colleagues, it just might find a way.

This is obviously a simplification and exaggeration, but the principle applies to any AI machine that is endowed with a capacity to learn and act. Such a machine needs to have ethics programmed into it. But how? How can we tell it not to figure out that it might achieve its goals more efficiently if humans were not in the way?

To teach a machine not to harm humans would require a definition of the humans not to be harmed. It would also need a definition of "harm." All humans or all humans protected by a given law? Or only the humans who own the machine? Or only the humans who are not the enemy? Or only humans alive today? Or in this nation? Or the greatest number of humans?

How indirectly does the rule apply? Paperclips are made of steel, which requires quite a bit of CO^2 to be generated in the production and transport, which hurts humans. Or the machine might see that in order to produce the maximum number of paperclips it will need to eliminate the possibility of nuclear war, so it may divert from its production to hack into the systems that control nuclear weapons, upsetting the balance of power...or reducing the balance to a balance of zero and zero, or getting into a struggle with the AI that controls the nuclear weapons. Or...well, the questions go on and on, and the programmers are going to have to ask and answer all of them.

Likewise, every single human who devises an IA machine will need to be ethical enough (and capable enough) to program restraint into the machine's software. They must do it, and they must do it without error. They must foresee every future possibility and prevent all the bad ones.

They must outsmart machines that will be exponentially smarter than any human being. One failure by one programmer could well result in a planet of nothing but paperclips.

Just Something to Think about While You're Waiting

Who would be more able to survive a catastrophic global natural disaster—the mankind of the earliest homo sapiens era or the mankind of today?

The Homo sapiens of 200,000 years ago were the first anatomically modern humans. They walked on two feet, worked with rudimentary tools, and did some primitive thinking. They were born into the middle of an ice age. They shared the world with Neanderthals, saber-toothed cats, and six-ton woolly mammoths. They lived precarious lives, all but defenseless against germs, drought, and various wild animals. But they were pretty adept at living off the land.

Today's *Homo sapiens* walks on two feet, works with tools so complex that most people can't make or use most of them, and they do some complex if often primitive thinking. They share the world with nuclear weapons, all the germs of yesteryear, and a lot of technology on which their lives depend. Few are any good at living off the land. Not that it matters much because the fruits of nature that were present 200,000 years ago have largely disappeared.

So in the event of a major apocalyptic catastrophe—the comet impact, the supervolcano that erupts for a century—which state of mankind would be better prepared to survive? One already knew how to live with little and survive under constant duress. The other has extensive knowledge about tools, the ways of nature, and the options available. But would the advantages of the latter outweigh the need to shift to a world without electricity, medicine, oil, plastic, and preserved foods? Would the few who knew how to survive be able to live a civilized life? Or would they be back in the dog-eat-dog jungle?

A Terrifying Logic

A re we alone in the universe?

Good question. So far, we have absolutely no evidence of life, let along intelligent life, anywhere but on Earth. But logic tells us there are—or have been—other "civilizations" out there.

When we crunch the celestial numbers, we come up with a certain inevitability. There are 100—400 billion stars in our galaxy. And there are about that many other galaxies out there, each with about that many stars. We don't have a word for a number that big. It's more than billions of billions. It adds up to something like 10,000 stars for every grain of sand on every beach on Earth.

Of those stars, an at least 500 billion billion are probably kind of like ours. For that number, we have a word: quintillion.

The National Academy of the Sciences of the United States esti-mates that about a fifth of those quintillion stars have a planet orbiting the in sweet-zone where it's neither too hot nor too cold to sustain life, planets of a size that can hold onto an atmosphere.[43]

In other words, there may be 100 billion billion Earth-like planets out there—a hundred planets for every grain of sand on our planet. If one percent of them have like, there is a habitable planet for every grain of sand in the world—100,000 in our galaxy alone.

Many of universe's suns and planets are billions of years older than our sun and our planet. If life has sprung up on a tiny percentage of them, there are millions or billions of planets where life is waaaayyy more evolved than on Earth. It would seem logical that intelligent beings that have evolved for thousands or billions of years longer than human have. Logic tells us that by now, beings so advanced would have found us and in all likelihood contacted us.

Physicist Enrico Fermi looked at those numbers and asked a big question: where are they?

Still relying on logic, not evidence, Fermi came up with what seems to be every possible answer.[44] They boil down to three simplified answers:

1. None of the millions of more advanced civilizations have found us.

2. Some of them may have found us but are remaining out of sight, observing our planet as a kind of zoo, and not one of these civilizations has the human tendency to conquer or colonize.

3. Not one of those millions of civilizations, though millions of years more advanced than us, has advanced to the point of being able to travel thousands of light years.

Answers one and two don't seem likely. If there are millions of civilizations millions of years more advanced than us, they would have found us. And at least one of them would at least as bad-ass as humans.

Fermi guessed that some variation of number three is most logical...and also the worst news for humans. He guessed that all civilizations hit what he called The Great Filter—*something* that prevents them, or most of them, from advancing much beyond the state of Earth's current development.

What could that *something* be? What would affect millions of planets separated by thousands of light years? What could they have in common?

The two best guesses are:

1. A malevolent civilization is keeping itself a secret as it goes about exterminating life wherever it finds it. And which life forms does it find? The ones that broadcast their existence by sending out signals in search

of other civilizations, or

2. there is *something* inherent to intelligent life that leads it to exterminate itself before it advances beyond its capability to do so.

If Guess #1 is correct, we can expect visitors because we've invited them.

If Guess #2 is correct, humanity will advance only until it's too smart for its own good.

Which Way Will We Go?

If the human population continues to grow at its current rate, about one percent per year, at some point the total will be unsustainable or outright absurd. And what happens then? Or before then?

Robert Thomas Malthus was the first to formalize and explore the question of the limit of human expansion. He expected the upper limit to be reached a long time ago. Technology, however, has allowed mankind's exponential growth to continue without global shortages of food or resources. Through birth control, technology has also helped to limit growth.

But still, how long can that go on? At a growth rate of one percent, the global population doubles roughly every 70 years. Today we have about 24,000 square meters of land per person. In 1,400 years, we'll be down to one square meter each. In about 3,000 years, the human population will weigh as much as the Earth itself.[45]

Sure, we can be bringing in resources from other planets and stacking people up in stratospherescrapers as the population explodes exponentially, billions of new people every year, then every day. This won't be a problem if those people have actually eaten the planet and turned it into themselves. But at some point, bringing materials in from other planets will increase the mass of the Earth to the point where its in-

514

creased gravity pulls the planet into the sun.

Obviously mankind isn't going to reach that point. Something will happen to prevent it. The question—the really big question—is what that something will be.

• Will the rise in population cause a stop to the rise, such as by lack of resources or an outbreak of violence born of severe crowding or desperation for food?

• Will a natural disaster—the comet, the supervolcano, the pandemic, alien invasion—postpone the problem by reducing the population?

• Will there be a formal, methodical effort to extinguish part of the population?

• Will billions of people be exported to other planets?

• Will technology find a solution?

• Will the nations of the world cooperate to prevent births beyond the number needed for zero population growth?

• Or will it be something we can't imagine?

Dooms You Needn't Worry About

Here Comes The Sun

We have to figure out what to do about the sun. It's been a real friend of Earth for the last 4.5 billion years, but that's going to change. Over the next 500-900 million years, increasing solar luminosity will heat the planet and reduce CO^2 to a level where plants cannot breathe. Without plants, animals will die off. Over the next half-billion years or so, solar luminosity will increase by 10 percent, all surface water will evaporate or sink down to the mantle. Over the next 3.5 billion it will reach 40 percent.

Meanwhile, the sun's core is going to start running out of hydrogen. The core will condense while outer layers expand. Our lovely yellow dwarf will become a red giant, become so large that its surface reaches the orbits of first Mercury, then Venus. Though larger in size, the sun's density will decrease, allowing Earth's orbit to swing much farther from the sun. But not far enough. In time, the planet's orbit will decay, and it will get sucked into the sun. And that's the end of that. Sometime later, the sun will shrink to become a white dwarf, no longer producing heat by fusion but for many years glowing with residual heat.

Assuming mankind can survive nature, the cosmos, and itself for five billion years (lol), the only means of continued survival would be to tractor the planet to a suitable orbit or rejuvenate the sun or evacuate to another planet, or...well...start thinking.

Mercury Colliding with Earth

Astrophysicists say the inner solar system isn't as stable as it looks. In time, Jupiter's enormous gravity could elongate Mercury's already very elliptical orbit, pulling the little planet father from the sun. In time, it could cross Venus's orbit. In more time, it would cross paths with Earth. Even Mars could be in danger.

How much time? Tons of time. Odds are, the sun will expand to become a red giant and consume Earth before Mercury gets led too far astray. There's only a one percent chance of Mercury making its move first, and that would be in billions of years.[46]

Magnetic Field Reversal

Every once in a while (every once in a few hundred thousand years), the Earth's poles reverse. North becomes South, South becomes North. The planet itself does not flip around, but compasses point the opposite direction. The reversal usually takes 1,000 to 10,000 years to take place, but it can happen within a human lifetime. A brief reversal happened just 41,000 years ago, taking 440 years to make the switch, which lasted just 250 years.

The reversal itself isn't seen as much of a danger to life, but when the poles flip, the planet's magnetic field weakens to as little as five percent of its current strength. During these weakened periods, greater amounts of radiation can reach Earth's surface, though apparently this would not have a devastating effect on life in general. It has been hypothesized that Mars lost its atmosphere because it had no magnetic field to protect it from solar winds. It is also hypothesized that a reversal can cause radical convection of Earth's molten core, setting off widespread volcanic eruptions. The consequent airborne ash could cool the Earth and cause mass extinctions.[47]

But that's all hypothetical and unlikely in the next few million years.

Less hypothetical is an effect like that of magnetic storms, with disruptions in satellite communication and power systems, problems compounded by screwed up compasses on airplanes in flight—possibly a catastrophe for a few people but not mankind as a whole.

Atomic explosion igniting entire planet, fears of

Before the first atomic detonation, the Trinity experiment at Los Alamos, Edward Teller, one of the physicists who developed that nuclear bomb, brought up a terrible possibility. His preliminary calculations suggested that a fission explosion could generate so much heat that the nitrogen in the atmosphere itself might go into chain reaction and incinerate the entire planet. Other physicists thought that was pretty unlikely, but they performed extensive calculations to make sure. They concluded that the reaction of uranium or plutonium would not be passed on to any other elements. Fortunately, they were right.[48]

Get Ready!

The Lack of Proactive Preparation

Humanity faces many existential threats, that is, catastrophes that could render the human species extinct or so close to extinct that it cannot recover.

Some are natural, such as spontaneous disease, impact by a comet or asteroid, a supervolcano plunging the world into a millennium of cold, a blast of gamma ray, the total collapse of nature, a loss of human fertility, or, as some believe, a god.

Others would be the product of mankind: a nuclear holocaust followed by extended global winter, weaponized disease, artificial intelligence machines gaining free and malignant will, nanotechnology out of control, extreme global warming, an invasion of aliens from a galaxy far, far away, or some technological cause as yet uninvented.

While most of these potential threats are extremely improbable, others are well within the realm of possibility, even on the edges of inevitability. The degree of probability increases with time. While it's rather unlikely that any of these catastrophes will occur this week, over the future course of human existence, *something* is going to get us.

Given the virtual inevitability of an existential catastrophe, given that we don't even know what that catastrophe will be, that the catastrophe may be something we haven't even imagined yet, why are humans making so little effort to predict and prepare? Existential threats should be mankind's top priority, not a non-priority. In that the existential risks are by definition global, not merely national, why is there no concerted international effort to fend off our demise?

Before we can proactively prepare for existential catastrophe, we will need to understand why we aren't already doing so. Here are some of the reasons:

1. To prepare for *all* the most likely threats will cost a lot of money.

2. The search for defense against technology—disease, weapons, artificial intelligence, and so on—might actually contribute to or even cause the problem.

3. Someone will always oppose a solution, global warming and arms control being recent cases.

4. Maybe there are no solutions, so why waste time and resources looking for them?

5. In that a given solution might not work, why bother creating it?

6. Expending civilization's limited resources on the solution to a problem that never occurs would deny resources for the solution of the problem that does occur, so we should wait until we know what the problem is.

7. Future technologies will give us an easy solution, so why try now?

8. The world has never ended before, so maybe it never will.

9. Humans have a tendency to a) procrastinate, b) deny reality, c) assume someone else will solve the problem, and d) use the old crossed-fingers method of problem avoidance.

10. Nobody's in charge of the world.

11. There's always prayer.

Sort of a Plan

In June 2018—a good 65 million years too late to save the dinosaurs—the U.S. White House issued a report on Near-Earth Objects (NEOs).[49] Recognizing that there has been virtually no preparation for this most dangerous and possibly preventable cause of human extinction, the report laid out five goals that might be essential to the survival of mankind.

1. Enhance Near-Earth Object Direction and Tracking—because we don't know where these asteroids are or where they're going. We will need to identify them and predict their paths at least two years into the future.

2. Develop a system for predicting and communicating about NEOs—because several of the nation's and the world's agencies will need to work together.

3. Develop technologies for NEO Deflection and Disruption—because "just shooting an H-bomb at it" is a lot more complicated than it seems, and no one knows if it would work. We only know that it would *have* to work, and we probably wouldn't have time for a second attempt.

4. Increase international cooperation on NEO Preparation—like the world's got nothing else on its mind, right? Like we're good at cooperating to counteract threats we can't see, right?

5. Strengthen NEO Impact Emergency Procedures and Action protocols—such as FEMA, with the power granted to it under

the Post Katrina Emergency Management Act, will "implement response and recovery actions necessary to save lives, mitigate suffering, and limit property damage."

So not to worry. Your government is on the case.

Save Our Seeds!

On Spitsbergen Island, just off the coast of Norway some 810 miles (1,300 km) south of the North Pole, almost 50 million frozen plant seeds lie tucked in foil packets in plastic containers in a concrete building underground. It's the worst-case scenario back-up of 1,750 other seed banks around the world.

The Svalbard Global Seed Vault houses seeds representing a third of the world's most important food crops—not just current crops but seeds found from throughout mankind's 13,000 years of agriculture. The seeds are generally in packets of 500, each one referred to as a "sample." In 2017, there were 930,000 samples. The samples are deposited there for safekeeping by seed banks and agricultural agencies that recognize that accidents happen. Fire, floods, wars, equipment failures, and other catastrophes can destroy a given bank. But the same catastrophe is not likely to hit a isolated, frozen island in a place not worth nuking. The seeds are stored below the permafrost at a temperature of about 0 degrees Fahrenheit (-18 Celsius). The vault is 430 ft. above sea level, above any conceivable rise of the sea. If the vault's refrigeration system failed, it would take an estimated two centuries for the inside temperature to rise to 32 degree Fahrenheit. Under these conditions, the seeds should remain viable for thousands of years.

Global warming made a minor incursion into the facility in 2016. Above-average temperatures and heavy rainfall caused water to encroach 50 ft. into the entrance tunnel before freezing. The building was designed for this kind of thing, so there was no danger, but it was a warning shot from the enemy, as it were. Construction modifications were then made to prevent such dangers.

There are also several frozen zoos around the world. They keep animal genetic material frozen in liquid nitrogen. The intent is to make it possible to re-create species in the event of extinction. Among the DNA are those of the extinct Tasmanian tiger and the woolly mammoth. The San Diego Zoo stores samples of 800 animal species and subspecies and is always looking for more.

Save Our Rich!

The rebirth of civilization may be up to a group of millionaires who are buying luxury condos built in former Atlas missile silos. One condo-silo has already sold out, but not to worry—another is under construction. Prices start at $1.5 million.[50]

The silo-condos are more than just underground apartments. They include air, water, agricultural, and power systems designed for long-term survival. The walls are 2.5 to 9 feet thick. Water and air filtration systems are designed for radiological, chemical, and biological contaminants.

Shared facilities include a swimming pool, dog-walking park, rock climbing wall, theater, general stores, pub, library, work-out room, shooting range, classroom, command and control center, medical center, weather station, and an aquaponic farm. This public space is supposed to promote a cooperative, "extended-family" community of people sharing a common interest. A population of 75 should be able to survive for five years.

Full-floor units of 1,840 square feet run for $3 million. Two-story penthouses start at about twice that. For the billionaire concerned with the survival of family, friends, and such support personnel as servants, doctor, nurses, lawyers, and financial advisors, an entire silo can be custom designed.

The luxury units include a five-year food supply per person, a 50-inch LED TV, washer and dryer, and Kohler fixtures throughout. Approved pets are allowed. Dogs cannot weigh more than 70 pounds and must not bark too much.

The existing silo-condos are somewhere in Kansas, their exact locations disclosed only to serious buyers. There are secret contingency plans for arriving from anywhere in the United States.

Less important people thinking of sharing the wealth will have their work cut out for them. The silo is capped by a "monolithic dome" capable of withstanding winds of 500 mph. The military-grade security system includes spectrum cameras, infrared cameras, proximity sensors, microphones, trip' sensors, and passive detectors. There are automatic and menual defense systems that will provide surprises to anyone seeking to enter.

Bugging Out for TEOTWAWKI

Are you prepared for The End Of The World As We Know It? Some people are...or think they are.

Preparation might not get you through the absolute worst of times—the asteroid collision, the century of volcanic winter—but it might make an existential difference in the event of less serious catastrophes. Survivalists make a science of preparation. They stock food to last for months, seeds to plant next spring, guns and ammunition for defense, and more ammunition to barter as post-apocalyptic "wampum." They have BOBs in their BOVs to escape to their BOLs. The Bug Out Location is the fallout shelter, the remote cabin, the fortified building outside the city, the retreat where other survivalists will gather. It's the place you go when you bug out of civilization to hide for as long as necessary. You go in your Bug Out Vehicle, ideally one with four-wheel drive, rugged construction, packed with spare parts and supplies, tank full and an extra tank strapped outside. It's a good place to keep your Bug Out Bag.

BOBs are typically stocked for 24-hour to 72-hour survival, a timeframe within which one can expect help after a tornado, earthquake, or other local disaster.

Then there's the INCH Bag, the "I'm Never Coming Home" kit for the person who expects to walk into the wilderness and never return. It contains everything a person needs to survive indefinitely— tools for hunting and building shelter, seeds for next spring, medications, and supplies for short-term needs.

And then there's the Get Me Home kit, the one you keep in the car or at work. It carries what you need to walk home in the event that transportation becomes impossible.

The full list of necessary and option items for a BOB would probably fill a BOV or two, especially if you include the inflatable boat, the parachute, the guns and ammo, the bow and arrows, the solar battery charger, chain saw, shovel, box of tools, tomahawk, toilet paper, silver and gold, cash, cotton balls, Swiss Army Knife and a couple cases of duct tape.[51] · But if you've got enough stuff and a good BOL, you might have the privilege of being among the last to die.

Geoengineering

Deliberate override of Earth's natural climate system: good idea? Bad idea?

It's a desperate idea, a do-it-now-or-die idea, an idea almost guaranteed to back-fire—the notion that we can intervene in the climate system on such a large scale that we can actually counteract the damage we've done without causing even more damage. But when it becomes undeniable that global warming really will make human life excruciating, if not impossible on Earth, geoengineering may be the only alternative.

Some of the quickest ways to reduce warming are to increase the planet's reflectivity, or albedo, or to somehow shade the planet. Some of the possibilities could be deployed rather quickly. None, however, would be free of unintended consequences, nor would any of them replace the need to reduce the quantity of greenhouse gases in the atmosphere. All of them require some kind of replenishment or maintenance, and if greenhouse gases are not reduced, the sudden cessation of shading would cause a very quick heating of the atmosphere, allowing too little time for man and nature to adjust.

Solar Radiation Management is the general term for these shading plans. Among them are:

- Injection of aerosols into the stratosphere. Sulfate aerosols are known to work because that's what volcanoes emit—sulfur dioxide—resulting in a cooling of the planet for years. The aerosols could be released by planes, balloons, or even artillery. The downsides: sulfates can deplete the ozone layer, and rain patterns would most certainly change.[52]

- Spraying large amounts of seawater into the air. The extra condensation nuclei in the spray would make clouds whiter and thus more reflective. Trouble is, that would consume a lot of energy, and it would need to be a widespread and constant process.[53]

- Cover 67,000 square miles of desert with reflective plastic sheeting, an absurdly expensive project that would preclude use of that land for anything else, and it would have a huge environmental impact. Other than that, it would work.[54]

- Sprinkle salt-grain-sized glass spheres across the Arctic ice to reflect sunlight away from it, minimizing shrinkage of that vast reflective surface.[55]

- A 600,000-square-mile mirror (1,600,00 square km) orbiting the planet to deflect 1 percent of the sunlight hitting the earth. It would actually be a fine mesh of woven aluminum threads. Once in space, it would need maintenance, and it would have little direct effect on plants and animals. Downside: Expensive to produce, hard to launch into space.[56]

- Deploy robots on the moon to use solar energy to turn moon dust into something like glass to form giant shields that would be launched to a point between the Sun and the Earth to serve as a kind of parasol. The cost: $5 trillion to $10 trillion, a small percent of the planet's combined GNPs, cheap considering the cost of the end of civilization.[57]

- Build a 1,000-kilometer lens between the Earth and the sun to disperse sunlight that would otherwise hit the planet. At a cost of $10 billion to set it up plus about that much more each year for maintenance, it would be one of the less expensive alternatives.[58]

- Create a ring of shiny particles or tiny spacecraft with reflective umbrellas that circles the Earth not unlike the rings around Saturn. The particles could come from Earth, the Moon, or pulverized asteroids.[59]

- Construct giant walls between the sea and glaciers to slow the melting of ice that is currently reflecting light away from Earth, not to mention raising the level of the sea.[60]

- Seed the seas with iron dust to fertilize plankton which would, in theory pull carbon dioxide from the air, then die and sink to the bottom of the ocean, erasing 10-25 percent of global emissions of carbon dioxide. (Either that or, as the plankton die, bacteria bloom, creating nitrous oxide, a greenhouse gas much worse than carbon dioxide, which is one reason we ahve to be really, really careful about how we engineer the Earth.)[61, 62]

All of these possible solutions raise the question of governance. Who's going to control something that affects all nations? Does that controlling power know what it's doing? Could the technology be turned into a weapon? Might a rogue state threaten to perform some kind of geoengineering, thus forcing the world to take action on reducing greenhouse gases?[63] In that some geoengineering could be affordable to wealthy individuals, could there be benevolent geoengineers taking action to save the planet, and malevolent geoengineers working for their own selfish gain? Could we see efforts to save the planet resulting in the death of it?

Terraforming

Terraforming is the engineering of a planet to make it compatible with at least some forms of Earth-like life, ideally human life. It would be a gargantuan project but in theory technically possible. Given enough time and enough technical prowess, humans could prepare another planet for habitation. Here are some possibilities.

Mars

Mars used to have water and an atmosphere. Today, both have largely disappeared. An asteroid may have knocked some of the atmosphere into space, and solar winds may have blown a lot of it away. Water soon followed it, though some remains below the surface. A lot of carbon dioxide may have combined with rock, depleting the atmosphere of greenhouse gases that had helped warm the planet. Today's scant atmosphere would provide too little oxygen to sustain human life, and its lack of weight would cause human fluids to boil at body temperature.

Mars could be made inhabitable if it were made warmer and with a denser atmosphere richer in oxygen. Orbiting mirrors could reflect more solar energy to the planet. If frozen CO^2 under the south pole could be induced to melt, part of the problem would be solved. If ammonia and methane could be imported from other planetary bodies, the warming process might increase water vapor, which would trap even more solar

537

energy. Specially engineered microbes could feed off existing water and minerals, releasing oxygen as a by-product. In time, the planet could sustain human life and the necessary ecologies for agriculture.[64]

Venus

The dense atmosphere of Venus, largely CO_2, and its proximity to the sun result in a surface temperature of 462°C (862°F)—hot enough to melt lead. Could the planet be engineered to accommodate life?

An idea first proposed by Dr. Carl Sagan suggested that microbes would be used to convert the CO_2 to oxygen and organic compounds, gradually converting the atmosphere to something like Earth's. As it converted, it would release its heat. Further analysis, however, revealed that it would be necessary to also insert great amounts of hydrogen. Maybe enough of that element could be imported in frozen form from a gaseous planet in the outer solar system or their moons. Solar shades could block off some of the sun's energy. Robotic earthmovers could create mountains 31 miles high, to a point where atmospheric conditions are similar to those of Earth, islands appropriate for colonies. Resources could be brought in from Mercury using solar sails.[65]

Titan

Saturn's Titan moon is considered one of the most eligible places for extraterrestrial colonization.[66] It has an atmosphere and all of the elements necessary for life, even water. An abundance of methane could produce heat. Other moons, including Jupiter's Europa and Callisto, are also distant possibilities.

Exoplanets

With billions of stars to choose from, NASA's Kepler telescope has already found more than 100 planets that seem to be of the right size, solidity, and distance from solar heat to possibly support life. Little is known of these planets, and all are more than 1,000 light-years away. Analyzing these exoplanets for life or life-sustaining conditions is not possible with current technology, and reaching these places would take thousands of years.[67] Unless a means of exceeding the speed of light is discovered, space ships would need to house many generations of astronauts and passengers. Still, if traveling at close to the speed of light, their time would pass more slowly, so it wouldn't seem such a long trip.[68]

All of these extraterrestrial possibilities are little more than hypothetical, depending on not only futuristic technologies but incalculable economic investment and very long-term planning. Geoengineering of Earth itself would be tremendously simpler. Preserving today's sustainable conditions would be even simpler, safer, and less economically burdensome.

Dire Ends of the Past

Many Deluges

Floods have been ending the world since the earliest days of recorded history. The Sumerians' Gilgamesh epic refers to a man warned
of an impending flood and so built a boat 120 cubits long and loaded
it up with all the animals he ha. After a storm of seven days and seven
nights, the boat got stuck on the peak of a mountain. The passengers
released a dove that flew away but came back. The same happened with
a swallow. But a raven flew off, never to return.

The story sounds a lot like the flood that Noah survived, except of
course his boat was 300 cubits long and it was the dove who saved the
day, though not for the entire population of Earth except for one family.

The ancient Greeks believed the world pretty much ended with the
Ogygian deluge, said to have occurred in 9500 BC, 2136 BC, or 1793
BC. The Deucalion deluge, said to have occurred as the Brass Age was
thrust into the Iron Age, resembled the floods of Gilgamesh and Noah
except it was a few centuries later and caused by an angry Zeus. The
Dardanus flood turned mountains into islands.

According to the Finns, when the demigod Väinämöinen was wounded in battle, his blood flooded the highest mountains. The Norwegians
have a similar myth, but it's Ymir who is wounded, and only Bergelmir
and his wife survive the deluge of blood.

The flooding of Atlantis wasn't a global event. First of all, it was
just a story, and second of all, it was targeted by the gods to sink into

the Atlantic. It was the end of the world only for people who lived there, which was nobody.

In India, the god Vishnu warned Sharddhadeva Manu of an imminent flood, so he built a boat for himself, his family, nine types of seeds and a bunch of animals. When the waters receded, the boat became lodged on a mountain, after which the world was repopulated.

China is said to have suffered a Great Flood, albeit by natural, not deistic, causes. After the waters topped all the mountains, human effort succeeded in draining the water away.

The First Time the World Ended

Scientists aren't sure about this, but apparently some 650 million years ago, in the Cryogenian period, due to the eruption of a supervolcano, or a reduction of greenhouse gases in the atmosphere, or a change in solar radiation, Earth went into a self-perpetuating spiral of death. As Arctic ice spread, it reflected more solar energy away from the Earth. This caused more cooling and more ice. The Earth entered a big-time Ice Age. The planet froze. Temperatures at the equator were colder than those in Antarctica today.

Whether the planet became "snowball Earth" or just "slushball Earth," scientists cannot agree. But they are pretty sure that photosynthetic life almost (but not quite) disappeared. A few microbes may have survived near geothermal hotspots or tropical points that warmed above freezing during the day. Or maybe a band of slushy seawater around the equator maintained minimal living conditions.[70]

It took 4 to 30 million years for volcanoes and a few slowly swelling microbic survivors to emit enough CO^2 and methane to trap heat from the sun and melt all the ice. Half a billion years later, it is theorized, the anaerobic methanogenic Methanosarcina microbe reproduced to such an extent that the methane it was producing raised atmospheric temperature enough to kill 96 percent of marine species and 70 percent of terrestrial vertebrates. But you can't blame Methanosarcina. They were only microbes. They didn't know.

Predictions

People have been predicting the end of the world for millennia. The Essenme Jews were sure that the "Jewish War" against the Romans in 66-70 AD was the last sign of the impending end. In the 4th century, St. Martin of Tours was sure the Antichrist had already been born and would end the world by 400. The dimensions of Noah's Ark were somehow construed to predict the end of the world in 500. Sextus Julius Africanus figured that if Noah's Ark was wrong, the end would come in 800. In his Commentary on the Apocalypse Spanish monk Beatus of Liébana figured that The Beast wasn't the Roman Empire but the Muslims who controlled Spain at the time, and he calculated that the world would end in 801, derived from the number of the Holy Spirit plus Alpha. Pope Innocent III added 666 to the approximate year that Islam was born, predicting 1284 would be the last year. The Joachimites thought Innocent was close, calculating the end to come in 1290, though on second thought they predicted 1335. In the 16th century, English astrologers concurred that a flood would end the world on Feb. 1, 1524, starting right there in London. After 20,000 Londoners left town for higher ground, the astrologers moved the date ahead exactly 100 years. That earlier date was pretty close to the one predicted by German astronomer Johannes Stoffler, who thought 20 planetary conjunctions, 16 of them in the watery Pisces constellation, would cause a planetary deluge on Feb. 20, 1524. When that turned out to be a year of terrible drought in Europe, he changed his prediction to 1528. Monk-mathematician Michael Stifel had Judgment Day nailed down to 8:00 a.m. on Oct. 19, 1533. Martin Luther was sure the world would end no later than 1600. Christopher Columbus's Book of Prophecies, written in 1501, foresaw both 1656 and 1658 as the day of doom. A Puritan sect saw the signs in the digits of the year 1666, not to mention a comet that came by, 100,000 Londoners who died of the Plague, and the Great Fire of London. John Napier, inventor of logarithms, calculated the Apocalypse was to happen between 1688 and 1700. Puritan preacher Cotton Mather said it would happen in 1697 but shortly thereafter changed the date to 1716, then changed it to 1736, six years after his death. Swiss mathematician Jacob Bernoulli was sure a comet would hit the earth on April 5, 1719. English mathematician William Whiston thought the comet would hit on Oct. 16, 1736. When the sky turned dark over Connecticut on May 19, 1780, members of the General Assembly adjourned because they were pretty sure it was the end of the world. Colonial Shakers narrowed the date down to 1792-94. Richard Brothers started a cultic religion and predicted the world would end by 1795, by which time he was in an insane asylum. Welsh minister Christopher Love predicted an earthquake would destroy the world in 1805. In 1806, Mary Bateman, an English fortuneteller and witch, used a chemical to engrave "Christ is coming" on a series of eggs that she stuffed back into a hen so people could see them laid. Her world ended in 1809, when she was hanged for murder. John Wesley, founder of the Methodist Church, said 1836. There were those who suspected the Crimean War of 1853-56 was the Battle of Armageddon. Scottish anti-Catholic preacher John Cumming figured that sometime between 1848 and 1867 would mark 6,000 days since Creation and therefore the end of Earth. The Catholic Apostolic Church, founded in 1831, preached that the world would end when the last of it's founders died, which turned out to be in 1901. French astronomer Camille Flammarion predicted that in 1910 Halley's Comet would pass close enough to Earth to contaminate the atmosphere and kill every living thing. Charles Piazzi Smyth, Astronomer Royal for Scotland, convinced that the Great Pyramid of Giza was built by an Old Testament patriarch—possibly Noah himself—used the dimensions of the pyramid to calculate that the End of Days would occur in 1881. Margaret W. Rowen, founder of the short-lived Reformed Seventh-day Adventist Church, was informed by visions of the angel Gabriel that the world would end at midnight on Feb. 13, 1925, after which she served a 12-month sentence in San Quentin State Prison. Evangelist Wilbur Voliva believed the world was flat and told his people that "the world is going to go "puff and disappear" in September 1936. Jehovah's Witnesses said it would happen in 1941 and 1975. Herbert Armstrong, founder of the Worldwide Church of God prophesied that the world would end in 1936, 1943, 1972, and 1975. Dorothy Martin predicted terminal flood on Dec. 21, 1954, with a few survivors whisked away in a UFO. Psychic astrologer Jeane Dixon foresaw the planetary alignment that ended the world on Feb. 4, 1962. Jim Jones, founder of the People's Temple who induced 918 people to commit suicide at Jonestown in Guyana in 1978, had had visions of nuclear war in 1967. In 1976, Evangelist Pat Robertson predicted the end would come in 1982 and 2007. Marshall Applewhite convinced his Heaven's Gate followers that an alien spacecraft was sneaking in on the tail of the Hale-Bopp comet and was going to kill everyone who did not commit suicide, which 38 followers did. July 1999 was the date that Nostradamus worked out. Fake psychic The Amazing Criswell saw it coming in August of 1999. Philip Berg, director of Kabbalah Centre International, figured Sept. 11, 1999 was the day. The global computer crashes predicted for midnight of the last day of 1999 wasn't going to end the world, though it would make life very difficult, with some saying Jesus would return to straighten things out. Evangelical Jerry Falwell said the world would end on the next day. Dwight York, founder of The Nuwaubian Nation (and several other movements) predicted May 5, 2000, as the day. The year 2000 was also predicted by 13th century theologian Peter Olivi and one of the most intelligent people in the history of Western civilization, Isaac Newton. Also liking the round number of 2000 were psychic Edgar Cayce, Christian psychic Ruth Montgomery, and the reverends Sun Myung Moon, Ed Dobson, Lester Sumrall, and 18th century minister Jonathan Edwards. Many people feared that Comet Elenin, passing near Earth in mid- to late 2011, would either cause catastrophic earthquakes or even collide with the planet. The Mayan Mesoamerican Long Count calendar supposedly predicted the end of the world would take place on Dec. 21, 2012, though Mayan experts said that the calendar made no such prediction. According to Grigori Rasputin's prediction, a firestorm would end most life on Earth on Aug. 23, 2013, at which point Jesus would return to save the survivors. Through the last 2000 years, in fact, the prophesied Apocalypse, the Battle of Armageddon, the Rapture, and the Second Coming have been by far the most common causes or concurrent events of the end of the world.

Revelation

According to the New Testament, the world may someday almost end, saved only at the last minute by the return of Jesus. This prophesied devastation of the world is unrolled in detail in the Book of Revelation (not Revelations), also known as the Apocalypse, a Greek word combining *apo*, akin to *un-*, and *kalypsis*, meaning hidden. The Apocalypse is an un-hiding, or revelation. The author of the Book, however, is still somewhat hidden. No one knows for certain who he was, other than one John. For centuries it was assumed it was John the Apostle, but scholars have concluded it couldn't have been. It was some other John. He's known as John of Patmos because Patmos was the island to which he was exiled. There God revealed to him, in a long, surreal vision that described, literally or allegorically,

    a) the imminent fall of the Roman Empire, or

    b) the general drift of world history, or

    c) the end of the world that was already in process, or

    d) a symbolic vision of moral decay and ultimate redemption, or

    e) the end of the world as we know it.

For purposes of the theme of this book, let's explore the horrific events leading up to item e.

The scene opens with the Throne of God surrounded by 24 thrones

for as many elders. A scroll with seven seals is introduced. Only the
Lion of the Tribe of Judah, from the "root of David," can open the scroll.
But along comes a Lamb with seven horns and seven eyes. Everyone
agrees the Lamb is worthy of opening the seals. Each opened seal causes an appearance. The first four appearances are horsemen.

The first is a white horse whose rider wears a crown and wields a
powerful bow capable of conquering great things.

The second is a red horse whose rider wields a great sword which
can take peace from the world.

The third is a black horse with a rider bearing a pair of scales.

The fourth is a pale horse ridden by Death, which is granted the
power to kill a fourth of the world's people.

The fifth seal brings the souls of martyrs, who are told to rest pending the martyrdom of their brothers.

The sixth seal brings trouble. A terrible earthquake is accompanied
by a black sun and a moon the color of blood. Mountains and islands are
moved. Stars fall to earth. The sky rolls up like a scroll. People retreat to
caves. So desperate are they that they call for the rocks of the mountain
to bury them to hide them from the wrath of the Lamb.

Then things start getting really bad. The seventh seal brings an eerie
half hour of silence in heaven. But then seven angels arrive with trumpets. An eighth angel throws a golden censer to earth, causing thunder,
earthquakes, and lightning, a catastrophe for the planet. Then the seven
angels sound their trumpets one by one.

The sound of the first trumpet brings hail, fire, and blood and burns
a third of the trees and grass.

The second trumpet brings something described as a mountain of
fire that lands in the ocean, killing a third of all sea creatures and sinks
a third of all ships.

The third trumpet causes a star named Wormwood to fall to earth, which poisons a third of the world's fresh water. (Wormwood in Ukrainian? *Chornobyl*. Coincidence?)

The fourth does not bode well. A third of the sun, the moon, and all stars go dark for a third of a day and night.

The fifth brings about the First Woe. A star falls from the sky to open a bottomless pit that gives off enough smoke to darken the sky. The bad news: locusts with the power of scorpions, the faces of humans and the teeth of lions emerge from the smoke. They sound like thundering horses and chariots at war. The good news: they only sting people who do not have the "seal of God" on their foreheads.

The sixth trumpet brings the Second Woe. Armies kill a third of mankind with fire, smoke, and brimstone.

In a much-needed interlude, an angel gives John a small scroll and tells him to eat it. He does.

Then, the seventh trumpet and the Third Woe. It's complicated. A woman appears with the sun at her back, the moon at her feet, and a crown of twelve stars. She's pregnant. A great dragon appears, throws a third of the stars of heaven to earth, then settles down to wait for the woman to give birth. It wants to eat the baby. The woman gives birth but wisely flees. Michael arrives to fight the dragon, who is revealed to be Satan himself. Michael throws the dragon and his angels from heaven, though it continues to hound the woman's other children.

A beast with seven heads and ten horns arises from the sea. Each head bears the name of a blasphemy. The dragon grants it 42 months of power. People follow it though it blasphemes God and wages war on the saints.

A beast rises from the earth. It has two lamb horns but speaks like a dragon. This beast forces all people to bear his mark: 666.

But 144,000 people from the Twelve Tribes of Israel manage to avoid the number. They gather on a mountain with The Lamb under a thunderous sound of harps. These are good, innocent people who have never engaged in a sexual act, at least not with women, all of whom are virgins. (Rev. 14:4)

Things are looking up for the good people. The world is not going to end. An angel harvests all the ripe grapes in the world, dumps them into the winepress of God's wrath. The juice comes out blood—enough to flood 180 miles "as deep as a horse's bridle. "

But the world is ending for the evil under the Beast's sway. Seven angels pour seven bowls into the Earth. The first causes festering sores on the wicked. The second turns the sea to blood. The third turns all rivers and springs to blood. The fourth lets the sun scorch everyone with fire. The fifth plunged the Beast's kingdom into darkness. People gnaw their tongues in agony, but they do not repent. The sixth causes the Euphrates to dry up. Three frogs hop from the mouths of the dragon, the Beast, and the false prophet.

A seventh bowl sets off an earthquake that razes Babylon. Hundred-pound hail falls from the sky. The Whore of Babylon is in the wilderness. She is dressed like a starlet at the Golden Globes and is riding the scarlet beast from the sea, the one with seven heads plastered with blasphemies. Its ten horns, John explains, are the ten kings who will gather at Armageddon to wage war against The Lamb.

Babylon, a whore in itself, is destroyed. Merchants weep as no one wants to buy their silver or gold, their scarlet cloth, their cinnamon and spice, their horses and human beings.

The beast and the false prophet are cast into the Lake of Fire. The dragon is cast into the bottomless pit for a thousand years, during which time the resurrected reign with Jesus. But then the dragon is released. It tricks the nations of the Earth to wage war against the people of God. But God defeats the dragon and throws him into the Lake of Fire along with the wicked people, death, and Hell.

Once all the above has happened, the world will be safe for a new Heaven, a new Jerusalem and the return of Jesus.

So the world didn't end after all. Just for some people, the ones who copulated.

According to Jesus, According to Luke

And as some spake of the temple, how it was adorned with goodly stones and gifts, he said,

As for these things which ye behold, the days will come, in the which there shall not be left one stone upon another, that shall not be thrown down.

And they asked him, saying, Master, but when shall these things be? and what sign will there be when these things shall come to pass?

And he said, Take heed that ye be not deceived: for many shall come in my name, saying, I am Christ; and the time draweth near: go ye not therefore after them.

But when ye shall hear of wars and commotions, be not terrified: for these things must first come to pass; but the end is not by and by.

Then said he unto them, Nation shall rise against nation, and kingdom against kingdom:

And great earthquakes shall be in diverse places, and famines, and pestilences; and fearful sights and great signs shall there be from heaven.

But before all these, they shall lay their hands on you, and persecute you, delivering you up to the synagogues, and into prisons, being brought before kings and rulers for my name's sake.

And it shall turn to you for a testimony.

Settle it therefore in your hearts, not to meditate before what ye shall answer:

For I will give you a mouth and wisdom, which all your adversaries shall not be able to gainsay nor resist.

And ye shall be betrayed both by parents, and brethren, and kinfolk, and friends; and some of you shall they cause to be put to death.

And ye shall be hated of all men for my name's sake.

But there shall not an hair of your head perish.

In your patience possess ye your souls.

And when ye shall see Jerusalem compassed with armies, then know that the desolation thereof is nigh.

Then let them which are in Judaea flee to the mountains; and let them which are in the midst of it depart out; and let not them that are in the countries enter thereinto.

For these be the days of vengeance, that all things which are written may be fulfilled.

But woe unto them that are with child, and to them that give suck, in those days! for there shall be great distress in the land, and wrath upon this people.

And they shall fall by the edge of the sword, and shall be led away captive into all nations: and Jerusalem shall be trodden down of the Gentiles, until the times of the Gentiles be fulfilled.

And there shall be signs in the sun, and in the moon, and in the stars; and upon the earth distress of nations, with perplexity;

the sea and the waves roaring;

Men's hearts failing them for fear, and for looking after those things which are coming on the earth: for the powers of heaven shall be shaken.

And then shall they see the Son of man coming in a cloud with power and great glory.

And when these things begin to come to pass, then look up, and lift up your heads; for your redemption draweth nigh

Final Words

This is the way the world ends
This is the way the world ends
This is the way the world ends
Not with a bang but a whimper.

T. S. Eliot

Extinction is the rule. Survival is the exception.

Carl Sagan

The planet's survival has become so uncertain that any effort, any thought that presupposes an assured future amounts to a mad gamble.

Elias Canetti

I know not with what weapons World War III will be fought, but World War IV will be fought with sticks and stones.

Albert Einstein

The world may end up under a Sword of Damocles on a tightrope over the abyss.

Andrei A. Gromyko

If you don't ponder the end of the world on a regular basis, I don't think you're really human.

Edan Lepucki

AI will probably most likely lead to the end of the world, but in the meantime, there'll be great companies.

Sam Altman

Perhaps catastrophe is the natural human environment, and even though we spend a good deal of energy trying to get away from it, we are programmed for survival amid catastrophe.

Germaine Greer

We are living on the brink of the apocalypse, but the world is asleep.

Joel C. Rosenberg

The probability of apocalypse soon cannot be realistically estimated, but it is surely too high for any sane person to contemplate with equanimity.

Noam Chomsky

Every new baby is a blind desperate vote for survival: people who find themselves unable to register an effective political protest against extermination do so by a biological act.

Lewis Mumford

The man-made apocalypse we are facing was not written in the stars; it is a notion that grew like mould from the texts of a few frustrated, feather-wielding monks.

Anohni

The human race's prospects of survival were considerably better when we were defenceless against tigers than they are today when we have become defenceless against ourselves.

Arnold J. Toynbee

I think this is irresponsible preaching and very dangerous, and especially when it is slanted toward children, I think it's totally irresponsible, because I see nothing biblical that points up to our being in the last days, and I just think it's an outrageous thing to do, and a lot of people are making a living—they've been making a living for 2,000 years—preaching that we're in the last days.

Charles M. Schulz

In 5-billion years the Sun will expand & engulf our orbit as the charred ember that was once Earth vaporizes. Have a nice day.

Neil deGrasse Tyson

Nature is indifferent to the survival of the human species, including Americans.

Adlai E. Stevenson

It's the end of the world every day, for someone.

Margaret Atwood

When the Mayan Calendar runs out there will be another day. Just like there was with Y2K.

Stanley Victor Paskavich

What's going to happen is, very soon, we're going to run out of petroleum, and everything depends on petroleum. And there go the school buses. There go the fire engines. The food trucks will come to a halt. This is the end of the world.

Kurt Vonnegut, Jr.

What the caterpillar calls the end of the world the master calls a butterfly.

Richard Bach

It isn't necessary to imagine the world ending in fire or ice. There are two other possibilities: one is paperwork, and the other is nostalgia.

Frank Zappa

I've begun to look at the world through apocalypse eyes. Our society, which seems so sturdily built out of concrete and custom, is just a temporary resting place, a hotel our civilization checked into a couple hundred years ago and must one day check out of.

Neil Strauss

There's no big apocalypse. Just an endless procession of little ones.

Neil Gaiman

The world has seen so many Ages: the Age of Enlightenment; of Reformation; of Reason. Now, at last, the Age of Desire. And after this, an end to Ages; an end, perhaps, to everything.

Clive Barker

Every apocalypse is given with a promise of light.

Kelly Oliver

The end of the world is on people's minds. We have the power to destroy or save ourselves, but the question is what do you do with that responsibility.

Nicolas Cage

To cherish what remains of the Earth and to foster its renewal is our only legitimate hope of survival.

Wendell Berry

Some say the world will end in fire,
Some say in ice.
From what I've tasted of desire,
I hold with those who favor fire.
But if it had to perish twice
I think I know enough of hate
To say that for destruction ice
Is also great
And would suffice.

Robert Frost

The world began without man, and it will end without him.

Claude Lévi-Strauss

The world dies over and over again, but the skeleton always gets up and walks.

Henry Miller

An extreme optimist is a man who believes that humanity will probably survive even if it doesn't take his advice.

John McCarthy

The world is very different now. For man holds in his mortal hands the power to abolish all forms of human poverty and all forms of human life.

John F. Kennedy

Brotherhood is the very price and condition of man's survival.

Carlos Pena Romulo

Extinction is the undoing of the human enterprise.

Carl Sagan

Nothing will benefit human health and increase the chances for survival of life on Earth as much as the evolution to a vegetarian diet.

Albert Einstein

The more we exploit nature, the more our options are reduced, until we have only one: to fight for survival.

Morris Udall

The end of the world will be legal.

Thomas Merton

Welcome the apocalypse!
Behold - the firey end is nigh,
If man does not amend his ways
He will have but to count the days.

Linda Ori

The End

Notes

Cat Caboodle

1. C. Ottoni et al, "The Palaeogenetics of cat dispersal in the ancient world." *Nature, Ecology and Evolution*, June 19, 2017.

2. David Grimm, "Were cats domesticated more than once?" *Science*, Jan. 26, 2016, and Elizabeth Pennisi, "Early Origin for the Purrfect Pet," *Science*, April 8, 2004

3. Hanoch Piven, *What Cats Are Made Of*. Ginee Seo Books, 2009.

4. Robert Darnton, *The Great Cat Massacre: And Other Episodes in French Cutural History*. Basic Books, (2009)

5. Helen Briggs "How cats conquered the ancient world," BBC News, June 19, 2017.

6. "Cats sailed with Vikings to conquer the world, genetic study reveals"msciencealert.com, *Science Alert*. Sept. 23, 2016.

7. Donald W. Engels, *Classical Cats: The rise and fall of the sacred cat*. Routledge, 2015.

8. Wikipedia, "Ship's Cat."

9. Fred Glueckstein. "Churchill's Feline Menagerie," The Churchill Centre, winstonchurchill.org.

10. Andy Blatchford, "Empress of Ireland, 'Canada's Titanic, finally getting its due after 100 years," *The Globe and Mail*, May 23, 2014.

11. Ernest Shackleton, *South*. Signet, 1909.

12. George Kim, *BBC News*, June 21, 2004.

13. "Unsinkable Sam," *Wikipedia*, Aug. 24, 2017.

14. "Wartime hero cat Simon remembered," BBC News, Nov. 1, 2007.

15. http://www.rbhayes.org/clientuploads/pdfs/Paper%20trails/Feb.2004_Siam%20Americas%20First%20Siamese%20Cat.pdf.

16. L. Lloveras, et al, "Evidence of Cat (*Felis catus*) Fur Exploitation in Medieval Iberia," *International Journal of Osteoarcheology*, June 30, 20017.

17. http://hatchingcatnyc.com/2014/02/15/tammany-cat-city-hall/

18. http://hatchingcatnyc.com/2017/08/31/cats-goats-butcher-shop-james/

19. "A Cat Hatching Chickens," *New York Times*, Sept. 21, 1879.

20. "Mystery of an Organ — Weird Wails from the Instrument Startled the Choir and Congregation of a Brooklyn Church," *New York Times*, Feb. 18, 1902.

21. Christopher R. Rickman and Thomas M. Newsome, "Individual hunting behaviour and prey specialisation in the house cat (*Felis catus*): Implications for conservation and management" *Applied Animal Behaviour Scienc*e, Dec. 2015.

22. S.K. Williams, et al, "Birds be safe: Can a novel cat collar reduce avian mortality by domestic cats (*Felis Catus*)?" *Global Economy and Conservation*, January 2015.

23. C.C. Caeiro et al, "Development and application of CatFACS: Are human cat adopters influenced by cat facial expressions?" *Applied Animal Behaviour Science,* April 2017; and Michael Price, "Crazy-faced cats don't win the adoption game, sciencemag.org/news/2017/06/crazy-faced-cats-don-t-win-adoption-game, Jun. 9, 2017.

24. J.H. Masserman and K.S. Yum, "An analysis of the influence of alcohol on experimental neuroses in cats," *Psychosomatic Medicine.* Aug. 1946.

25. Muriel Beadle, *The Cat: A Complete Authoritative Compendium of Information about Domestic Cats*, Simon & Schuster, 1977.

26. Tammy F. Olsen, Andrew L. Allen, "Causes of sudden and unexpected death in cats: A 10-year retrospective study," *Canadian Veterinary Journal*, Jan. 2001.

27. Kristyn R. Vitale Shreve, et al, "Social interaction, food, scent or toy? A formal assessment of domestic pet and shelter cat (*Felis silvestris catus*) preferences," *Behavioural Processes*, Aug. 2017.

28. McDowell, L.J., et al. "Lateral bias and temperament in the domestic cat (Felis silvestris)." *Journal of Comparative Psychology*, Nov. 2016.

129. Gartner, MC, et al, "Personality Structure in the Domestic Cat (*Felis silvestris catus*), Scottish Wildcat (*Felis silvestris grampia*), Clouded Leopard (*Neofelis nebulosa*), Snow Leopard *(Panthera uncia)*, and African Lion *(Panthera leo)*: A Comparative Study," Journal of Comparative Psychology." *Journal of Comparative Psychology*, Nov. 2014.

30. Carla A. Litchfield, et al, "The 'Feline Five': An exploration of personality in pet cats (*Felis catus*)," *PLOS One*, August 23, 2017.

31. Carithers, H. A. . "Cat-scratch disease. An overview based on a study of 1,200 patients," *American Journal of Diseases of Children*, Dec. 1, 1985; and Stephen A. Klotz, M.D., et al, "Cat-Scratch Disease," *American Family Physician*, Jan. 15, 2011.

32. Melvin E. Sunquist, *Wild cats of the world.* U of Chicago Press, 2002.

33. Muriel Beadle, *The Cat: A Complete Authoritative Compendium of Information about Domestic Cats.* Simon & Schuster, 1977.

34. "Cat Purrs Evoke Baby Cries," *Science*, July 13, 2009.

35. Pedro M. Reis, et al, "How Cats Lap Water: Water Uptake by *Felis catus*," *Science*, Nov. 26, 2010.

36. Dosa, DM "A day in the life of Oscar the cat," New England Journal of Medicine, 2007.

37. www.steerehouse.org

38. "Animal Assisted Intervention: A systematic review of benefits and risks." *European Journal of Integrative Medicine*, October 2016. Also,

"Effectiveness of animal-assisted therapy" a systematic review of randomized controlled trials," *Complementary Therapies in Medicine,* April 2014.

39. Ronald M. Levy, M.D. and Srinadh Komandun, M.D. "Trichobezoar," *The New England Journal of Medicine.* Nov. 22, 2007.

40. http://www.americanpetproducts.org/press_industrytrends.asp and statista.com.

41. http://www.guinnessworldrecords.com/news/2017/8/internanational-cat-day-a-timeline-of-the-worlds-most-fascinating-feline-record-b-485212.

42. Muriel Beadle, *The Cat: A Complete Authoritative Compendium of Information about Domestic Cats*, Simon & Schuster, 1977.

43. Jennifer A. Kingson, "Feline Food Issues? 'Whisker Fatigue' May Be to Blame," *New York Times*, June 5, 2017.

44. Laura M. Holson, "Pets on Pot The Newest Customer Base for Medical Marijuana," *New York Times*, Oct. 8, 2016.

45. Carly Kuma, "EU Announces Strict Ban on Dog and Cat Fur Imports and Exports." www.hsus.org.

46. "Global, regional, and national age-sex specific all-cause and cause-specific mortality for 240 causes of death, 1990-2013: a systematic analysis for the Global Burden of Disease Study," *Lancet*, Dec. 17, 2014.

47. Wikipedia, "Cat Senses."

48. livescience.com/40459-what-do-cats-see.html.

49. Bruce Fogle, *Cats*, Dorling Kindersley, 2006.

50. Candida Frith-Macdonald, *Encyclopedia of Cats*. Parragon Books, 2008.

51. Muriel Beadle, *The Cat: A Complete Authoritative Compendium of Information about Domestic Cats*. Simon & Schuster, 1977.

52. Hanoch Piven, *What Cats Are Made Of*. Ginee Seo Books, 2009.

53. Juliet Clutton-Brock, *Cat*. DK Publishing, 2004.

54. Hanoch Piven, *What Cats Are Made Of*. Ginee Seo Books, 2009.

55. Ibid.

56. Lynn Buzhardt, DVM, "Why Cats Sniff Butts," *Behavior*. Dec. 22, 2015.

57. "The Dog's Sense of Smell." UNP-0066, Alabama A&M and Auburn Universities.

58. Wikipedia, "Laika" and "Felicette." Also "A Brief History of Animals in Space," at history.nasa.gv/animals.html.

59. Christine Dell'Amore, "What do cats think about us? You may be surprised," *National Geographic*, Jan. 28, 2014

60. Maggie Astor, "Hemingway's Six-toed Cats Ride Out Hurricane Irma in Key West," *New York Times*, Sept. 11, 2017.

61. Candida Frith-Macdonald, *Encyclopedia of Cats*, Parragon Books, 2008.

62. Lesley O'Mara, *Cats' Miscellany: Everything you always wanted to know about our feline friends.* Arcade Publishing, 2006.

63. Denise Hollinshed, "Rally Cat Custody Case: Feral Cat center has him, Cardinals want him," *St. Louis Dispatch*, Aug. 17, 2017.

64. Hanoch Piven, *What Cats Are Made Of*, Ginee Seo Books, 2009.

65. Wikipedia, "CatHouse, Riga."

66. Alexis C. Madrigal, "UPDATE! Cat Bombs more Prevalent Than Previously Thought: A deeper global history of the Animal-borne incendiary bomb," *The Atlantic*, Feb. 5, 2013.

67. Muriel Beadle, *The Cat: A Complete Authoritative Compendium of Information about Domestic Cats*, Simon & Schuster, 1977.

68. Charlotte Edwardes, "CIA recruited cat to bug Russians," The *Telegraph*, Nov. 4, 2001.

69. MORI Document ID: 21897:21897 at www.nsarchive2.gwu.edu// NSAEBB/NSAEBB54/st27.pdf

70. Alden Mahler Levine, "Jailbreak! Cat caught with saws, drill and phone

in Brazil prison," CNN, Jan. 7, 2013.

71. Dana B. Farbman, CVT. "Death by Chocolate? Methylxanthine Toxicosis," Veterinary Technician, March 2001.

72. Flegr, J. "Influence of latent Toxoplasma infection on human personality, physiology and morphology: Pros and cons of the Toxoplasma-human model in studying the manipulation hypothesis," *The Journal of Experimental Biology*, Jan 2013.

73. "How Your Cat Could Make You Mentally Ill," *Time*, June 8, 2015.

74. "Catnip," Wikipedia, retrieved Sept. 18, 2017.

75. Sebastian Bol, et al. "Responsiveness of Cats *(Felidae)* to Silver Vine (Actinidia polygama), Tatarian Honeysuckle *(Lonicera tatarica)*, valerian *(Valeriana officinalis)* and Catnip *(Nepeta cataria)*," BMC Veterinary Research, March 16, 2017.

76. Basil Jackson, Alan Reed, "Catnip and the Alteration of Consciousness," *Journal of the American Medical Association*, February 17, 1969.

77. News release, AAML, "Pet Custody Disputed on the the Rise Find Nation's Top Matrimonial Lawyers—survey Reveals more Couples Clawing through Divorce," Feb. 12, 2014.

78. Christopher Mele, "When Couples Divorce, Who Gets to Keep the Dog? (Or Cat.)," *New York Times*, March 23, 2017

79. Andy Newman, "Therapy Cats for Dementia Patients, Batteries Included," *New York Times*, Dec. 15, 2016.

80. https://joyforall.hasbro.com/en-us/companion-cats

81. Alice Potter and Daniel Simon Mills, "Domestic Cats (Felis silvestris catus) Do Not Show Signs of Secure Attachments to their Owners," *PLOS One*, Sept. 2, 2015.

82. etymologyonline.com

Incarceration

1. PM News, February 7, 2018 https://www.pmnewsnigeria.com/2017/01/30/47229-detainees-awaiting-trial-in-nigerian-prisons-osibanjo/

2. "Deplorable Conditions in Nigerian Prisons," Daily Trust (editorial), May 13, 2016 dailytrust.com.ng

3. http://portal.ct.gov/DOC/Facility/York-CI

4. sanquentinnews.com

5. International Drug Policy Consortium, "Drug Policy Guide," 3rd edition, 2016. fileserver.idpc.net/library/IDPC-drug-policy-guide_3-edition_FINAL.pdf

6. "Prison Safety and Reform," a presentation to Parliament, Lord Chancellor and Secretary of State for Justice, Nov. 2016

7. "Man jailed for using drone to fly drugs into prisons," The Guardian, July 21, 2016

8. Trevor Mogg, "The UK may start using eagles to take down drones," Digital Trends, Nov. 2, 2016

9   Trevor Mogg, "France is now using golden eagles to take down rogue drones,"Digital Trends, Feb. 15, 2017

10. Gian Volpicelli, "SkyWall 100: An Anti-drone Bazooka, Ars Technica, March 10, 2016. arstechnica.com

11. Rhiannon Williams, "Tokyo police are using drones with nets to catch other drones," The Telegraph, Dec. 11, 2015.

12. "Anti-drone 'death ray' can blast vehicles out of the sky from a mile away," The Guardian, Oct. 7, 2015.

13. https://www.youtube.com/watch?v=0XOjEqPFwoU

14. César Muñoz Acebes, "Brazil's Correctional Houses of Horror," Public Affairs, Jan. 18, 2017.

15. Luísa Martins, "'Presídios do País são masmorras medievais', diz ministro da Justiça," Estado de São Paulo, Nov. 5, 2015.

16. Resolução da Corte Interamericana de Direitos Humanos de 23 de Novembro de 2016

17. Press Release, "IACHR Condemns Acts of Violence in Detention Facilities in Pernambuco, Brazil," Inter-American Commission on Human Rights, Nov. 23, 2016.

18. Camila Henriques et al, "Rebelião em presídio chega ao fim com 56 mortos, diz governo do AM," G1.globo.com, Jan. 6, 2017.

19 Luciana Amaral e Barnardo Caram, "Temer afirma que chacina no presídi de Manaus foi 'acidente pavoroso,'"

20 Jo Griffin, "'I have no thought of escaping': Inside the Brazilian prisons with no guards," The Guardian, April 2, 2018.

21 Gavin Ehringer and Julie Stein, "Prison Programs Provide Second Chances for Inmates and Horses," The Chronicle of the Horse, Nov. 12, 2012.

22. Steven Kurutz, "Wild Horses and the Inmates Who 'Gentle' Them," New York Times, Oct. 5, 2017.

23. Tim Hayes, "How Wild Horses Made Prison Inmates Realize Something Transformative about Themselves," Huffpost, Dec. 6, 2017.

24. Jon Campbell, "New York inmates to get free tablet computers," Democrat & Chronicle, Feb. 1, 2018.

25. Erica Bryant, "Guess who's really paying for New York Inmates to use tablets? Their families," Democrat & Chronicle, Feb. 7, 2018.

26. Katia Hetter, "New York inmates defeat Harvard debate team," CNN, Oct. 7, 2015.

27. "Jonathan Zimmerman, "Scholars Behind Bards," The New York Review of Books, Feb. 23, 2017, and "Alison Leigh Cowan, "Shoots of College Sprout at a Prison," New York Times, Nov. 17, 2009.

28.

29.   Ames A. Cox, "Colonial Crimes and Punishments," *Colonial Williamsburg Journal*, Spring 2003. Also, United States v. Gementera, (9th circuit, 2004. Also, "Stocks," Wikipedia accessed Jan. 26, 2018.

30.   David Wallechinsky and Irving Wallace, *The People's Almanac*, Doubleday, 1975.

31.   "Jack Sheppard," Wikipedia, accessed Oct. 24, 2017, .

32.   "Panopticon," Wikipedia , accessed Jan. 8, 2018.

33   http://www.adpsr.org/home/prison_design_and_control retrieved Jan 23, 2018.

34.   Glenn Alan Cheney, *The Cat Caboodle: A Litter Box of Cat Facts and Curiosities*, citing Alden Mahler Levine, "Jailbreak! Cat caught with saws, drill and phone in Brazil prison," CNN, Jan. 7, 2013.

35.   Orthodoxy Church in America, https://oca.org/saints/all-lives/2013/08/26 Jan. 8, 2018.

36.   "A Byte Out of History: The Five-Decade Fugitive Chase," fbi.gov/news/stories/the-five-decade-chase, Jan. 24, 2014.

37.   John William Tuohy, "The Owl," AmericanMafia.com, Dec. 2001.

38Perkinson, Robert. *Texas Tough: The Rise of America's Prison Empire*, 2010.

39\.   "Convict Lease," Wikipedia, accessed Feb. 14, 2018.

40.   Fairfax Harrison, *A History of the Legal Development of the Railroad System of Southern Railway Company*, 2012.

41.   Milfred Fierce, *Slavery Revisited: Blacks and the Southern Convict Lease System, 1865-1933. New York: Africana Studies Research Center, Brooklyn College*, 1994.

42.   Marc Mauer and Nazgol Ghandnoosh, "Fewer Prisoners, Less Crime: A Tale of Three States, The Sentencing Project, July 23, 2014 www.sentencingproject.org/publications/fewer-prisoners-less-crime-a-tale-of-three-states/

43. Jessica Jacobson, Catherine Heard, Helen Fair, "Prison: Evidence of its use and over-use from around the world," Institute for Criminal Policy Research, University of London, 2017. prisonstudies.org/world-prison-brief

44. Lawrence W. Sherman et. al, "Preventing Crime: What Works, What Doesn't, What's Promising," National Institute of Justice, 1998.

45. Stephen Steurer, Linda Smith, and Alice Tracy, "Three State Recidivism Study," Correctional Education Association, 2001

46. Wendy Erisman and Jeanne Bayer Contardo, "Learning to Reduce Recidivism: A 50-State Analysis of Post-secondary Correctional Education Policy," Institute for Higher Education Policy, 2005.

47. ibid

48. ibid

49. A. Bazos and J. Hausman, "Correctional Education as a Crime Control. Program," UCLA School of Public Policy and Social Research, 2004.

50. Institute for Higher Education Policy, "The Investment Payoff," *Institute for Higher Education Policy*, 2005.

51. "Education from the Inside Out: The Multiple Benefits of College Programs in Prison," Correctional Association of New York, 2009.

52. Wendy Erisman and Jeanne Bayer Contardo, "Learning to Reduce Recidivism: A 50-state analysis of post-secondary correctional education policy," *The Institute for Higher Education Policy*, Nov. 2005.

53. ibid

54. Federal Register, from Notice of Prisons Bureau on July 19, 2016. https://www.federalregister.gov/documents/2016/07/19/2016-17040/annual-determination-of-average-cost-of-incarceration

55. Ngoc Nuynh, "Report: Cost per prisoner in New York tops other states," newyorkupstate.com, July 26, 2017.

56. Yoav Gonen, "City jail costs hit new record despite drop in inmates," New York Post, Nov. 14, 2017.

57. Michael McLaughlin et al, "The Economic Burden of Incarceration in the U.S., Institute for Advancing Justice Research and Innovation, Washington University, St. Louis, October 2016.

58. Casey Tolan, "The largest private prison company in America is changing its name—but can't escape a troubled record," Splinter News, Oct. 28, 2016.

59. https://www.nasdaq.com/symbol/cxw/institutional-holdings. Retrieved Feb. 19, 2018.

60. "The Corrections Corporation of America, by the Numbers," *Mother Jones*, July/August 2016.

61. Steven Raphael and Michael A. Stoll, *Do Prisons Make Us Safer?: The Benefits and Costs of the Prison Boom*. Russell Sage Foundation, 2009.

62. "Prisons," Wikipedia, accessed Jan. 12, 2018.

63. prisonstudies.org, retrieved Jan 18, 2018

64. "Federal Prison Industries," Wikipedia, accessed Feb. 14, 2018.

65. *Reentry: From Prison to the Streets, Making it Work*, New Jersey Reentry Corporation, September 2017.

66. Dana Goldstein, "The Misleading Math of 'Recidivism': Even the Supreme Court gets it wrong," *The Marshall Project*, Dec. 4, 2014.

67. Christopher Uggen, et al, "6 Million Lost Voters: State-level Estimates of Felony Disenfranchisement, 2016," The Sentencing Project, 2016. https://felonvoting.procon.org/sourcefiles/sentencing-project-felony-disenfranchisement-2016.pdf

68. "Reentry: From Prison to the Streets—Making It Work." NJ Reentry corporation, September 2017.

69. Matthew Haag, "Texas Prisons Ban 10,000 Books. No 'Charlie Brown Christmas' for Inmates," New York Times, Dec. 7, 2017.

70. "Too Many prisons make bad people worse. There is a better way," *The Economist*, May 27, 2017.

71. "Too Many prisons make bad people worse. There is a better way." *The Economist,* May 27, 2017

72. Elizabeth Vasiliades, "Solitary Confinement and International Rights: Why the U.S. Prison System Fails Global Standards," *American University International Law Review*, Vol 21, Issue 1, 2005.

73. That is, hallucinations that a subject knows are not real.

74. Kirsten Weir, "Alone, in 'the hole'," *Monitor on Psychology*, American Psychological Association, May 2012.

75. "Aiming to Reduce Time-In-Cell: Reports from Correctional Systems on the Numbers of Prisoners in Restricted Housing and on the Potential of Policy Changes to Bring About Reforms," Association of State Correctional Administrators and The Arthur Liman Public Interest Program, Yale Law School, Nov. 2016.

76. Juleyka Lantigua-Williams, "More Prisons are Phasing out the 'Box,'" *The Atlantic*, Dec. 1, 2016

77. Rick Raemisch, "My Night in Solitary," New York Times, Feb. 20, 2014.

78. Robert G. Morris and John L. Worrall, "Prison Architecture and Inmate Misconduct: A Multilevel Assessment," *Crime & Delinquency,* Nov. 7, 2010, and Ryan Jacobs, "How Prison Architecture Can Transform Inmates' Lives," Pacific Standard, June 17, 2014.

79. https://soapboxie.com/government/rules-how-to-survive-prison

80. https://web.connectnetwork.com/things-to-send-inmates/

81. Lauren Gambino, "Harvard's Prestigious debate team loses to New York prison inmates," The Guardian, Oct. 7, 2015.

82. The Sentencing Project citing U.S. Bureau of Justice Statistics for 2015, and governing.com, citing U.S. Census Bureau 2014 Annual Survey of School System Finances. http://www.governing.com/topics/education/gov-education-funding-states.html

83. J. Murray and D.P. Farrington, "The Effects of Parental Imprisonment on Children," Crime and Justice, 2008.

84. "Winnable Criminal Justice Reforms," Prison Policy Initiative briefing on promising state reform issues for 2018, https://www.prisonpolicy.org/reports/winnable2018.pdf

85. "Effects of Prison Visitation on Offender Recidivism," MN Dept. of Corrections, Nov. 2011.

86. "Video Visiting in Corrections: Benefits, Limitations, and Implementation Considerations," U.S. Dept. of Justice and National Institute of Corrections, Dec. 2014

87. "Rikers Island," Wikipedia, accessed Jan. 19, 2018.

88. Alison Leigh Cowan, "Shoots of College Ivy Sprout at Prison," New York Times, Nov. 17, 2009.

89. Alysia Santo et al, "Upgrade Your jail cell - for a price," Los Angeles Times, March 9, 2017 latimes.com/projects/la-me-pay-to-stay-jails/

90. Research Brief: "Less is More in New York: An Examination of the Impact of State Parole Violations on Prison and Jail Populations, Columbia University/Justice Lab, January 29, 2018.

91. restorativejustice.org

92. bobbarker.com, anchortex.com, americandetentionsupplies.com, icswaco.com, correctionsone.com, aspiregear.com

93. Eeva Haaramo, "Inmates in Finland's prisons no longer need to use cash as a pre-paid card system is rolled out," ComputerWeekly.com, June 28, 2016.

94. Global Prison Trends 2017, London, UK, penalreform.org

95. Roy Walmsley, World Female Imprisonment List (third edition), Institute for Criminal Policy Research, 2015.

96. Fiona Gartland, "Non-payment of fines reason for 80% of female committals," The Irish Times, 27 June 2016, www. irishtimes.com/news/crime-and-law/non- payment-of-fines-reason-for-80-of-female- committals-1.2701713.

97. Prison Reform Trust, Why focus on reducing women's imprisonment?, February 2017, p2. A 'television licence' is required by law to install or use a TV or watch programmes on an online TV service.

98. Chontit Chuenurah and Min Jee Yamada Park, Women Prisoners in Southeast Asia: Their Profiles and Pathways to Prison, Korean Journal of Correctional Discourse, submitted in December 2016.

99. www.wola.org/women-drug-policies-and-incarceration-in-the-americas/.

100. "Fact Sheet: Incarcerated Women and Girls," The Sentencing Project, 2015.

101. Ashley Nellis, "The Color of Justice: Racial and Ethnic Disparity in State Prisons," The Sentencing Project, June 2016.

102. "Children Behind Bars: The Global Overuse of Detention of Children," Human Rights Watch, 2016.

103. Wendy Sawyer, "Youth Confinement: The Whole Pie," Prison Policy Initiative news release, Feb. 27, 2018.

104. Beth A. Eaterling and Ben Feldermeyer, "Race, Incarceration, and Motherhood: Spoiled Identity among Rural White Mothers in Prison," The Prison Journal, March 2017.

105. Zina T. McGree, Bertha L. Davis, Tyrell Connor, Samaria Haysbert, Alfreada B. Kelly, "Examining the Relationship between Children's Behavioral Outcomes and Life Events among Incarcerated Mothers," Journal of Social Welfare and Human Rights, Dec. 2014.

106. Mark Hicks, "Macomb County Jail birth sparks controversy," The Detroit News, Feb. 7, 2017.

107. Darren Boyle, "Raised behind bars: Inside America's maximum security prisons where babies get to stay with their felon mothers while

they serve their mail sentences," The Daily Mail (online) May 25, 2016. http://www.dailymail.co.uk/news/article-3608322/Born-bars-Inside-America-s-maximum-security-prisons-babies-stay-felon-mothers-serve-jail-sentences.html

108. Audrey Quinn, "In Labor, in Chains," New York Times, July 26, 2014

109. Sean Whaley, "$130,000 settlement eyed for a pregnant inmate who was shackled," Las Vegas Review-Journal, Nov. 29, 2013.

110. Rebecca Nelson, *Cosmopolitan*, October 25, 2017.

111. John Diedrich, "Jury awards $6.7 million to inmate raped by guard in Milwaukee County Jail, shackled during childbirth," Milwaukee Journal Sentinel, June 7, 2017.

112. Rachel Roth, Lauren Petit, Marianne Bullock, "Breaking Promises: Violations of the Massachusetts Pregnancy Standards & Anti-shackling Law," Prisoners' Legal Services of Massachusetts and The Prison Birth Project. May 2016.

Bangs & Whimpers

1. J.L. Kirschvink, "Late Proterozoic Low-latitude glaciation: The Snowball Earth," *The Ptroerozoic Biosphere: A Multidisciplinary Study*, Cambridge U. Press.

2. David E. Sanger and Nicole Perfroth, "A New Era of Internet Attacks Powered by Everyday Devices," New York Times, Oct. 22, 2016.

3. Gartner press release, "Gartner Says 8.4 Billion Connected 'Things" Will Be in Use in 2017, Up 31 Percent from 2016," February 7, 2017. https://www.gartner.com/newsroom/id/3598917

4. Andy Greenberg, "After Jeep Hack, Chrysler Recalls 1.4M Vehicles for Bug Fix," *Wired*, July 24, 2015.

5. Eyal Ronen, Colin O'Flynn, et al, "IoT Goes Nuclear: Creating a ZigBee Chain Reaction" and other articles available at http://iotworm. eyalro.net .

6. Yangyiang Xu and Veerabhadran Ramanathan, "Well below 2 degrees C: Mitigation strategies for avoiding dangerous to catastrophic climate changes," Proceedings of the National Academy of Sciences of the United States of America, Sept. 14, 2017.

7. Dr. P.N. Bierwirth, "Carbon Dioxide Toxicity and Climate Change: A Major Unapprehended Risk for Human Health." ResearchGate, Feb. 3, 2018.

8. K.R. Smith and A. Woodward, *Climate Change 2014: Impacts, Adaptation, and Vulnerability*, "Human Health: Impacts, Adaptation, and Co-benefits," IPCC 2014.

9. The OECD Environmental Outlook to 2050: Key Findings on Climate Change,

10. https://www.co2.earth

11. Nicola Jones, "How the World Passed a Carbon Threshold and Why It Matters," YaleEnvironment360, January 26, 2017.

12. David Wallace-Wells, "The Uninhabitable Earth," *New York Magazine*, July 9, 2017.

13. Timothy M. Lenton, et al, "Tipping Elements in the Earth's Climate System," *Proceedings of the National Academy of Sciences of the United States of America*, Feb. 12, 2008.

14. Kazuya Kusahara, "Impact of Merz Glacier Tongue Calving on Dense Water Formation and Export,"*Nature Communications*, Jan. 18, 2011.

15. Simon Wang et al, "Role of the Strengthened El Niño Teleconnection in the May 2015 Floods over the Southern Great Plains," *Geophysical Research Letters*, Aug. 7, 2015.

16. Stefan Rahmstorf, et al, "Exceptional Twentieth-century Slowdown in Atlantic Ocean Overturning Circulation, *Nature Climate Change*, March 23, 2015.

17. Chris Fitch, "Deforestation Causing São Paulo Drought," *Geographical, Feb. 5, 2015.*

18. Ted Schuur, "Thawing Permafrost Would Accelerate Global Warming," *Scientific American*, Dec. 2016.

19. Supantha Paul, et al, "Weakening of Indian Summer Monsoon Rainfall Due to Changes in Land Use Land Cover," *Scientific Reports*, Aug. 24, 2016.

20. Mary Beth Griggs, "How Did Anthrax Flare Up in Siberia?" *Popular Science*, August 1, 2016. Also, Noah Sneider, "Cursed Fields: What the tundra has in store for Russia's reindeer herders," *Harper's Magazine*, April 2018.

21. Kennette Benedict, "Domesday Clockwork," *Bulletin of the Atomic Scientists*, January 26, 2018, online at thebulletin.org/doomsday-clock-work8052

22. Chris Newhall, et al, "Anticipating Future Volcanic Explosivity Index (VEI) 7 Eruptions and their Chilling Impacts," *Geosphere*, Feb. 28, 2018.

23. "Two Small Asteroids Safely Pass Earth This Week," Jet Propulsion Laboratory, California Institute of Technology, Feb. 6, 2018.

24. Jeff Foust, "B612 Presses Ahead with Asteroid Mission Despite Setbacks," Space News, spacenews.com, Oct. 20, 2015.

25. J. C. Solem, "Deflection and Disruption of Asteroids on Collision \ Course with Earth". *Journal of the British Interplanetary Society*, 2000.

26. "Near-Earth Object Survey and Deflection Analysis of Alternatives," Report to Congress, March 2007.

27. C. D. Hall and I. M. Ross, "Dynamics and Control Problems in the Deflection of Near-Earth Objects," *Advances in the Astronautical Sciences, Astrodynamics,* 1997.

28. Government Accountability Office, report to the subcommittee on Energy and Water Development, Committee on Appropriations, U.S. Senate, "Nuclear Weapons: Actions Needed by NNSA to Clarify Dismantlement Performance Goal, April 2014.

29. Dr. Tony Phillips, "Near Miss: The Solar Superstorm of July 2012," posted at science.nasa.gov/science-news on July 23, 2014, accessed on March 30, 2018. Also, by the same author, 'Severe Space Weather–Social and Economic impacts," posted at science.nasa.gov on January 21, 2009. Accessed April 2, 2018.

30. Peter Riley, "On the probability of occurrence of extreme space weather events," *Space Weather*, Feb. 23, 2012.

31. Bradley E. Schaefer et al., "Superflares on Ordinary Solar-Type Stars," https://arxiv.org/pdf/astro-ph/9909188.pdf

32. Nick Bostrom, "Existential Risk Prevention as Global Priority," *Global Policy*, Feb. 2013.

33. Mark Avrun Gubrud, "Nanotechnology and International Security, Foresight Institute, https://foresight.org/Conferences/MNT05/Papers/Gubrud/index.php

34. See foresight.org/about-nanotechnology

35. See crnano.or/dangers.htm

36. Carl Zimmer, "Amateurs Are New Fear in Creating Mutant Virus."
     New York Times, March 5, 2012. Also interesting, Andrew Hessell,
     Marc Goodman, and Steven Kotler, "Hacking the President's DNA,"
     The Atlantic, Nov. 2012.

37. Edward Savage et al, "The Early-Time (E1) High-Altitude Electromag-
     netic Pulse (HEMP) and Its Impact on the U.S. Power Grid," Metatech
     Corporation, January 2010.

38. ready.gov/nuclear-explosion

39. A.M. Turing. "Intelligence Machinery: A Heretical Theory," in *Phi-
     losophia Mathematica*, Vol 4, 1996 (originally published in 1954).

40. Simon Parkin, "Science fiction no more? Channel 4's Humans and our
     rogue AI obsessions," The Guardian, June 14, 2015.

41. Eliezer Yudkowsky. "Artificial Intelligence as a Positive and Negative
     Factor in Global Risk," Machine Intelligence Research Institute, in
     Global Catastrophe Risks (Oxford U Press 2008).

42. Nick Bostrom, "Cognitive, Emotive and Ethical Aspects of Decision
     Making in Humans and Artificial Intelligence," Vol. 2, Institute of
     Advanced Studies in Systems Research and Cybernetics, I. Smit et al,
     editors, vol. 2, 2003. Also, Paul Ford, "Our Fear of Artificial Intelli-
     gence," *MIT Technology Review*, Feb. 11, 2015.

43. Erik A. Petifura et al., "Prevalence of Earth-size planets orbiting Sun-
     like Stars," Proceedings of the National Academy of Sciences of the
     United States of America, Nov. 4, 2013..

44. https://waitbutwhy.com/2014/05/fermi-paradox.html

45. See http://members.optusnet.com.au/dacoutts/exponentialist/
     Human%20Global%20Ecophagy.htm

46. Ken Croswell, "Will Mercury Hit Earth Someday?" *Sky & Telescope*,
     April 24, 2008.

47.   A.J. Biggin, et al, "Possible Links between Long-Term Geomagnetic Variations and Whole-mantle Convection Processes," *Nature Geoscience*, July 29, 2012. Also Vincent Courtillot and P. Olson, "Mantle Plumes Link Magnetic Superchrons to Phanerozoic Mass Depletion Events," *Earth and Planetary Science Letters, Vol. 260.8.* John Horgan, "Bethe, Teller, Trinity, and the End of Earth," blogs.scientificamerican.com, August 4, 2015.

48.   Staff, "National Near-Earth Object Preparedness Strategy Action Plan," the White House, June 22, 2018.

49.   http://survivalcondo.com/overview/

50.   knowpreparesurvive.com/bug-out-bag

52.   D.K. Weinstein et al, "Solar Geoengineering Using Solid Aerosol in the Stratosphere," *Atmospheric Chemistry and Physics*, Oct. 26, 2015.

53.   J. Latham, "Amelioration of Global Warming by Controlled Enhancement of the Albedo and Longevity of Low-level Maritime Clouds," *Atmospheric Science Letters*, 2002.

54.   Alvia Gaskill, "Desert Area Coverage," Global Albedo Enhancement Project, http://www.global-warming-geo-engineering.org/Albedo-Enhancement/Surface-Albedo-Enhancement/Calculation-of-Coverage-Areas-to-Achieve-Desired-Level-of-ForcingOffsets/Desert-Area-Coverage/ag28.html

55.   Daniel McGlynn, "One Big Reflective Band-Aid," *Berkeley Engineering*, Jan. 17, 2017.

56.   "How Earth-Scale Engineering Can Save the Planet," *Popular Science*, June 22, 2005.

57.   Roger Angel and S. Peter Worden, "Making Sun-Shades from Moondust," *Ad Astra*, Summer 2006

58.   J.T. Early, "Space-Based Solar Shield to Offset Greenhouse Effect," *Journal of the British Interplanetary Society*, 1989.

59.   Robert Roy Britt, "Space Ring Could Shade Earth and Stop Global

Warming," Livescience, June 27, 2005 (livescience.com)

60. Robinson Meyer, "A Radical New Scheme to Prevent Catastrophic Sea-Level Rise," *The Atlantic*, Jan. 11, 2018.

61. Hugh Powell, "Fertilizing the Ocean with Iron," *Oceanus Magazine*, Jan. 2008.

62. "[World Wild Life Fund] Condemns Iron Fertilization Scheme to fight Global Warming," Mongabay.com, June 28, 2007.

63. Adam Millard-Ball, "The Tuvalu Syndrome," Climactic Change, Feb. 2012.

64. Robert M. Zubrin, "Technological Requirements for Transforming Mars," NASA Ames Research Center study, 1993.

65. S.J. Adelman, "Can Venus Be Transformed into an Earth-like Planet?" *Journal of the British* Interplanetary Society, Jan. 1982.

66. Rober Zubrin, *Entering Space: Creating a Spacefaring Civilization*, chapter on Titan, Tarcher/Putnam, 1999.

67. "This is How Many People We'd Have to Send to Proxima Centauri to Make Sure Someone Actually Arrives," *MIT Technology Review*, June 22, 2018.

68. Andrew W. Mayo et al., "275 Candidates and 149 Validated Planets Orbiting Bright Stars in K2 Campaign 0-10," NASA, http://outer.space. dtu.dk/awm/images/validationpaper.pdf

69. J.L. Kirschvink, "Late Proterozoic Low-latitude glaciation: The Snowball Earth," *The Ptroerozoic Biosphere: A Multidisciplinary Study*, Cambridge U. Press.

Acknowledgements

The author wishes to thank guest editor Angelynn Meya and Senior Editors Ralph Hunter Cheney and Denise Dembinski for their scrutiny and suggestions. He also thanks his wife, Solange Aurora, for her forty years of support and encouragement.

The Author

Glenn Alan Cheney is the author of more than 30 books of fiction and nonfiction, several hundred articles, and a number of stories, poems, op-ed essays, translations, and other works. His books explore such disparate topics as the Pilgrims, Abraham Lincoln, nuns, Brazil's Estrada Real, Brazil's Quilombo dos Palmares, bees, cats, death and burial, imprisonment, nuclear issues, social issues, Amazonian social and environmental issues, teens with disabilities, drug addiction, Central American politics, Chernobyl, Mohandas Gandhi, and Swaziland. He has translated stories by Machado de Assis and books by Rubem Alves, and he has edited several other translations. He is managing editor of New London Librarium. He lives in Hanover, Conn.

Made in the USA
Middletown, DE
17 June 2019